P9-CAY-982

William Shakespeare's

KING LEAR

a graphic novel by Gareth Hinds

THECOMIC.COM

Cambridge, Massachusetts

In memory of my teacher
David Passalacqua, and my grandfather, Mel.

Preface

Shakespeare's plays were first published as a series of Quartos (small paperbacks) and then as a larger, more prestigious Folio volume. For most of the plays, there isn't much difference between the Quarto and Folio editions; but in the case of *King Lear*, there are many differences, including whole scenes that appear only in one or the other. Most modern editions of *Lear* are conflated texts, based primarily on the Folio but with scenes from the Quarto added. I found that I preferred the Quarto, so I based the text for this book primarily on the Quarto, adding selections from the Folio where I judged appropriate.

In the versions of *King Lear* that I consulted in preparing this text – including those from The Pelican Shakespeare, The Folger Library, Barron's Shakespeare Made Easy, and The Oxford University Press – the punctuation has been modernized to varying degrees and in somewhat different styles. For this book, I chose the punctuation that seemed most appropriate for readability and pacing in the comic medium.

Most of Shakespeare's writing is set in verse (iambic pentameter, specifically). Although I was able to preserve the original line breaks in some of the important speeches, in most cases I found it necessary to remove the line breaks and set the text as prose in order to maintain the flow of the dialogue. There are also numerous instances where I split lines or changed a particularly archaic word. In each of these cases I carefully considered the meter, and broke it only if I felt the impact was minimal.

Some readers may find Shakespeare's use of language difficult. To address this, I have written a short colloquial translation of the text, which you can download for free from THECOMIC.COM and use as a read-along guide. Mine is a loose, entertaining and idiomatic translation. For a more literal side-by-side translation, I recommend the *King Lear* volume in Barron's Shakespeare Made Easy series.

I would like to offer a huge "thank you" to all my friends who have proofread or given me feedback during the epic course of this project: Paul, lydia, Sean, Lynda, Dan & Laurie, Cat & Josh, Wes, Gretchen, Mat & Dianne, Bill, and my parents. I'd particularly like to thank my tireless editor, Alison, and my Shakespeare expert, Sarah.

– G.H.

Dramatis Personae

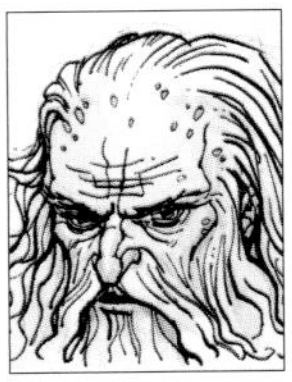

LEAR
King of Britain

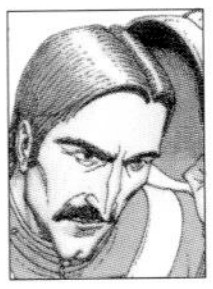

Earl of
KENT

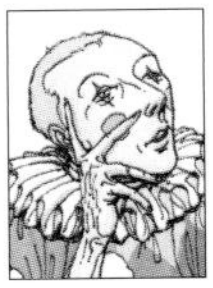

Fool
servant to Lear

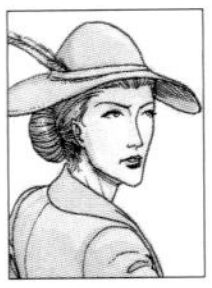

GONERIL
Lear's eldest daughter

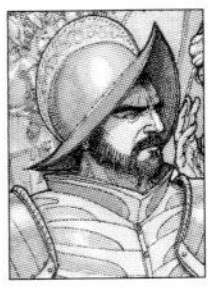

Duke of
ALBANY

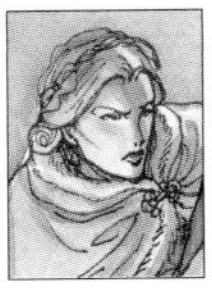

REGAN
Lear's second daughter

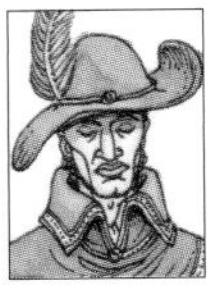

Duke of
CORNWALL

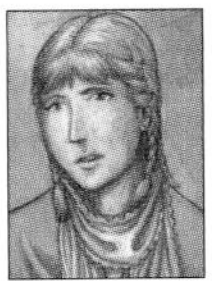

CORDELIA
Lear's youngest daughter

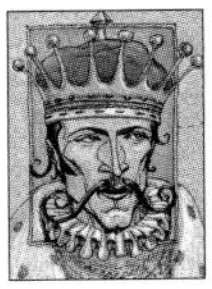

King of
FRANCE

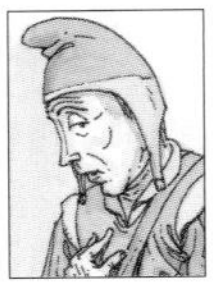

OSWALD
servant to Goneril

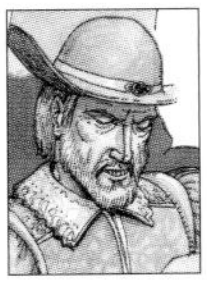

Earl of
GLOUCESTER

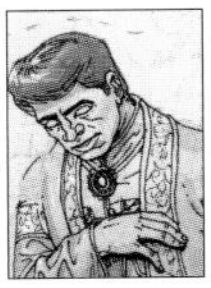

Duke of
BURGUNDY
suitor to Cordelia

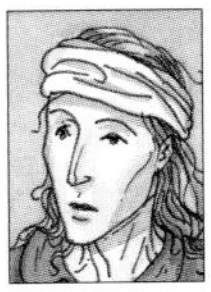

EDGAR
Gloucester's son

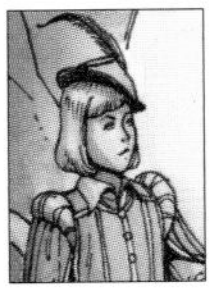

EDMUND
Gloucester's illegitimate son

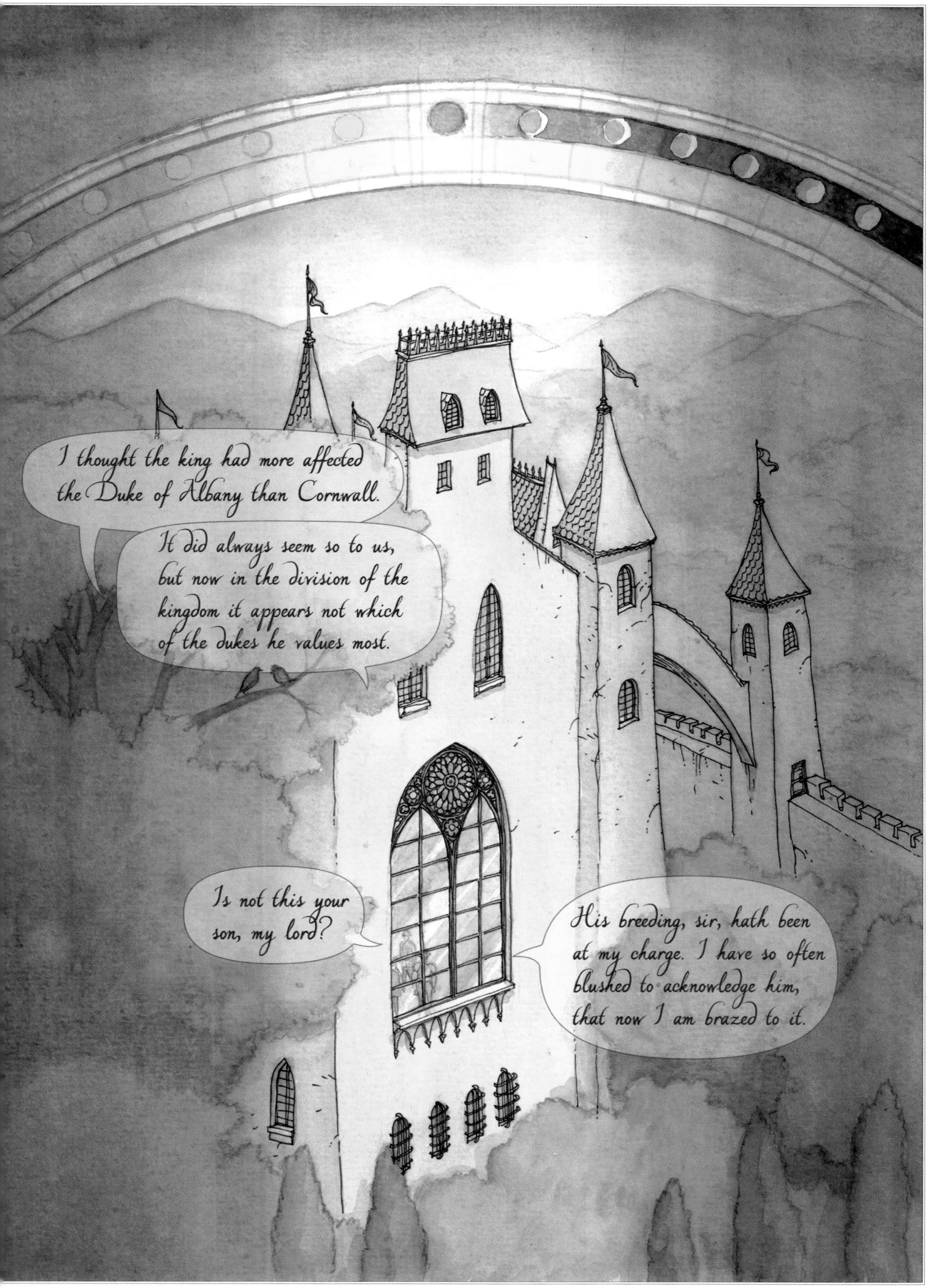
I thought the king had more affected the Duke of Albany than Cornwall.
It did always seem so to us, but now in the division of the kingdom it appears not which of the dukes he values most.
Is not this your son, my lord?
His breeding, sir, hath been at my charge. I have so often blushed to acknowledge him, that now I am brazed to it.

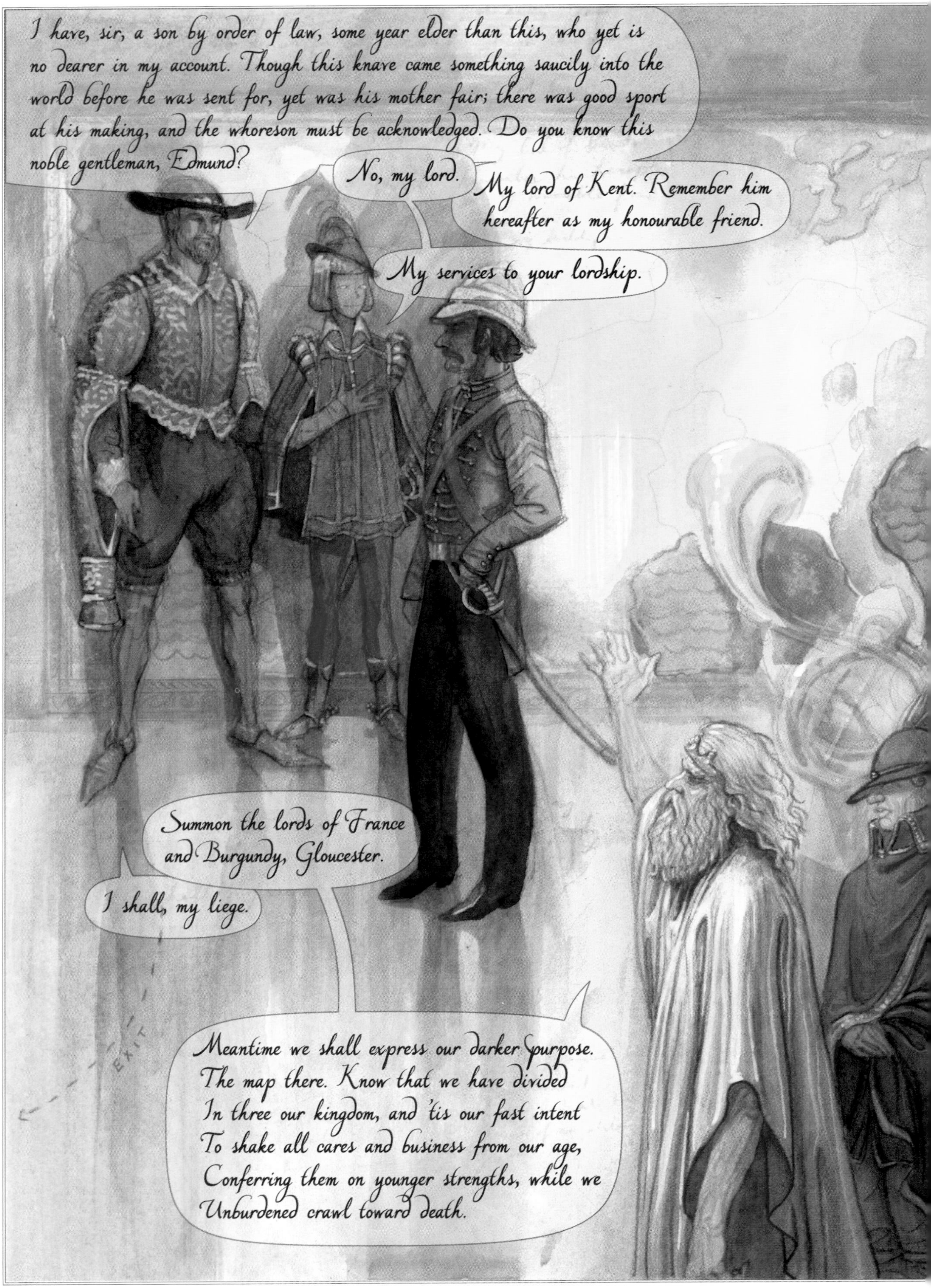
I have, sir, a son by order of law, some year elder than this, who yet is no dearer in my account. Though this knave came something saucily into the world before he was sent for, yet was his mother fair; there was good sport at his making, and the whoreson must be acknowledged. Do you know this noble gentleman, Edmund?
No, my lord.
My lord of Kent. Remember him hereafter as my honourable friend.
My services to your lordship.
Summon the lords of France and Burgundy, Gloucester.
I shall, my liege.
EXIT
Meantime we shall express our darker purpose.
The map there. Know that we have divided
In three our kingdom, and 'tis our fast intent
To shake all cares and business from our age,
Conferring them on younger strengths, while we
Unburdened crawl toward death.

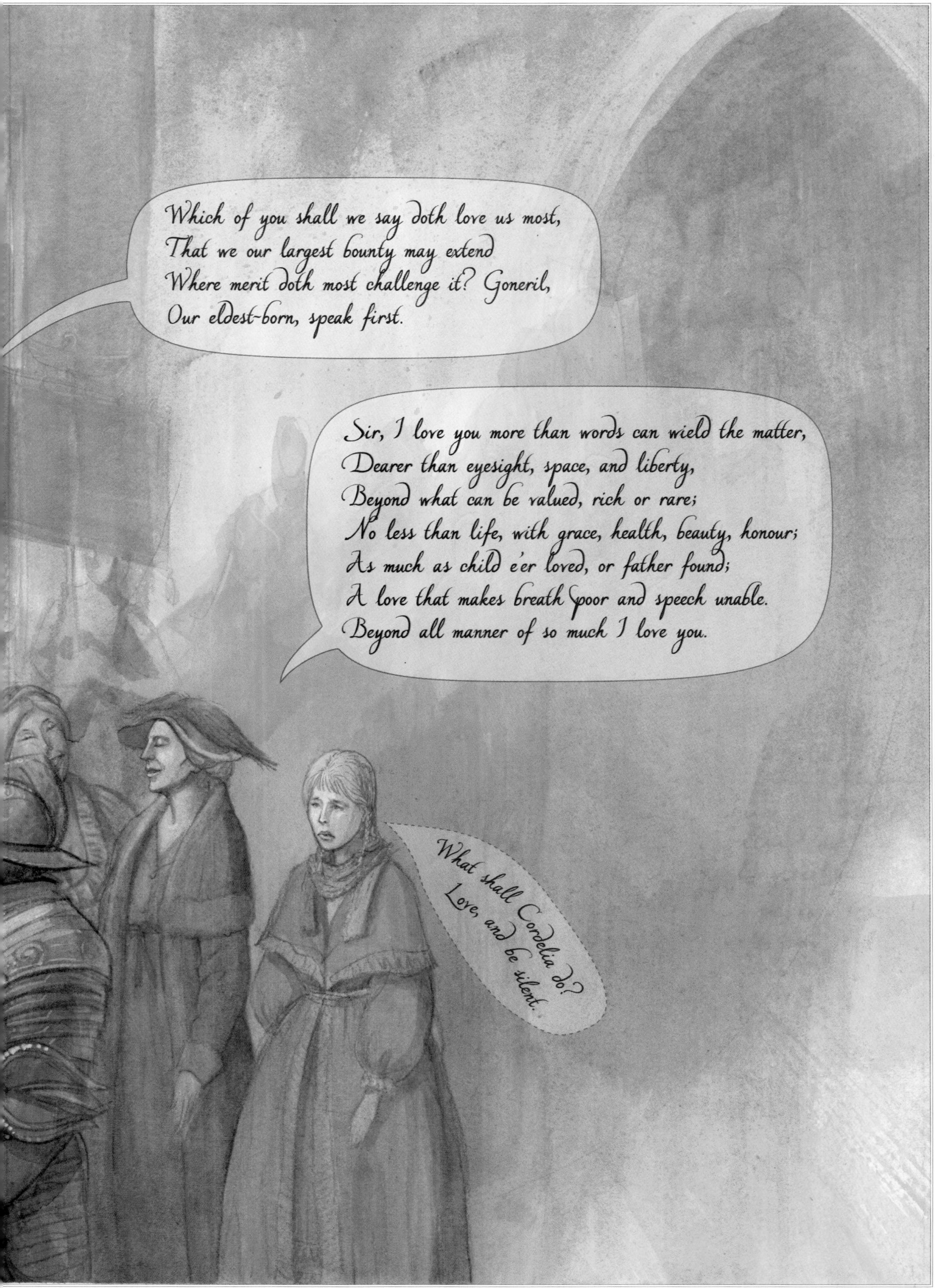
Which of you shall we say doth love us most, That we our largest bounty may extend Where merit doth most challenge it? Goneril, Our eldest-born, speak first.
Sir, I love you more than words can wield the matter, Dearer than eyesight, space, and liberty, Beyond what can be valued, rich or rare; No less than life, with grace, health, beauty, honour; As much as child e'er loved, or father found; A love that makes breath poor and speech unable. Beyond all manner of so much I love you.
What shall Cordelia do? Love, and be silent.

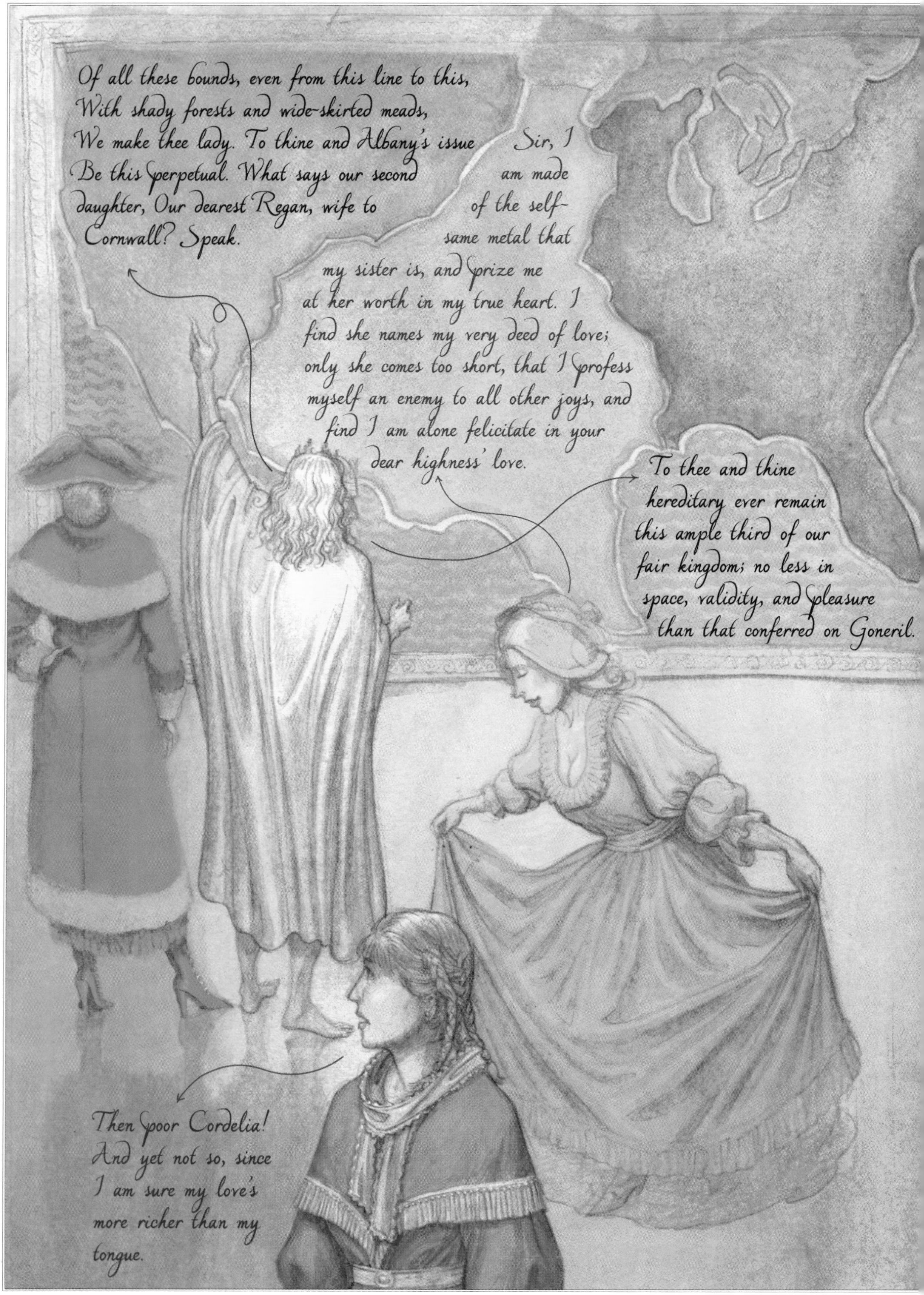
Of all these bounds, even from this line to this, With shady forests and wide-skirted meads, We make thee lady. To thine and Albany's issue Be this perpetual. What says our second daughter, Our dearest Regan, wife to Cornwall? Speak.
Sir, I am made of the self-same metal that my sister is, and prize me at her worth in my true heart. I find she names my very deed of love; only she comes too short, that I profess myself an enemy to all other joys, and find I am alone felicitate in your dear highness' love.
To thee and thine hereditary ever remain this ample third of our fair kingdom; no less in space, validity, and pleasure than that conferred on Goneril.
Then poor Cordelia! And yet not so, since I am sure my love's more richer than my tongue.

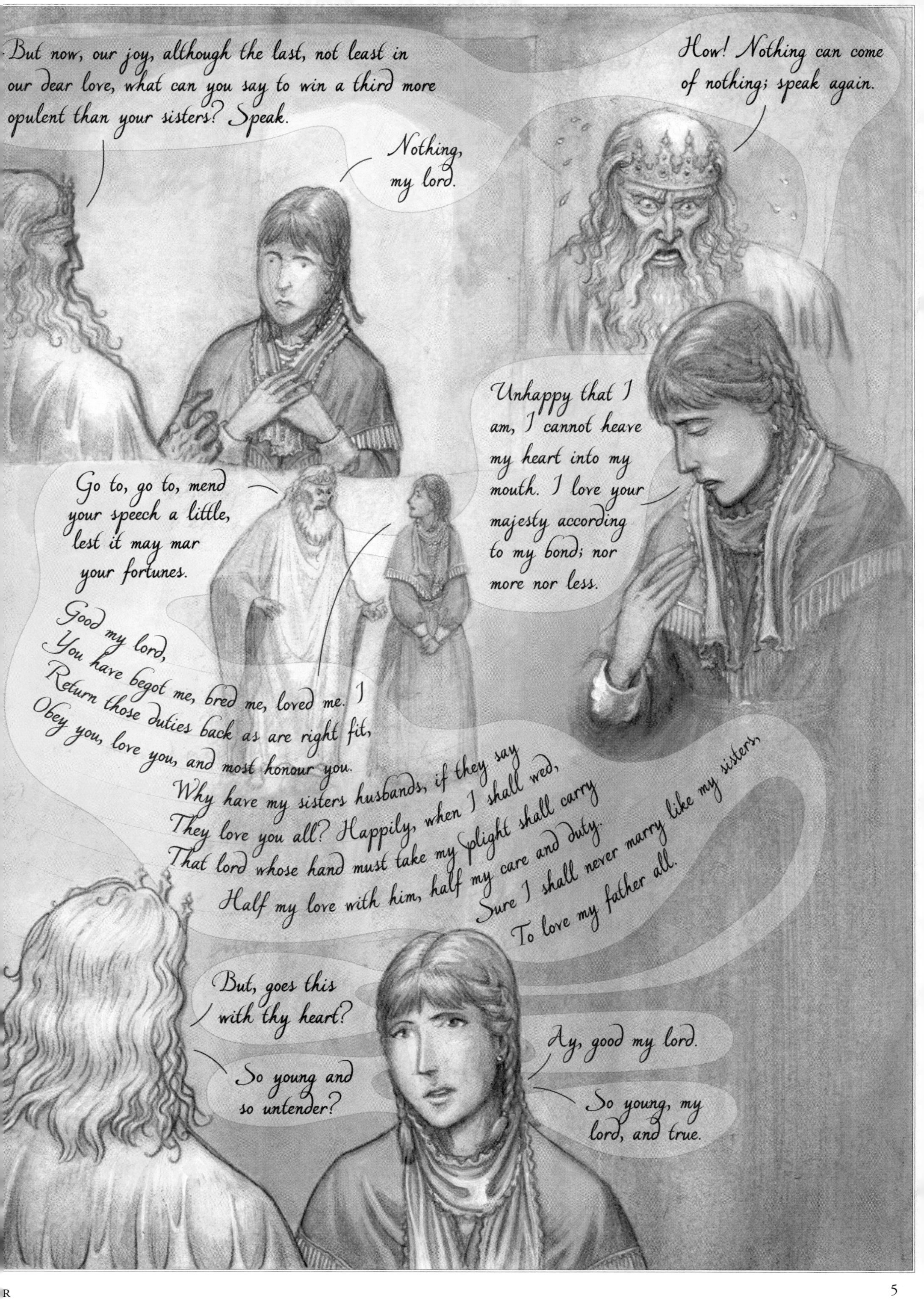
But now, our joy, although the last, not least in our dear love, what can you say to win a third more opulent than your sisters? Speak.
Nothing, my lord.
How! Nothing can come of nothing; speak again.
Unhappy that I am, I cannot heave my heart into my mouth. I love your majesty according to my bond; nor more nor less.
Go to, go to, mend your speech a little, lest it may mar your fortunes.
Good my lord,
You have begot me, bred me, loved me. I
Return those duties back as are right fit,
Obey you, love you, and most honour you.
Why have my sisters husbands, if they say
They love you all? Happily, when I shall wed,
That lord whose hand must take my plight shall carry
Half my love with him, half my care and duty.
Sure I shall never marry like my sisters,
To love my father all.
But, goes this with thy heart?
Ay, good my lord.
So young and so untender?
So young, my lord, and true.

R

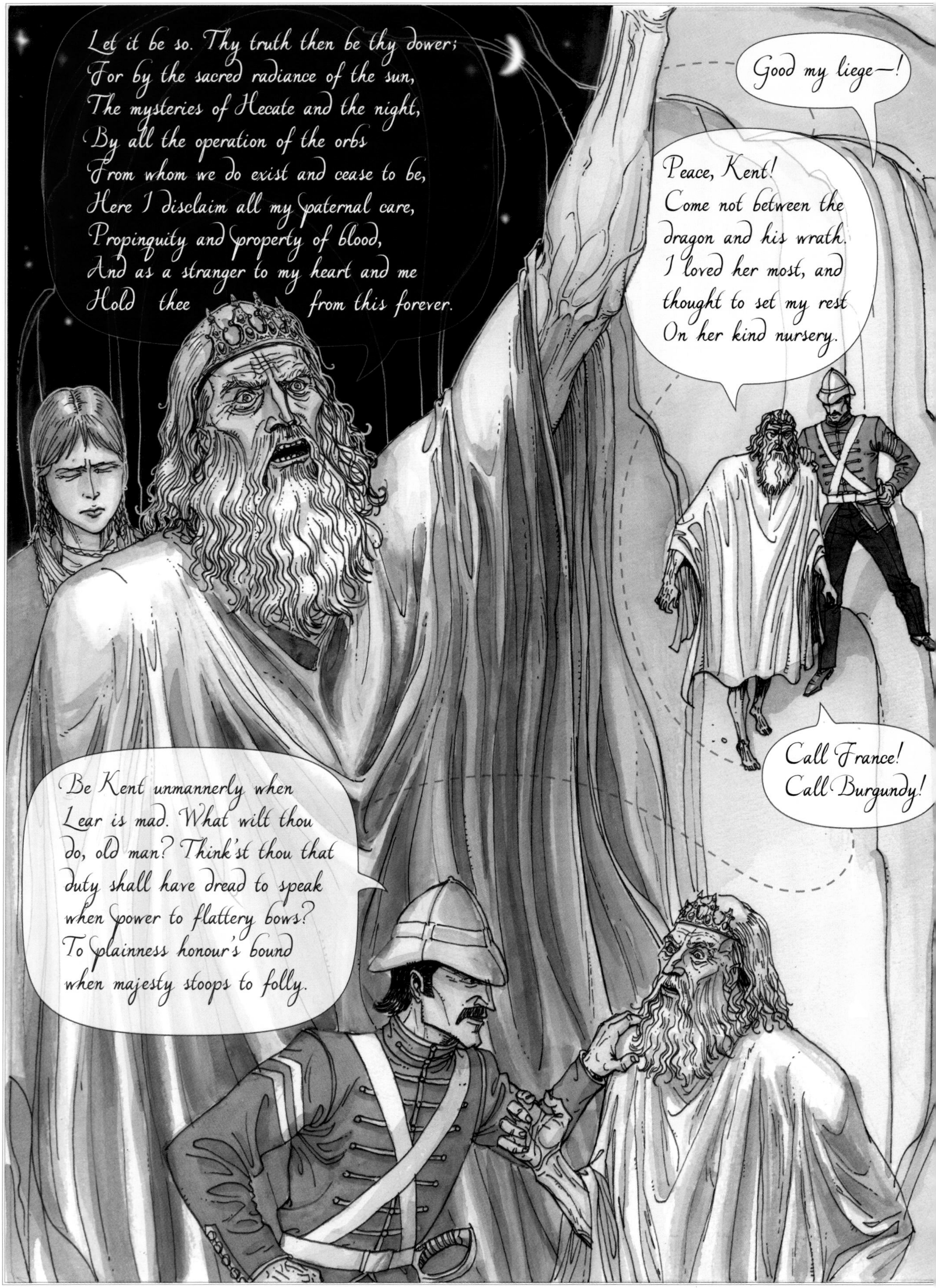
Let it be so. Thy truth then be thy dower;
For by the sacred radiance of the sun,
The mysteries of Hecate and the night,
By all the operation of the orbs
From whom we do exist and cease to be,
Here I disclaim all my paternal care,
Propinquity and property of blood,
And as a stranger to my heart and me
Hold thee from this forever.
Good my liege—!
Peace, Kent!
Come not between the dragon and his wrath.
I loved her most, and thought to set my rest
On her kind nursery.
Call France!
Call Burgundy!
Be Kent unmannerly when Lear is mad. What wilt thou do, old man? Think'st thou that duty shall have dread to speak when power to flattery bows? To plainness honour's bound when majesty stoops to folly.

K

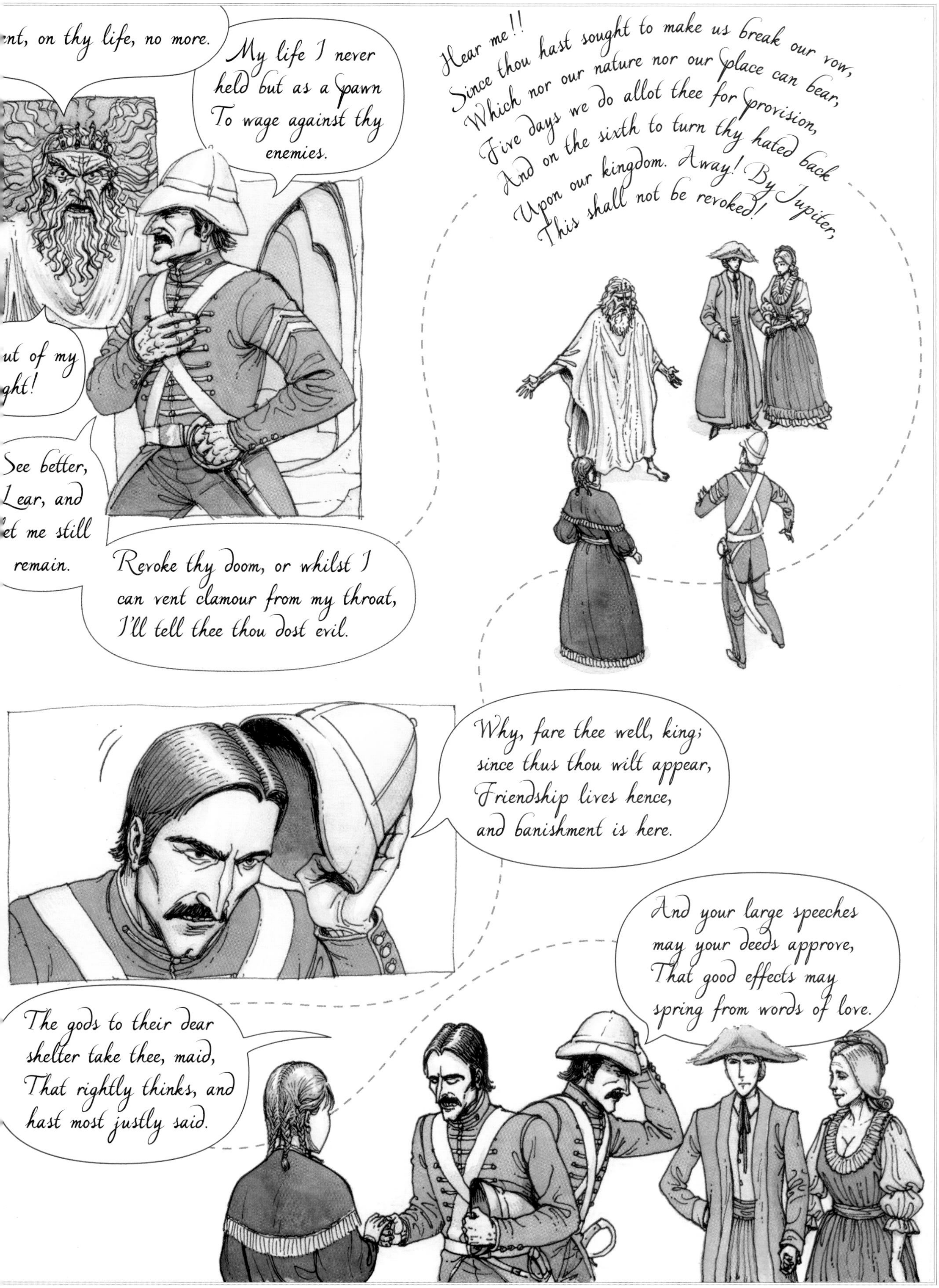

...nt, on thy life, no more.
My life I never held but as a pawn To wage against thy enemies.
...ut of my ...ght!
See better, Lear, and ...et me still remain.
Revoke thy doom, or whilst I can vent clamour from my throat, I'll tell thee thou dost evil.
Hear me!! Since thou hast sought to make us break our vow, Which nor our nature nor our place can bear, Five days we do allot thee for provision, And on the sixth to turn thy hated back Upon our kingdom. Away! By Jupiter, This shall not be revoked!
Why, fare thee well, king; since thus thou wilt appear, Friendship lives hence, and banishment is here.
The gods to their dear shelter take thee, maid, That rightly thinks, and hast most justly said.
And your large speeches may your deeds approve, That good effects may spring from words of love.

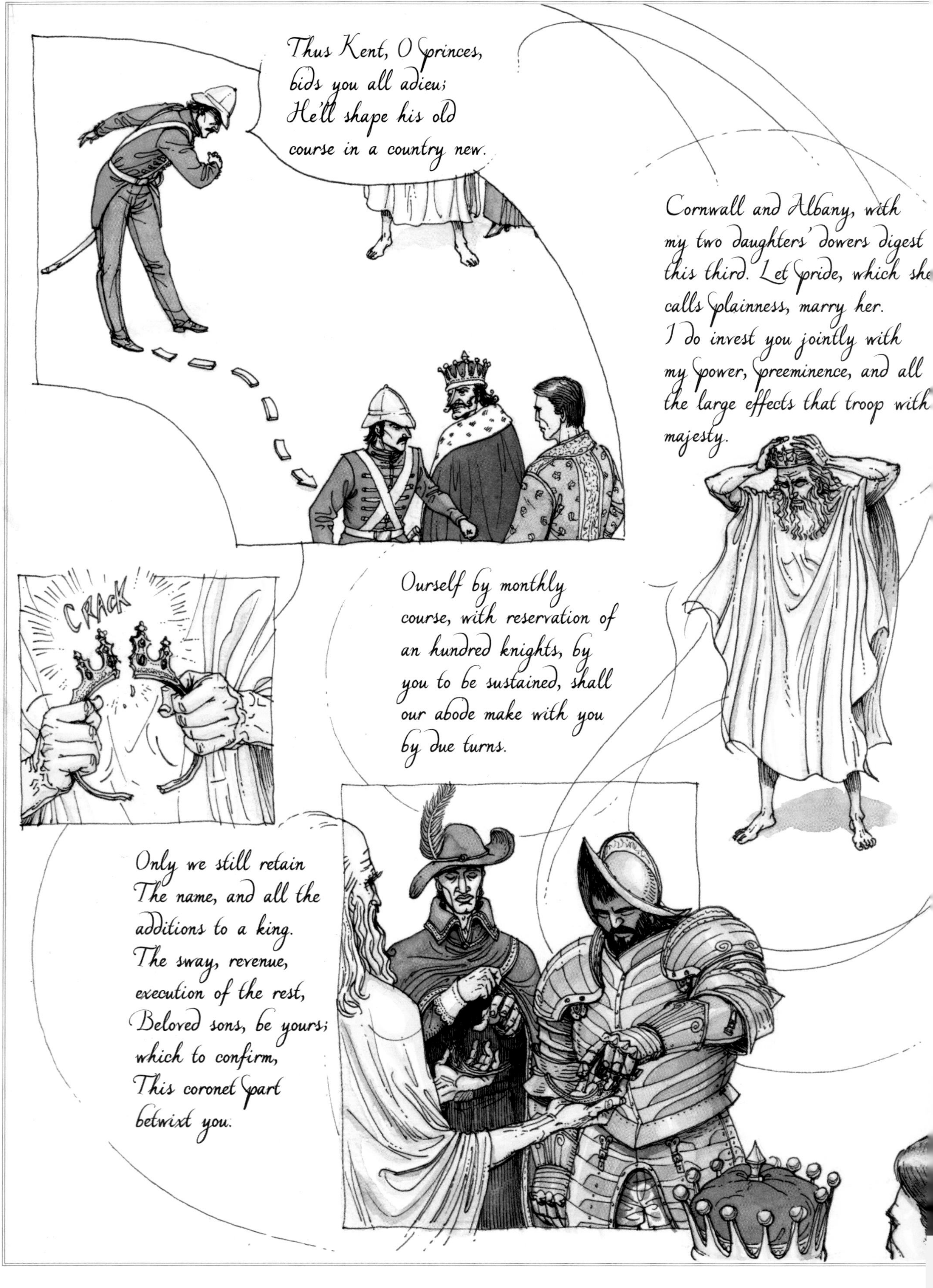
Thus Kent, O princes, bids you all adieu; He'll shape his old course in a country new.
Cornwall and Albany, with my two daughters' dowers digest this third. Let pride, which she calls plainness, marry her. I do invest you jointly with my power, preeminence, and all the large effects that troop with majesty.
Ourself by monthly course, with reservation of an hundred knights, by you to be sustained, shall our abode make with you by due turns.
CRACK
Only we still retain The name, and all the additions to a king. The sway, revenue, execution of the rest, Beloved sons, be yours; which to confirm, This coronet part betwixt you.

K

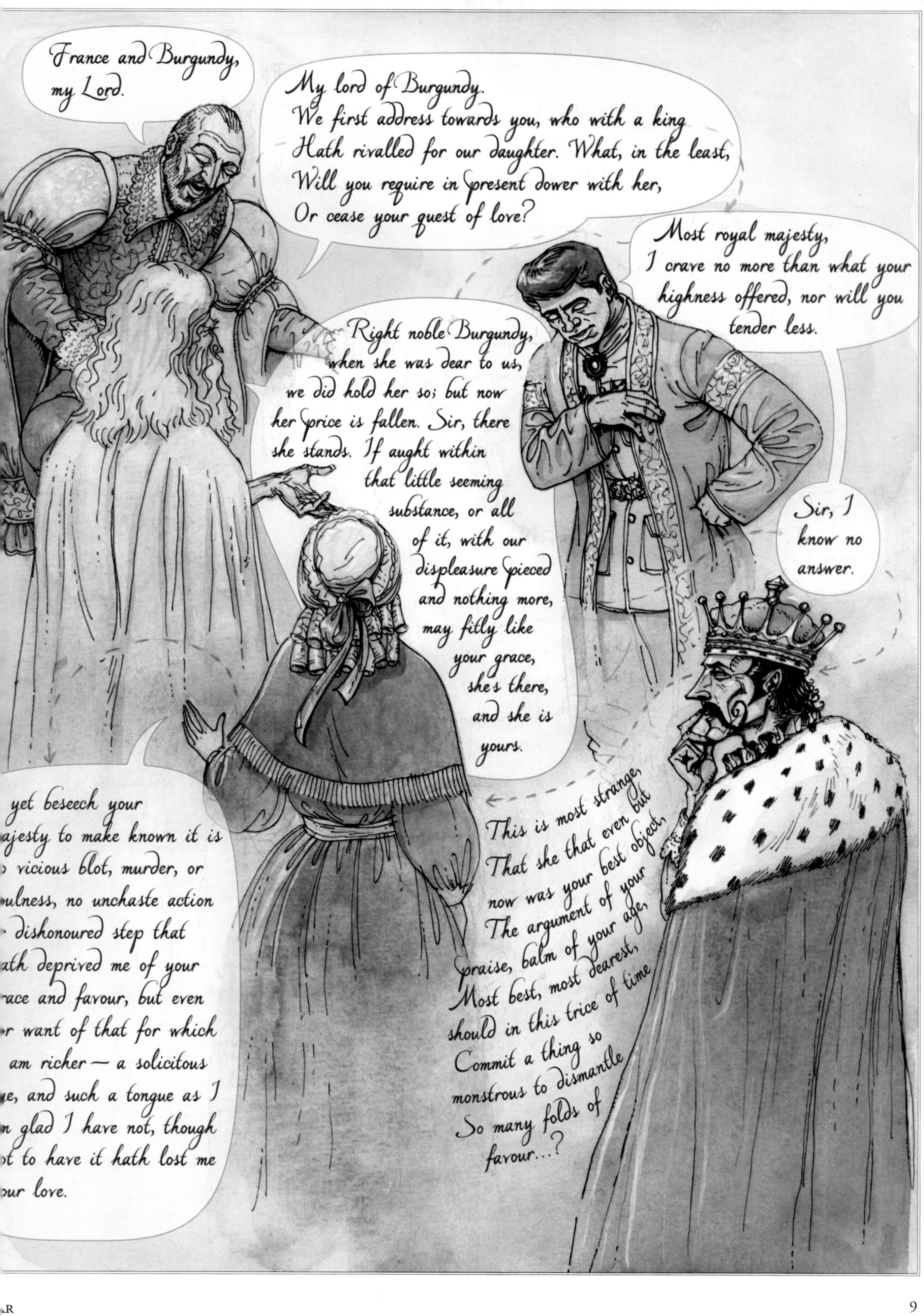
France and Burgundy, my Lord.
My lord of Burgundy. We first address towards you, who with a king Hath rivalled for our daughter. What, in the least, Will you require in present dower with her, Or cease your quest of love?
Most royal majesty, I crave no more than what your highness offered, nor will you tender less.
Right noble Burgundy, when she was dear to us, we did hold her so; but now her price is fallen. Sir, there she stands. If aught within that little seeming substance, or all of it, with our displeasure pieced and nothing more, may fitly like your grace, she's there, and she is yours.
Sir, I know no answer.
yet beseech your ajesty to make known it is vicious blot, murder, or ulness, no unchaste action dishonoured step that ath deprived me of your race and favour, but even r want of that for which am richer — a solicitous e, and such a tongue as I n glad I have not, though t to have it hath lost me ur love.
This is most strange, That she that even but now was your best object, The argument of your praise, balm of your age, Most best, most dearest, should in this trice of time Commit a thing so monstrous to dismantle So many folds of favour...?

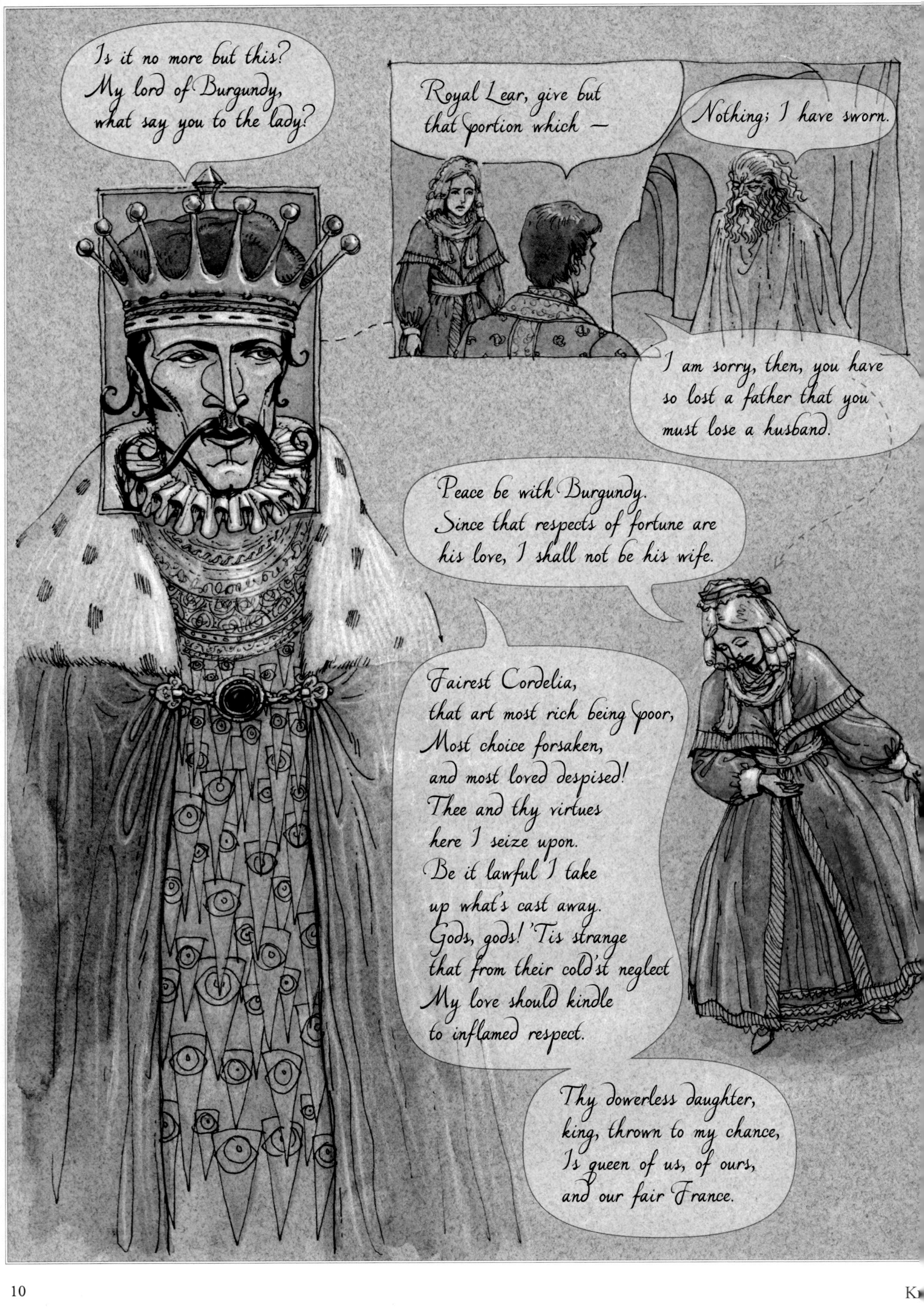
Is it no more but this? My lord of Burgundy, what say you to the lady?
Royal Lear, give but that portion which —
Nothing; I have sworn.
I am sorry, then, you have so lost a father that you must lose a husband.
Peace be with Burgundy. Since that respects of fortune are his love, I shall not be his wife.
Fairest Cordelia, that art most rich being poor, Most choice forsaken, and most loved despised! Thee and thy virtues here I seize upon. Be it lawful I take up what's cast away. Gods, gods! 'Tis strange that from their cold'st neglect My love should kindle to inflamed respect.
Thy dowerless daughter, king, thrown to my chance, Is queen of us, of ours, and our fair France.

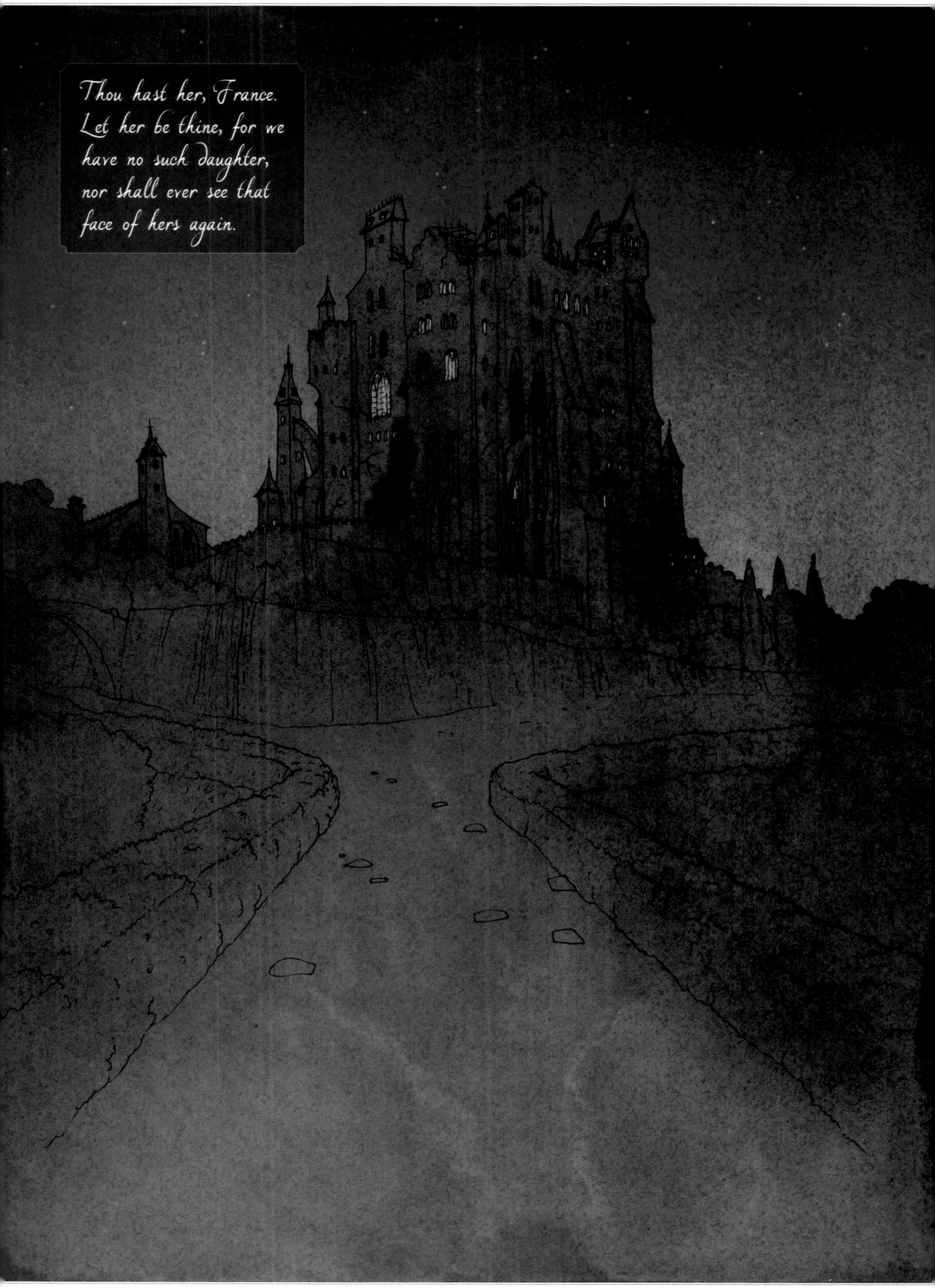
Thou hast her, France. Let her be thine, for we have no such daughter, nor shall ever see that face of hers again.

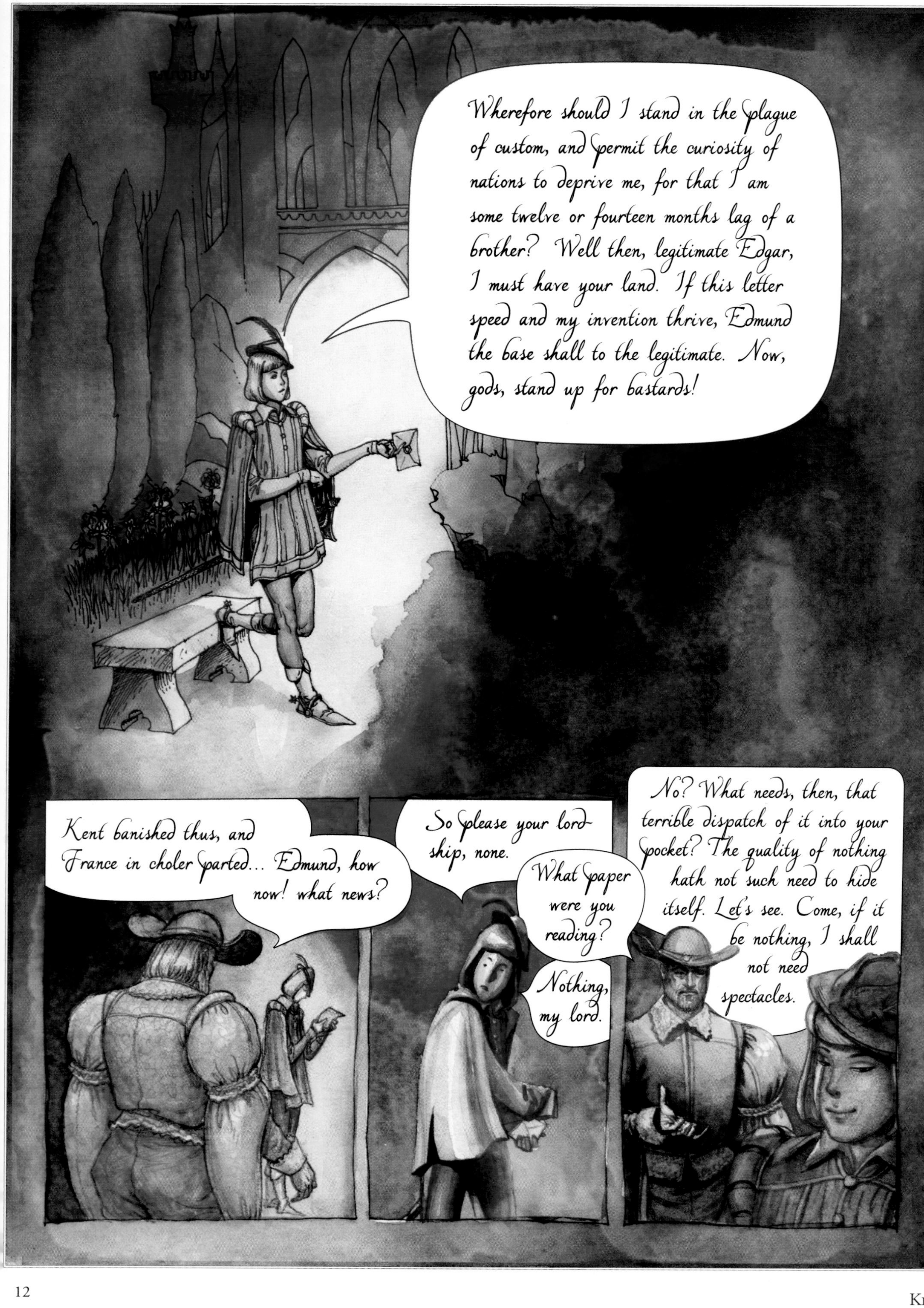
Wherefore should I stand in the plague of custom, and permit the curiosity of nations to deprive me, for that I am some twelve or fourteen months lag of a brother? Well then, legitimate Edgar, I must have your land. If this letter speed and my invention thrive, Edmund the base shall to the legitimate. Now, gods, stand up for bastards!
Kent banished thus, and France in choler parted... Edmund, how now! what news?
So please your lordship, none.
What paper were you reading?
Nothing, my lord.
No? What needs, then, that terrible dispatch of it into your pocket? The quality of nothing hath not such need to hide itself. Let's see. Come, if it be nothing, I shall not need spectacles.

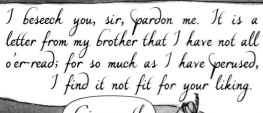

I beseech you, sir, pardon me. It is a letter from my brother that I have not all o'er-read; for so much as I have perused, I find it not fit for your liking.

Give me the letter, sir.

Hum, conspiracy! "Slept till I waked him, you should enjoy half his revenue" — my son Edgar! Had he a hand to write this, a heart and brain to breed it in? You know the character to be your brother's?

It is his hand, my lord, but I hope his heart is not in the contents.

Find out this villain, Edmund. It shall lose thee nothing. Do it carefully.

These late eclipses in the sun and moon portend no good to us. Though the wisdom of nature can reason thus and thus, yet nature finds itself scourged by the sequent effects. Love cools, friendship falls off, brothers divide; in cities mutinies, in countries discord, in palaces treason, and the bond cracked 'twixt son and father.

This is the excellent foppery of the world, that when we are sick in fortune, we make guilty of our disasters the sun, the moon, and the stars, as if we were villains by necessity, fools by heavenly compulsion. Tut! I should have been that I am had the maidenliest star in the firmament twinkled on my bastardy.

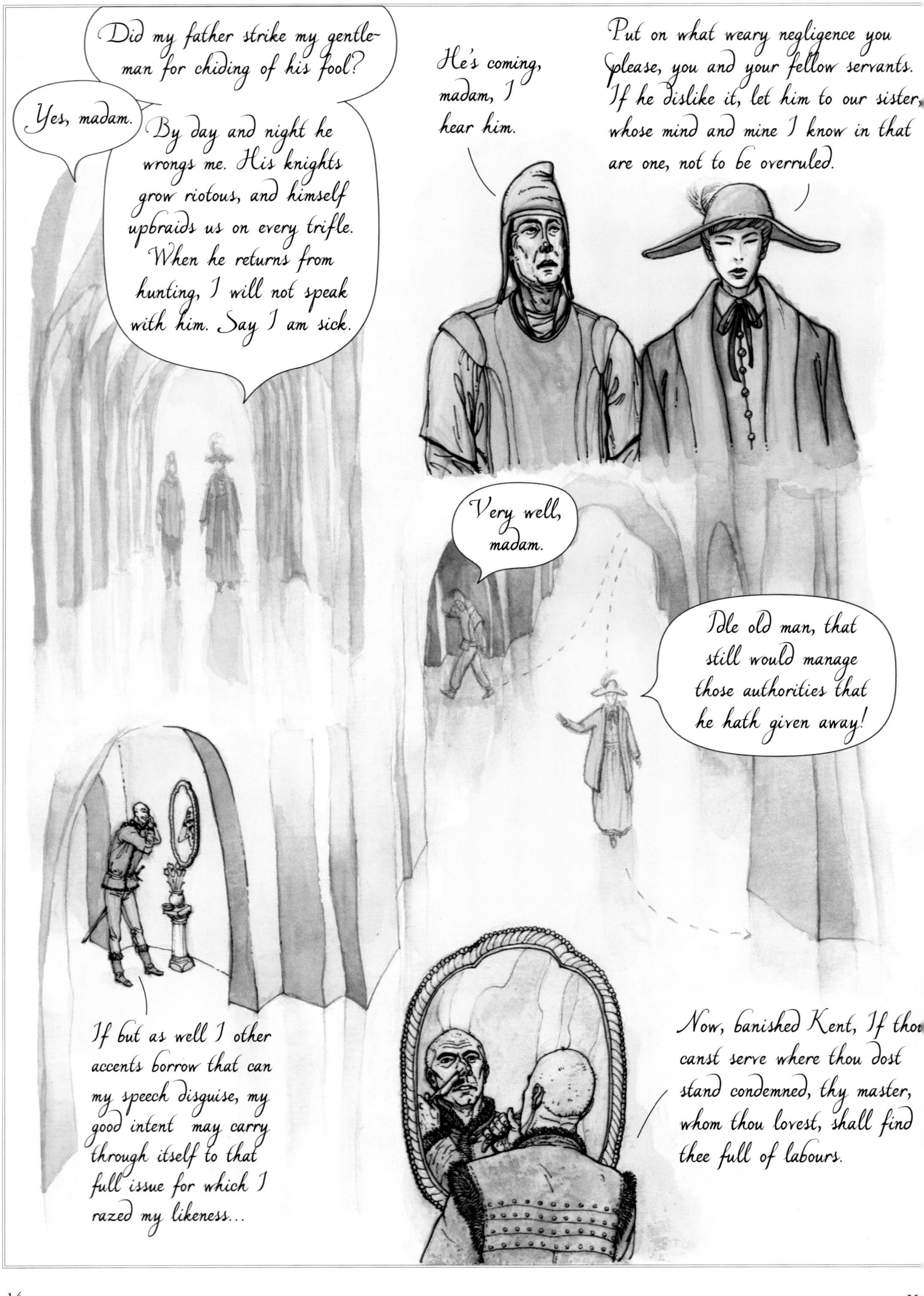
Did my father strike my gentleman for chiding of his fool?
Yes, madam.
By day and night he wrongs me. His knights grow riotous, and himself upbraids us on every trifle. When he returns from hunting, I will not speak with him. Say I am sick.
He's coming, madam, I hear him.
Put on what weary negligence you please, you and your fellow servants. If he dislike it, let him to our sister, whose mind and mine I know in that are one, not to be overruled.
Very well, madam.
Idle old man, that still would manage those authorities that he hath given away!
If but as well I other accents borrow that can my speech disguise, my good intent may carry through itself to that full issue for which I razed my likeness...
Now, banished Kent, If thou canst serve where thou dost stand condemned, thy master, whom thou lovest, shall find thee full of labours.

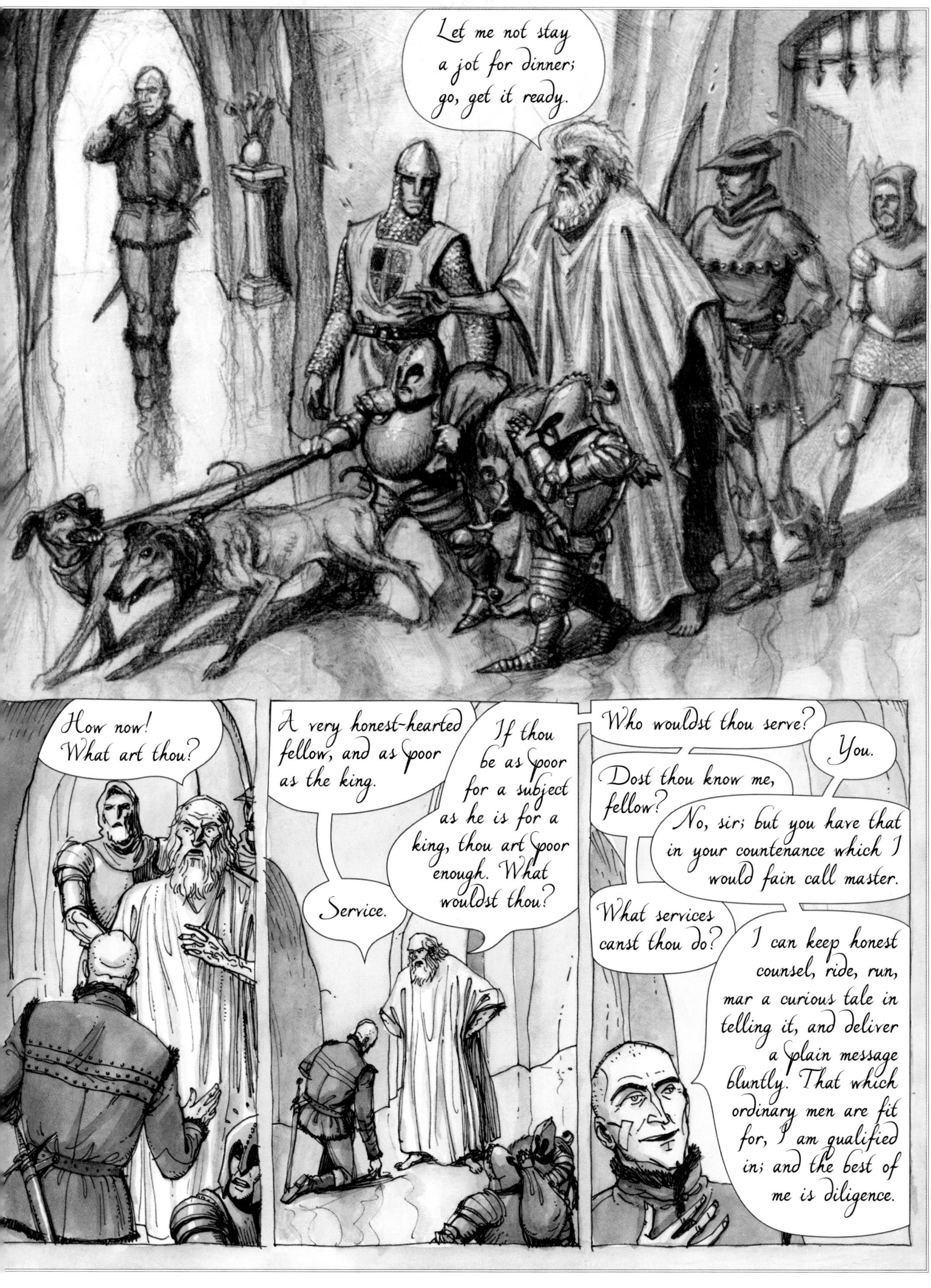
Let me not stay a jot for dinner; go, get it ready.
How now! What art thou?
A very honest-hearted fellow, and as poor as the king.
If thou be as poor for a subject as he is for a king, thou art poor enough. What wouldst thou?
Service.
Who wouldst thou serve?
You.
Dost thou know me, fellow?
No, sir; but you have that in your countenance which I would fain call master.
What services canst thou do?
I can keep honest counsel, ride, run, mar a curious tale in telling it, and deliver a plain message bluntly. That which ordinary men are fit for, I am qualified in; and the best of me is diligence.

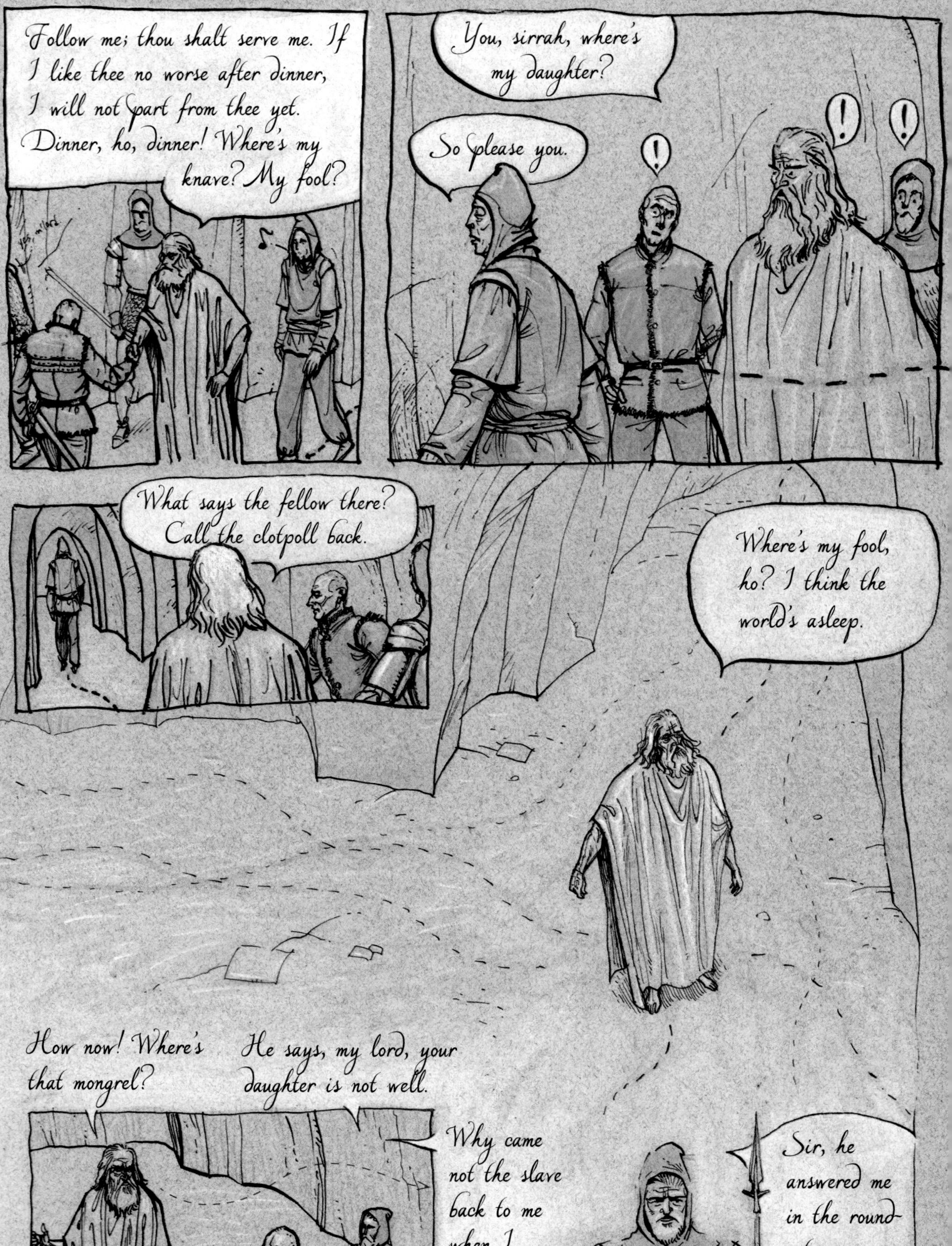

Follow me; thou shalt serve me. If I like thee no worse after dinner, I will not part from thee yet. Dinner, ho, dinner! Where's my knave? My fool?
You, sirrah, where's my daughter?
So please you.
What says the fellow there? Call the clotpoll back.
Where's my fool, ho? I think the world's asleep.
How now! Where's that mongrel?
He says, my lord, your daughter is not well.
Why came not the slave back to me when I called him?
Sir, he answered me in the roundest manner, he would not.

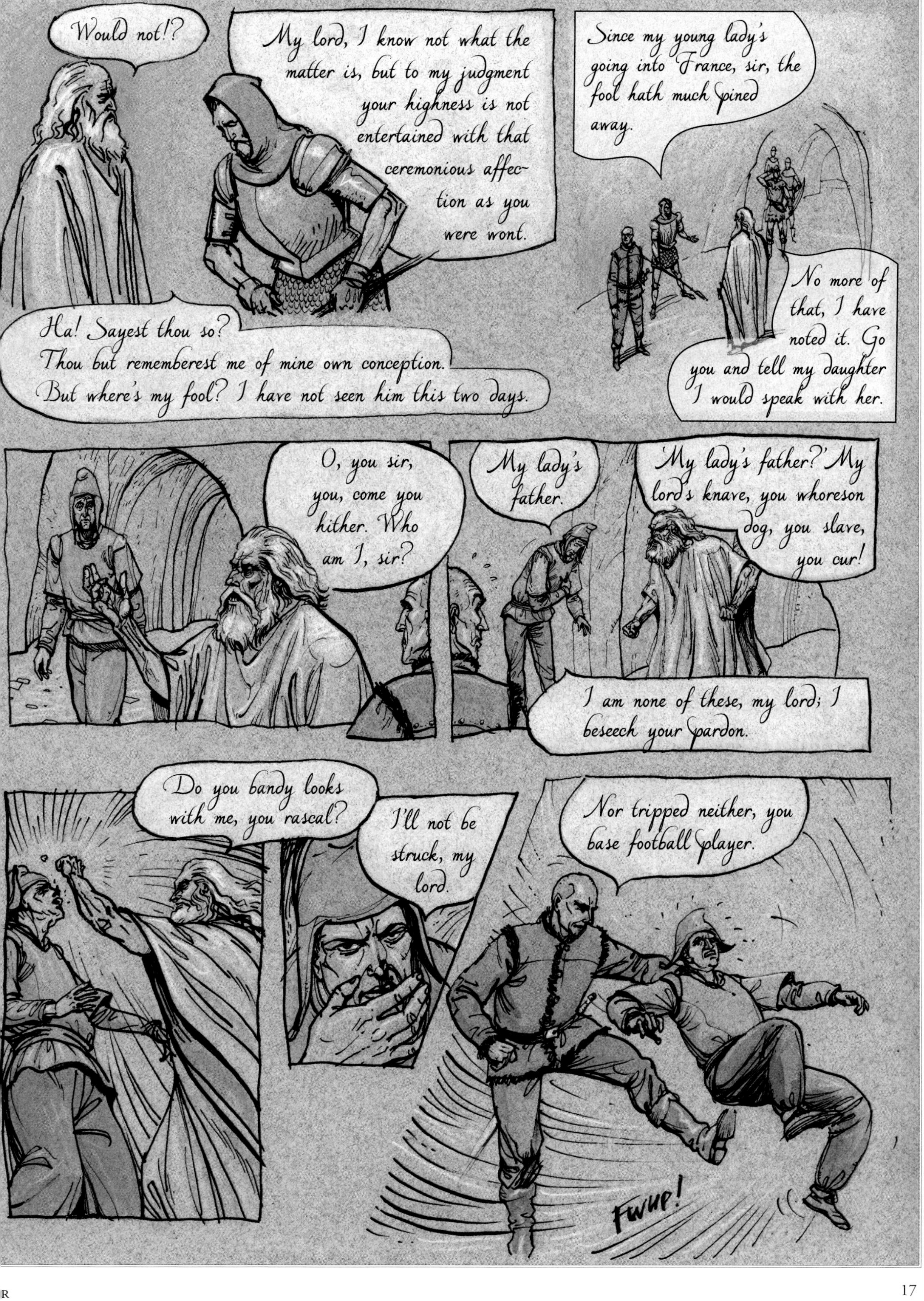
Would not!?
My lord, I know not what the matter is, but to my judgment your highness is not entertained with that ceremonious affection as you were wont.
Ha! Sayest thou so? Thou but rememberest me of mine own conception. But where's my fool? I have not seen him this two days.
Since my young lady's going into France, sir, the fool hath much pined away.
No more of that, I have noted it. Go you and tell my daughter I would speak with her.
O, you sir, you, come you hither. Who am I, sir?
My lady's father.
'My lady's father?' My lord's knave, you whoreson dog, you slave, you cur!
I am none of these, my lord; I beseech your pardon.
Do you bandy looks with me, you rascal?
I'll not be struck, my lord.
Nor tripped neither, you base football player.
FWUP!

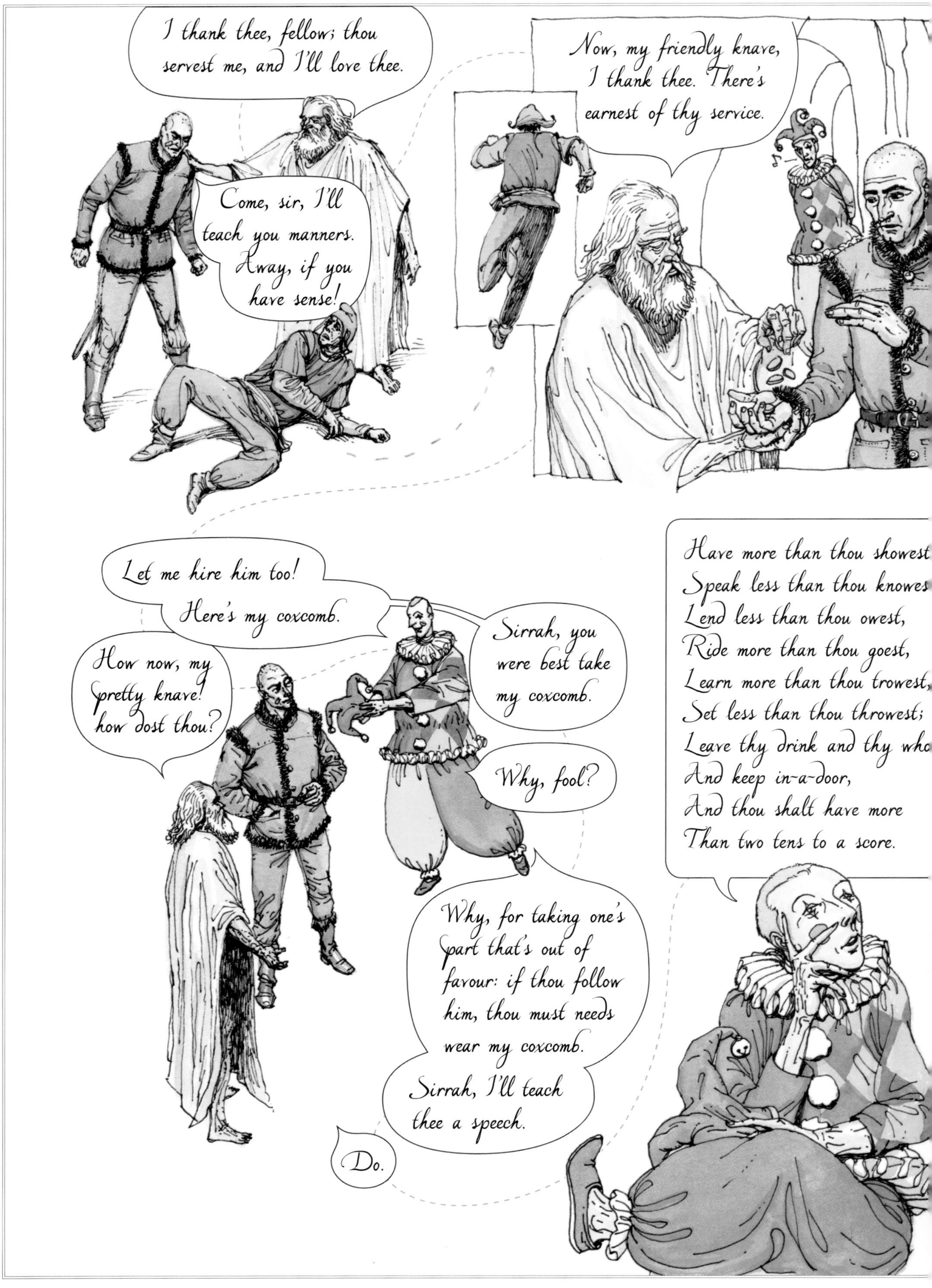
I thank thee, fellow; thou servest me, and I'll love thee.
Come, sir, I'll teach you manners. Away, if you have sense!
Now, my friendly knave, I thank thee. There's earnest of thy service.
Let me hire him too! Here's my coxcomb.
How now, my pretty knave! how dost thou?
Sirrah, you were best take my coxcomb.
Why, fool?
Why, for taking one's part that's out of favour: if thou follow him, thou must needs wear my coxcomb.
Sirrah, I'll teach thee a speech.
Do.
Have more than thou showest
Speak less than thou knowes
Lend less than thou owest,
Ride more than thou goest,
Learn more than thou trowest,
Set less than thou throwest;
Leave thy drink and thy who
And keep in-a-door,
And thou shalt have more
Than two tens to a score.

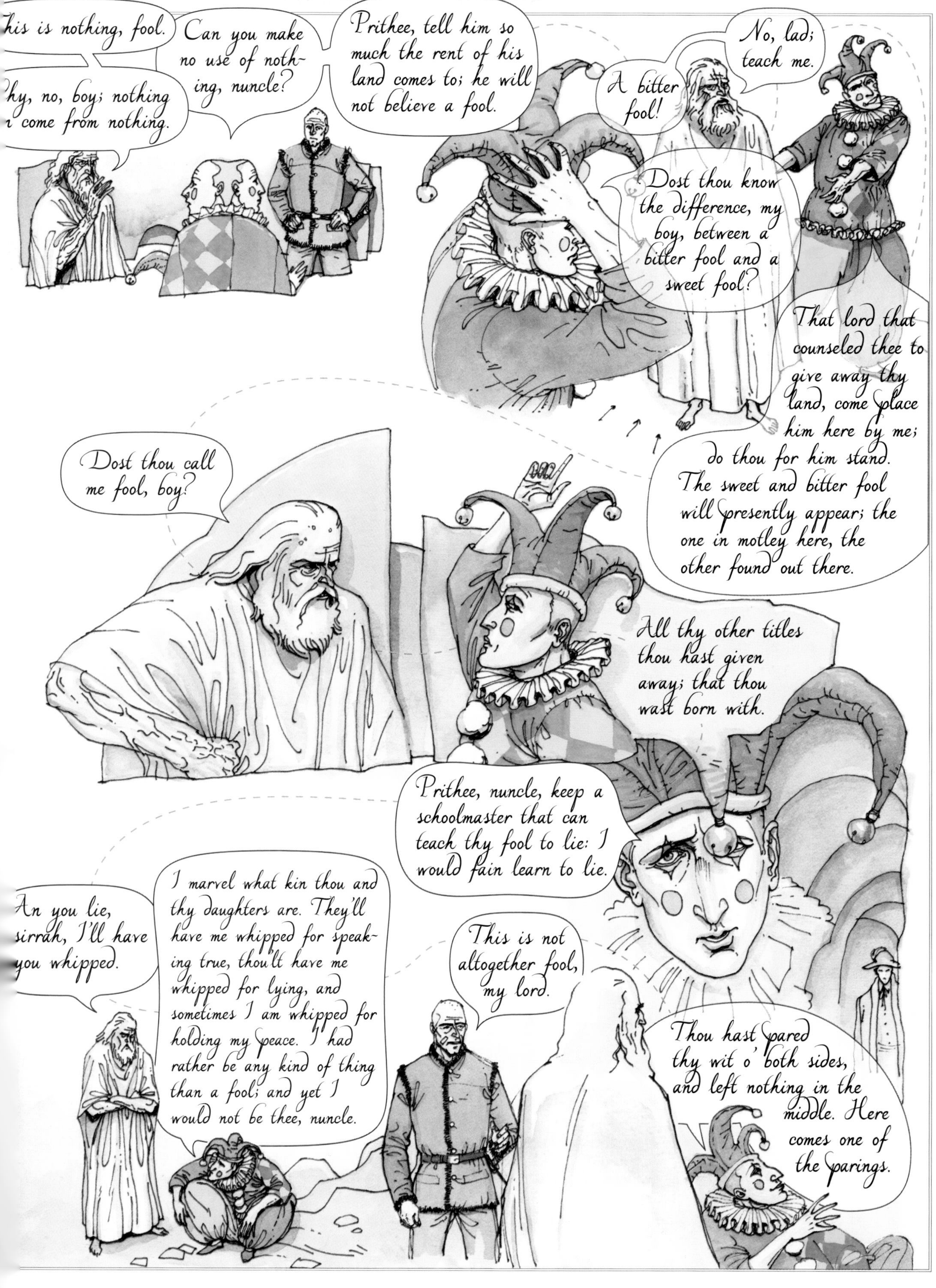
his is nothing, fool.
Can you make no use of nothing, nuncle?
hy, no, boy; nothing n come from nothing.
Prithee, tell him so much the rent of his land comes to; he will not believe a fool.
A bitter fool!
No, lad; teach me.
Dost thou know the difference, my boy, between a bitter fool and a sweet fool?
That lord that counseled thee to give away thy land, come place him here by me; do thou for him stand. The sweet and bitter fool will presently appear; the one in motley here, the other found out there.
Dost thou call me fool, boy?
All thy other titles thou hast given away; that thou wast born with.
Prithee, nuncle, keep a schoolmaster that can teach thy fool to lie: I would fain learn to lie.
An you lie, sirrah, I'll have you whipped.
I marvel what kin thou and thy daughters are. They'll have me whipped for speaking true, thou'lt have me whipped for lying, and sometimes I am whipped for holding my peace. I had rather be any kind of thing than a fool; and yet I would not be thee, nuncle.
This is not altogether fool, my lord.
Thou hast pared thy wit o' both sides, and left nothing in the middle. Here comes one of the parings.

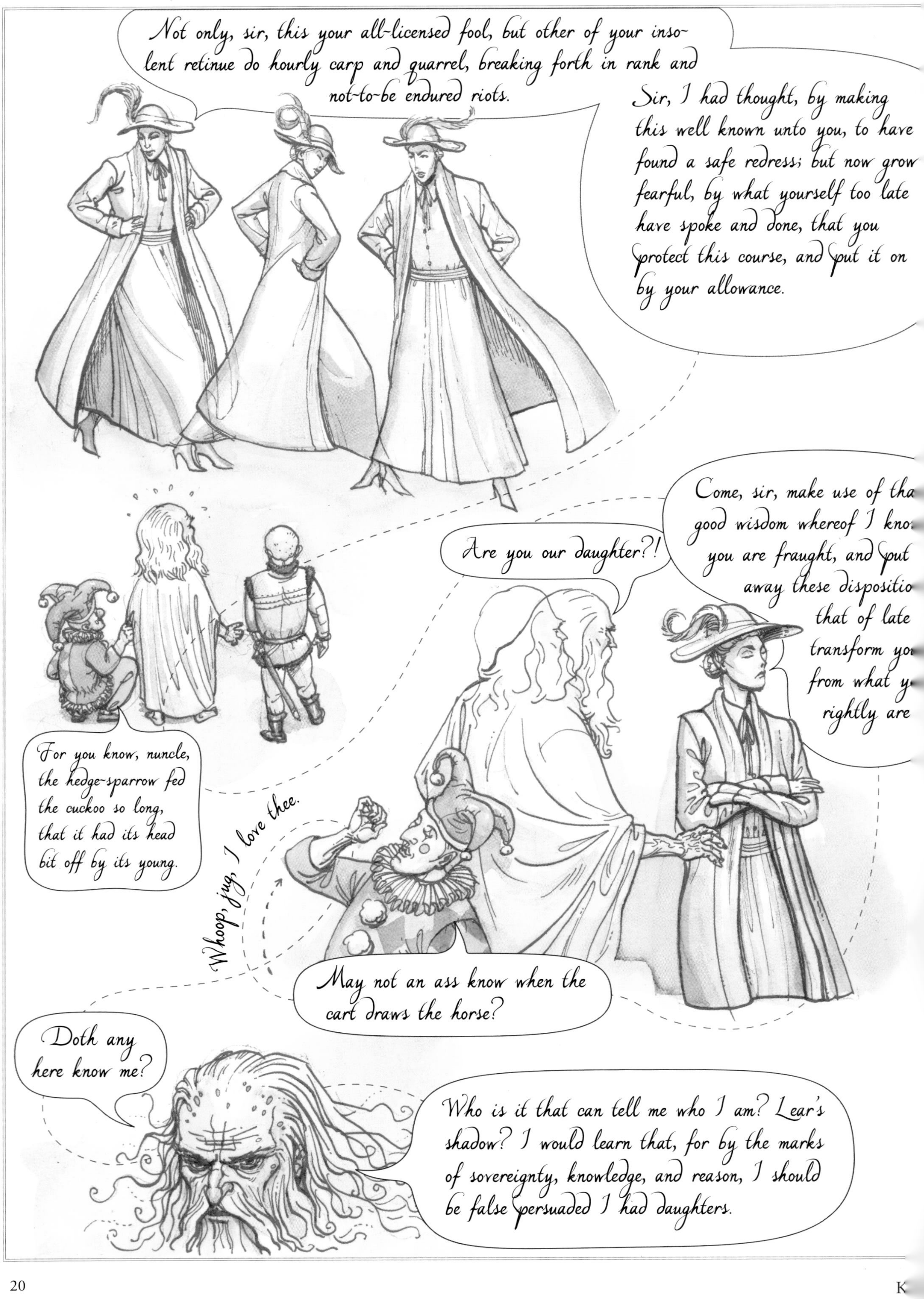

Not only, sir, this your all-licensed fool, but other of your insolent retinue do hourly carp and quarrel, breaking forth in rank and not-to-be endured riots.
Sir, I had thought, by making this well known unto you, to have found a safe redress; but now grow fearful, by what yourself too late have spoke and done, that you protect this course, and put it on by your allowance.
For you know, nuncle, the hedge-sparrow fed the cuckoo so long, that it had its head bit off by its young.
Whoop, jug, I love thee.
Are you our daughter?!
Come, sir, make use of tha good wisdom whereof I kno you are fraught, and put away these dispositio that of late transform yo from what y rightly are
May not an ass know when the cart draws the horse?
Doth any here know me?
Who is it that can tell me who I am? Lear's shadow? I would learn that, for by the marks of sovereignty, knowledge, and reason, I should be false persuaded I had daughters.

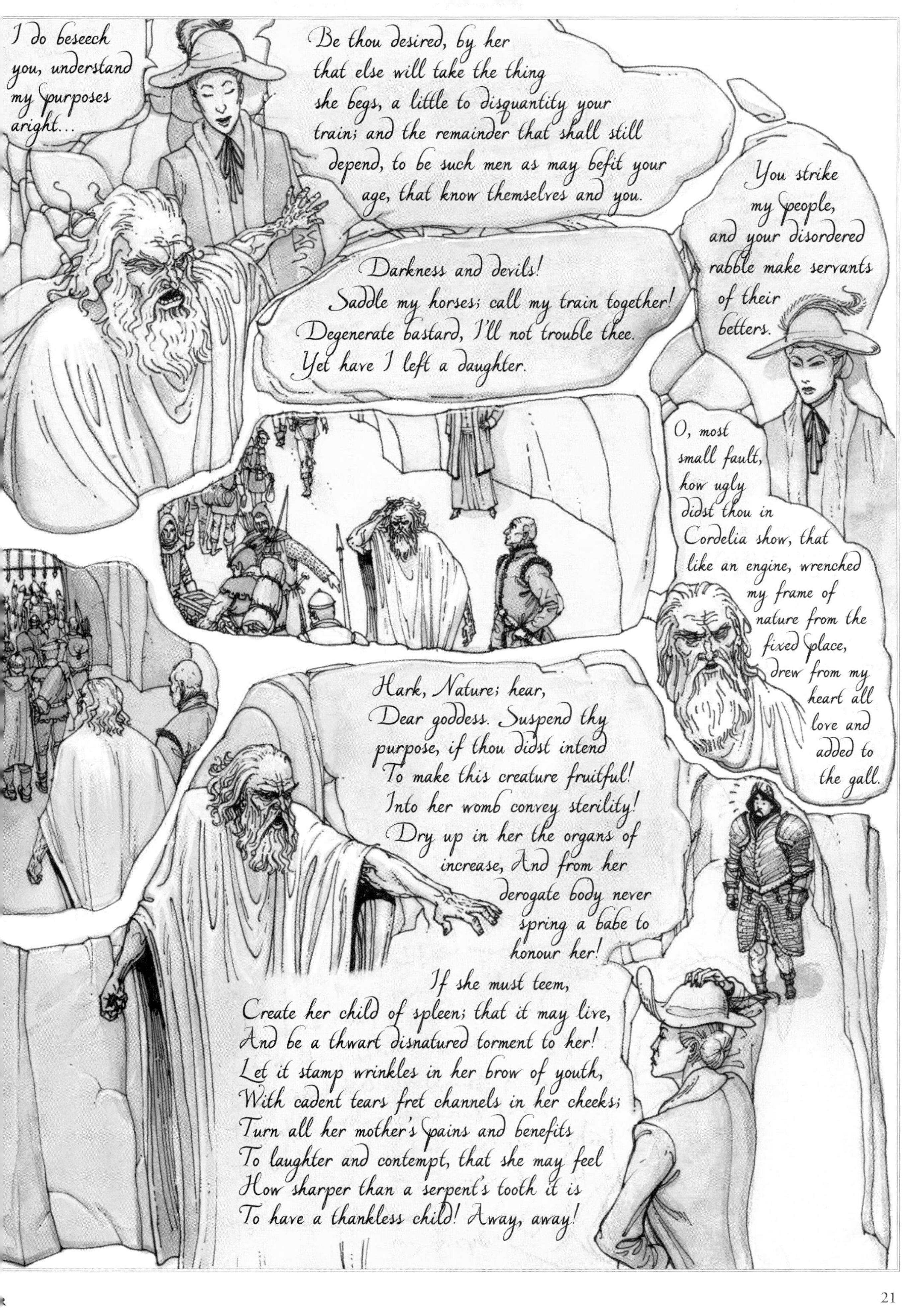

I do beseech you, understand my purposes aright...
Be thou desired, by her that else will take the thing she begs, a little to disquantity your train; and the remainder that shall still depend, to be such men as may befit your age, that know themselves and you.
Darkness and devils! Saddle my horses; call my train together! Degenerate bastard, I'll not trouble thee. Yet have I left a daughter.
You strike my people, and your disordered rabble make servants of their betters.
O, most small fault, how ugly didst thou in Cordelia show, that like an engine, wrenched my frame of nature from the fixed place, drew from my heart all love and added to the gall.
Hark, Nature; hear, Dear goddess. Suspend thy purpose, if thou didst intend To make this creature fruitful! Into her womb convey sterility! Dry up in her the organs of increase, And from her derogate body never spring a babe to honour her!
If she must teem, Create her child of spleen; that it may live, And be a thwart disnatured torment to her! Let it stamp wrinkles in her brow of youth, With cadent tears fret channels in her cheeks; Turn all her mother's pains and benefits To laughter and contempt, that she may feel How sharper than a serpent's tooth it is To have a thankless child! Away, away!

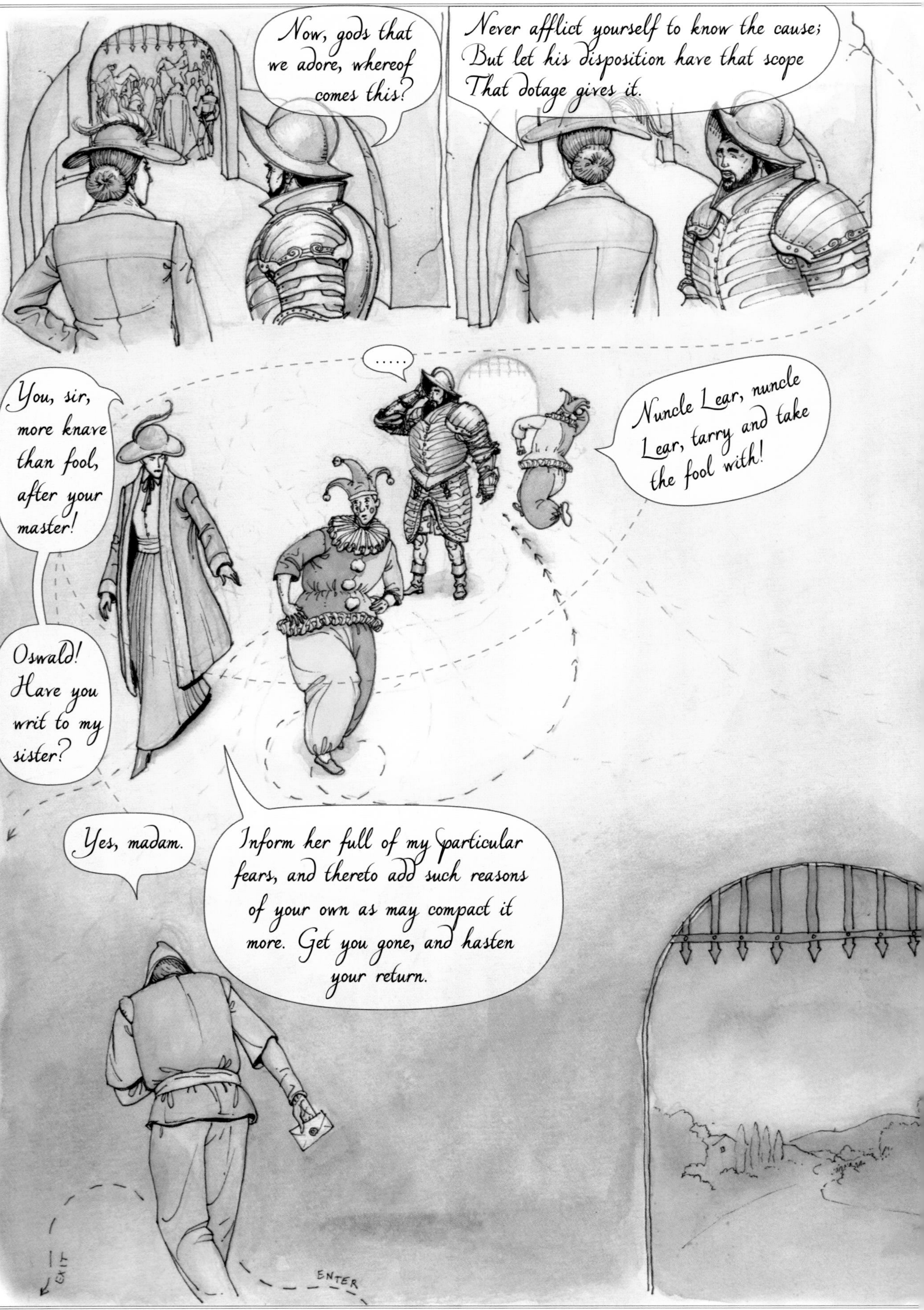

Now, gods that we adore, whereof comes this?
Never afflict yourself to know the cause; But let his disposition have that scope That dotage gives it.
.....
Nuncle Lear, nuncle Lear, tarry and take the fool with!
You, sir, more knave than fool, after your master!
Oswald! Have you writ to my sister?
Yes, madam.
Inform her full of my particular fears, and thereto add such reasons of your own as may compact it more. Get you gone, and hasten your return.
EXIT
ENTER

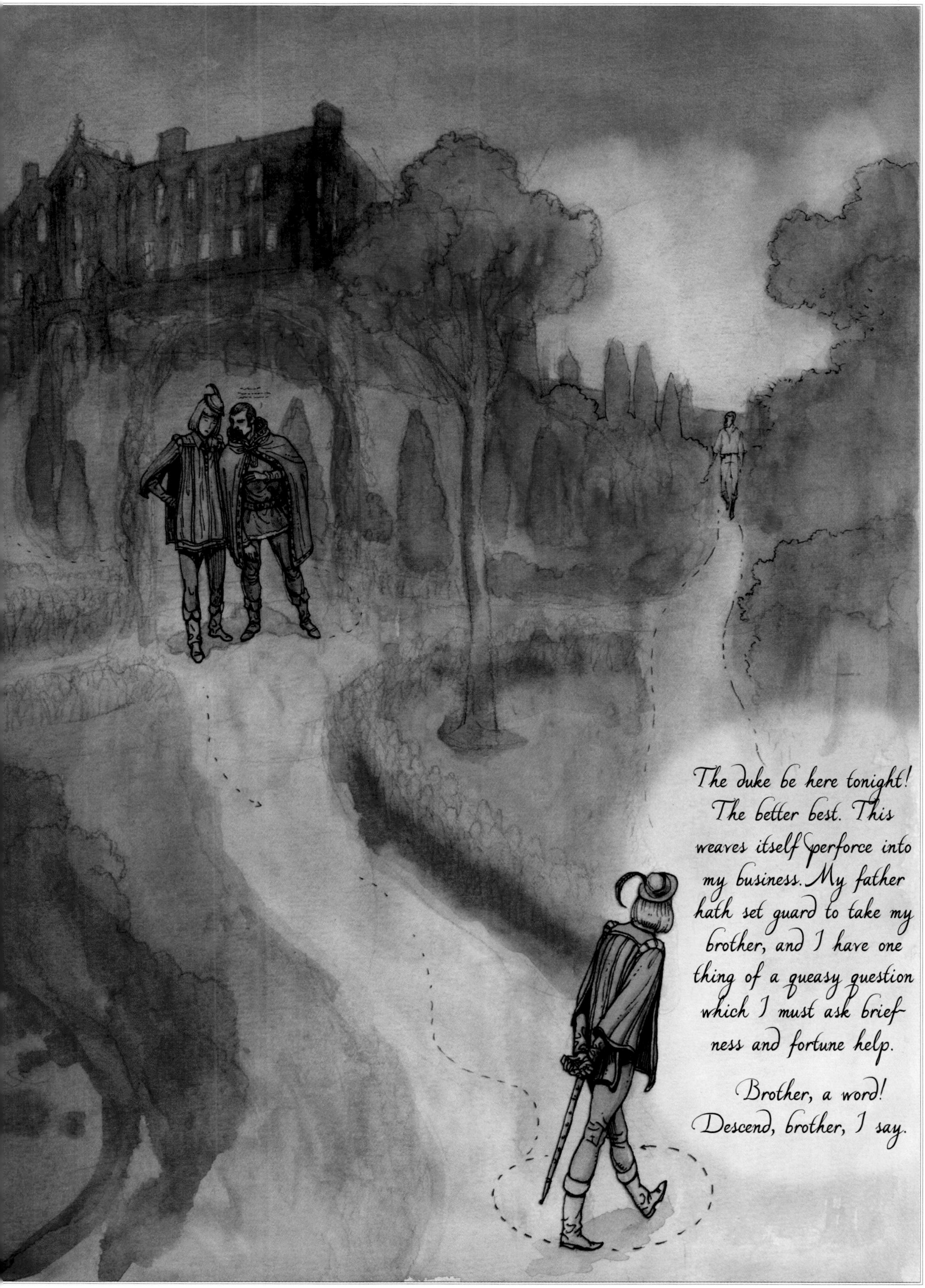
The duke be here tonight! The better best. This weaves itself perforce into my business. My father hath set guard to take my brother, and I have one thing of a queasy question which I must ask brief-ness and fortune help.
Brother, a word! Descend, brother, I say.

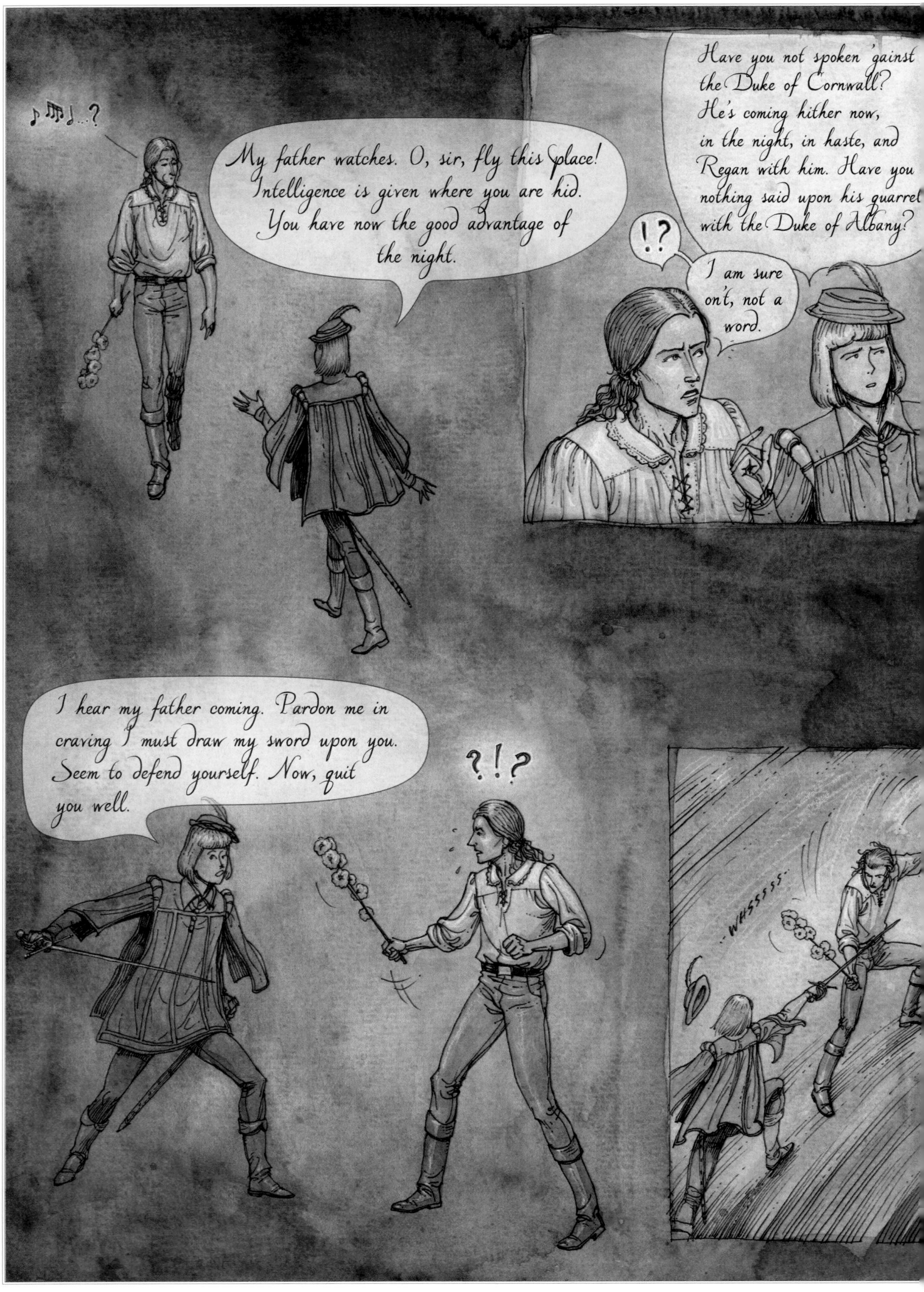

...?
My father watches. O, sir, fly this place! Intelligence is given where you are hid. You have now the good advantage of the night.
Have you not spoken 'gainst the Duke of Cornwall? He's coming hither now, in the night, in haste, and Regan with him. Have you nothing said upon his quarrel with the Duke of Albany?
!?
I am sure on't, not a word.
I hear my father coming. Pardon me in craving I must draw my sword upon you. Seem to defend yourself. Now, quit you well.
?!?
WHSSSSS...

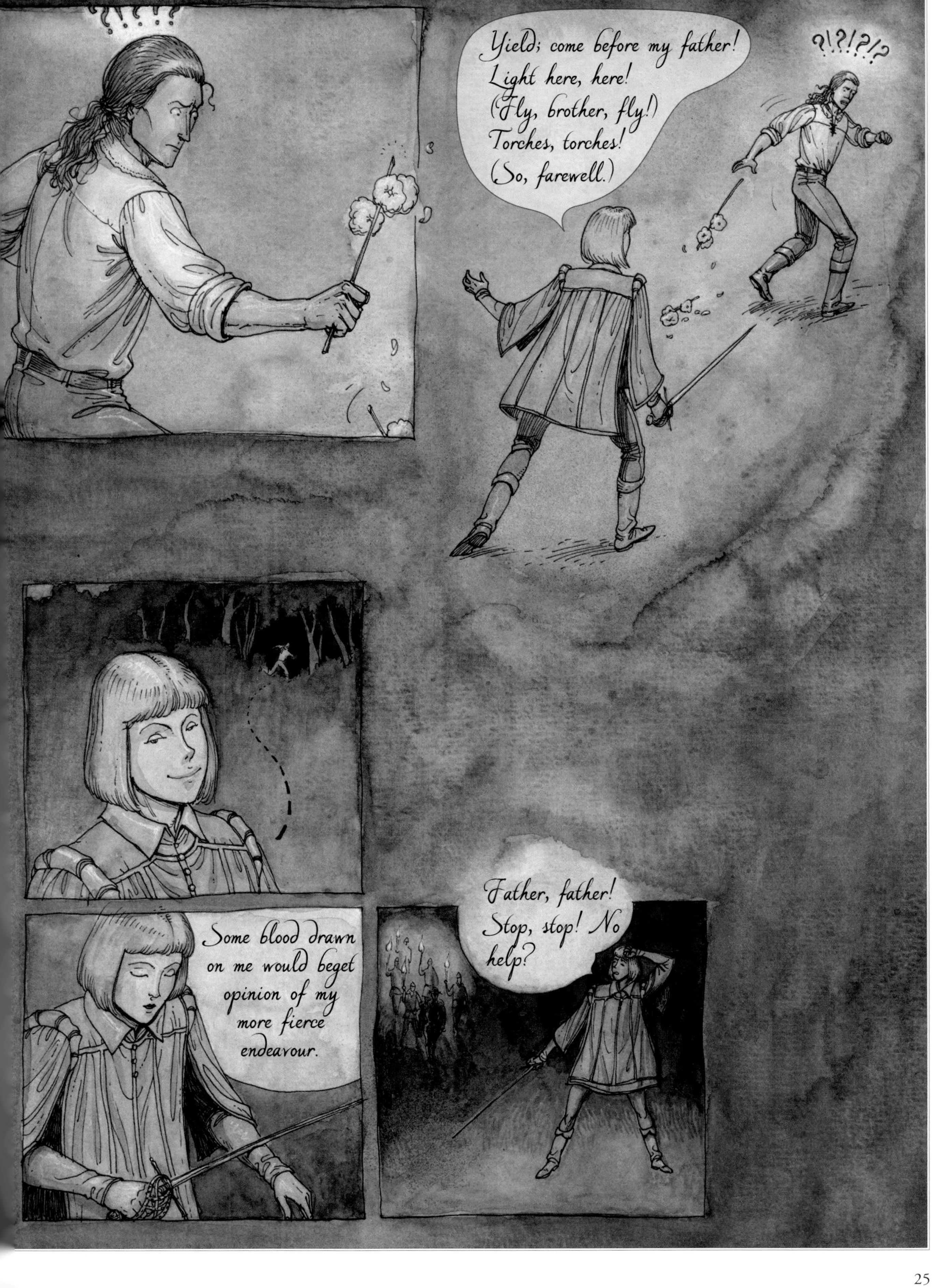
?!?!?
Yield; come before my father! Light here, here! (Fly, brother, fly!) Torches, torches! (So, farewell.)
?!?!?!?
Some blood drawn on me would beget opinion of my more fierce endeavour.
Father, father! Stop, stop! No help?

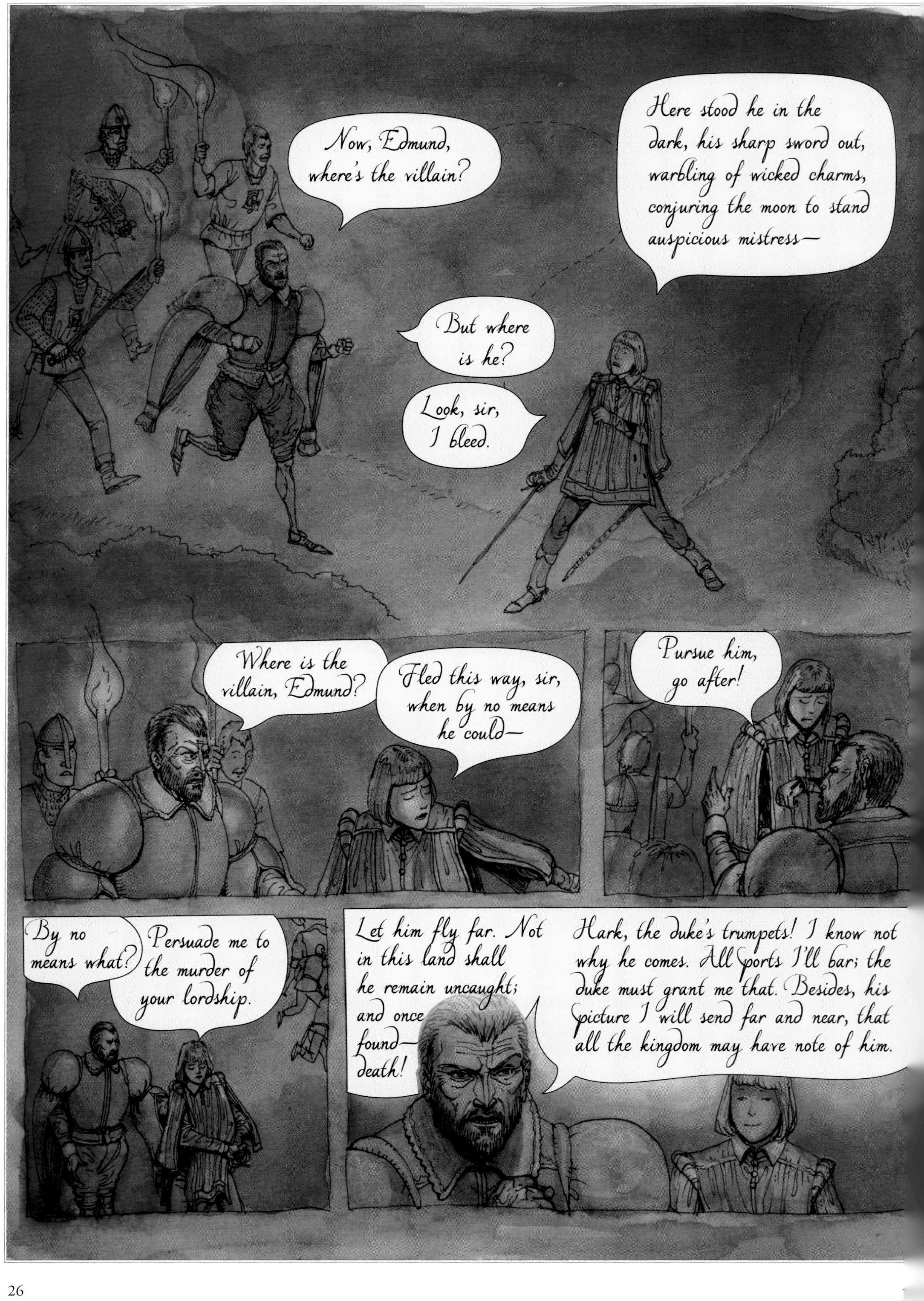
Now, Edmund, where's the villain?
Here stood he in the dark, his sharp sword out, warbling of wicked charms, conjuring the moon to stand auspicious mistress—
But where is he?
Look, sir, I bleed.
Where is the villain, Edmund?
Fled this way, sir, when by no means he could—
Pursue him, go after!
By no means what?
Persuade me to the murder of your lordship.
Let him fly far. Not in this land shall he remain uncaught; and once found—death!
Hark, the duke's trumpets! I know not why he comes. All ports I'll bar; the duke must grant me that. Besides, his picture I will send far and near, that all the kingdom may have note of him.

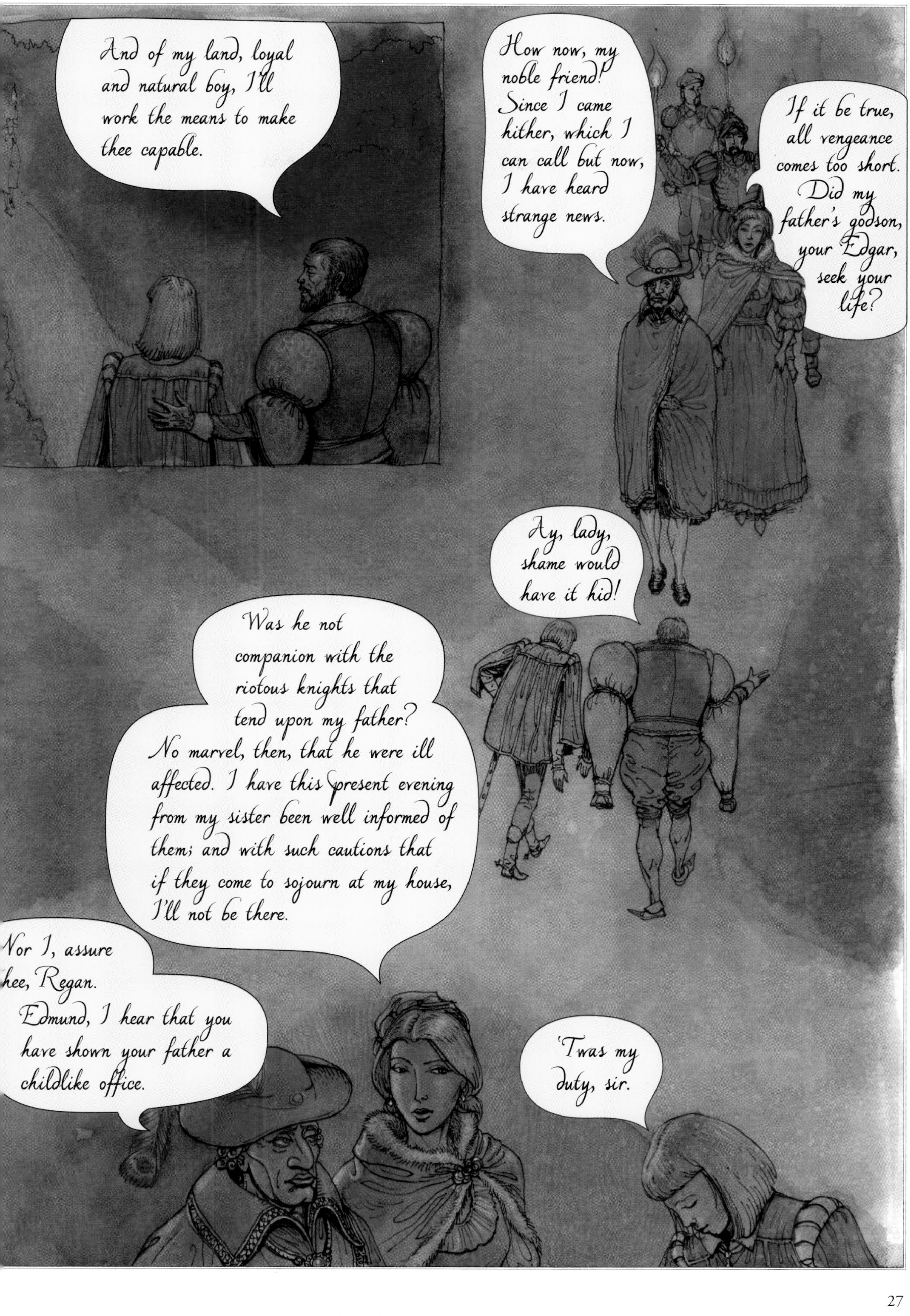

And of my land, loyal and natural boy, I'll work the means to make thee capable.
How now, my noble friend! Since I came hither, which I can call but now, I have heard strange news.
If it be true, all vengeance comes too short. Did my father's godson, your Edgar, seek your life?
Ay, lady, shame would have it hid!
Was he not companion with the riotous knights that tend upon my father? No marvel, then, that he were ill affected. I have this present evening from my sister been well informed of them; and with such cautions that if they come to sojourn at my house, I'll not be there.
Nor I, assure thee, Regan. Edmund, I hear that you have shown your father a childlike office.
'Twas my duty, sir.

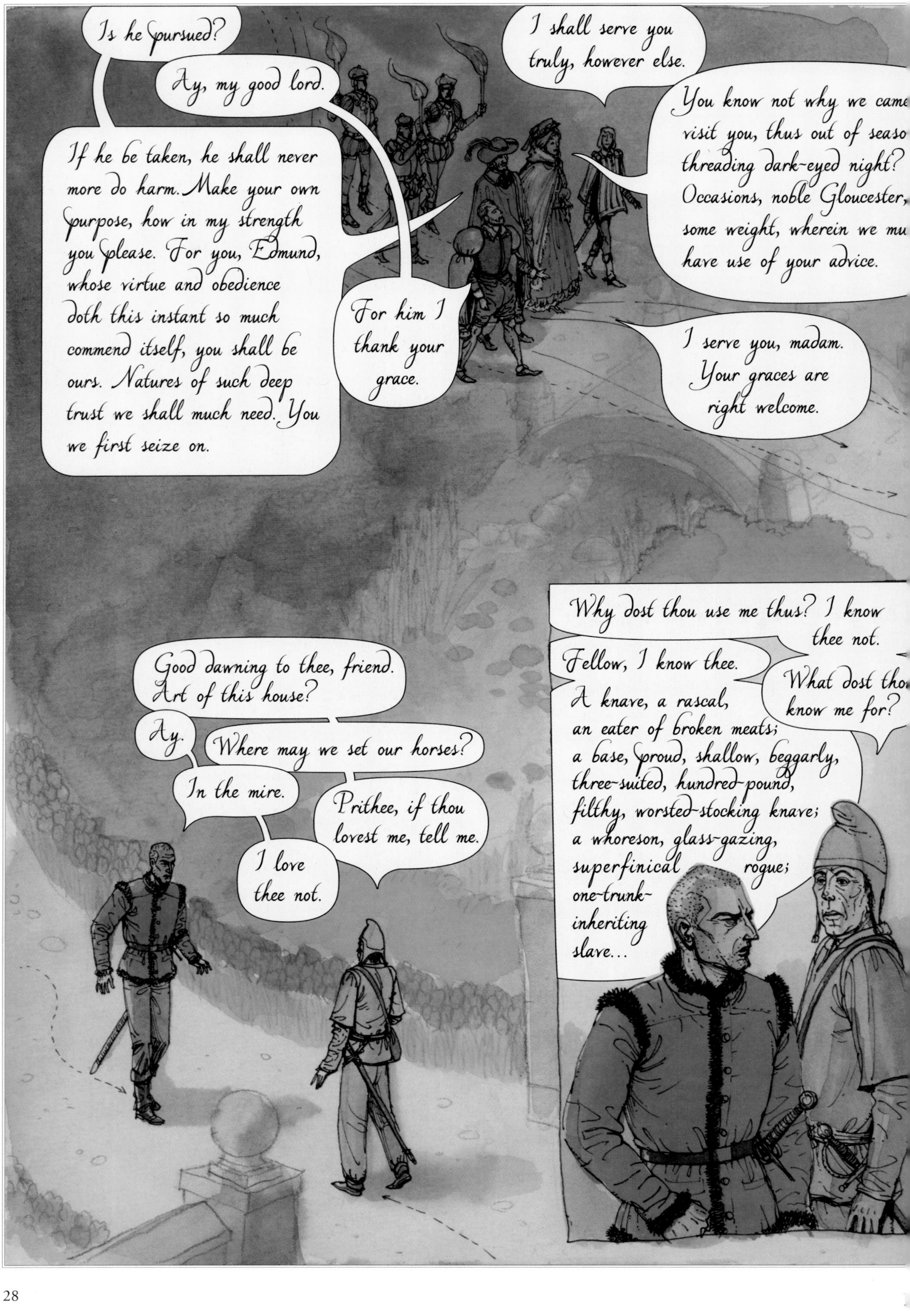
Is he pursued?
Ay, my good lord.
If he be taken, he shall never more do harm. Make your own purpose, how in my strength you please. For you, Edmund, whose virtue and obedience doth this instant so much commend itself, you shall be ours. Natures of such deep trust we shall much need. You we first seize on.
For him I thank your grace.
I shall serve you truly, however else.
You know not why we came
visit you, thus out of seaso
threading dark-eyed night?
Occasions, noble Gloucester,
some weight, wherein we mu
have use of your advice.
I serve you, madam. Your graces are right welcome.
Good dawning to thee, friend. Art of this house?
Ay.
Where may we set our horses?
In the mire.
Prithee, if thou lovest me, tell me.
I love thee not.
Why dost thou use me thus? I know thee not.
Fellow, I know thee.
What dost tho
know me for?
A knave, a rascal, an eater of broken meats; a base, proud, shallow, beggarly, three-suited, hundred-pound, filthy, worsted-stocking knave; a whoreson, glass-gazing, superfinical rogue; one-trunk-inheriting slave...

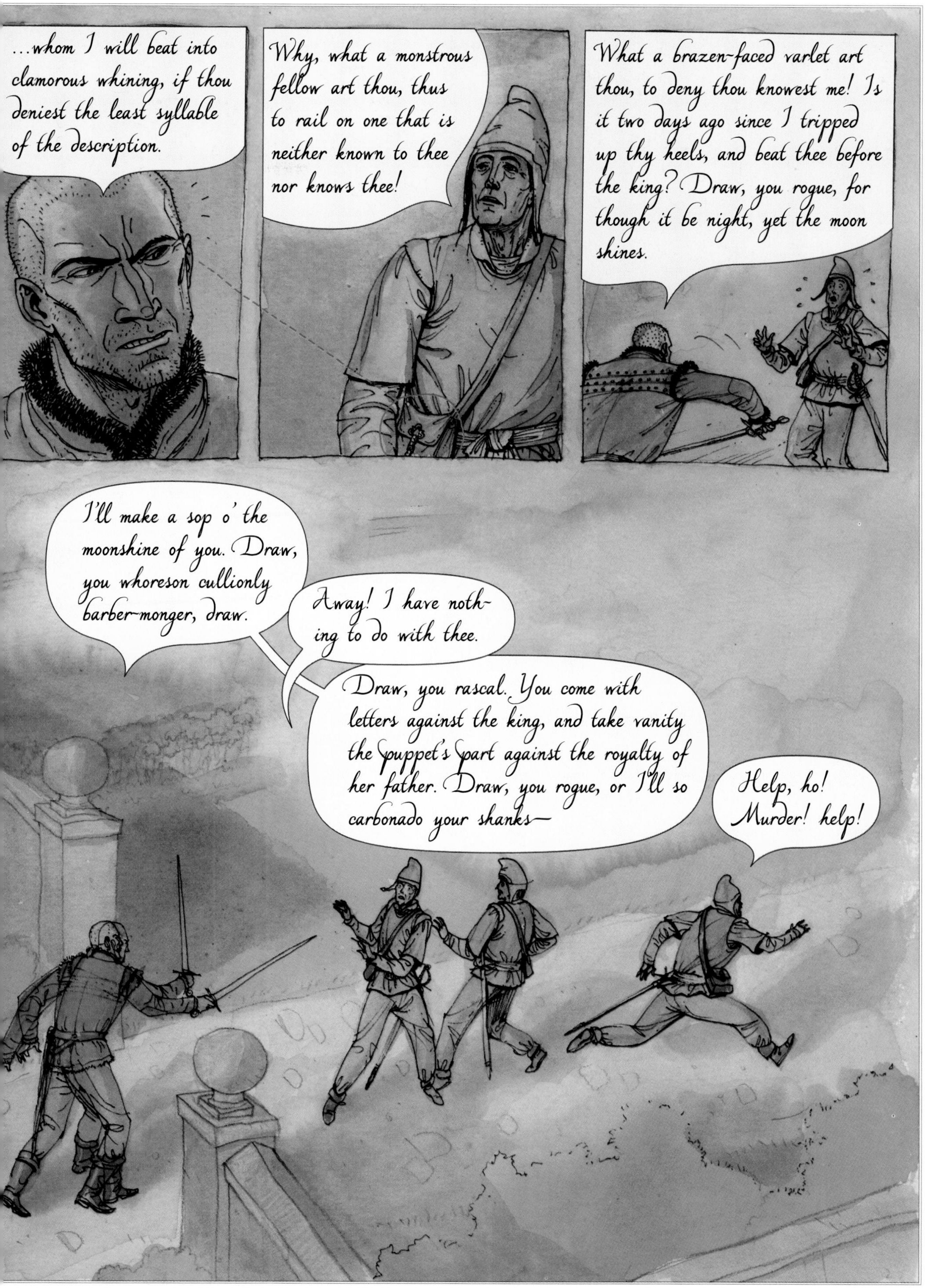
...whom I will beat into clamorous whining, if thou deniest the least syllable of the description.
Why, what a monstrous fellow art thou, thus to rail on one that is neither known to thee nor knows thee!
What a brazen-faced varlet art thou, to deny thou knowest me! Is it two days ago since I tripped up thy heels, and beat thee before the king? Draw, you rogue, for though it be night, yet the moon shines.
I'll make a sop o' the moonshine of you. Draw, you whoreson cullionly barber-monger, draw.
Away! I have nothing to do with thee.
Draw, you rascal. You come with letters against the king, and take vanity the puppet's part against the royalty of her father. Draw, you rogue, or I'll so carbonado your shanks—
Help, ho! Murder! help!

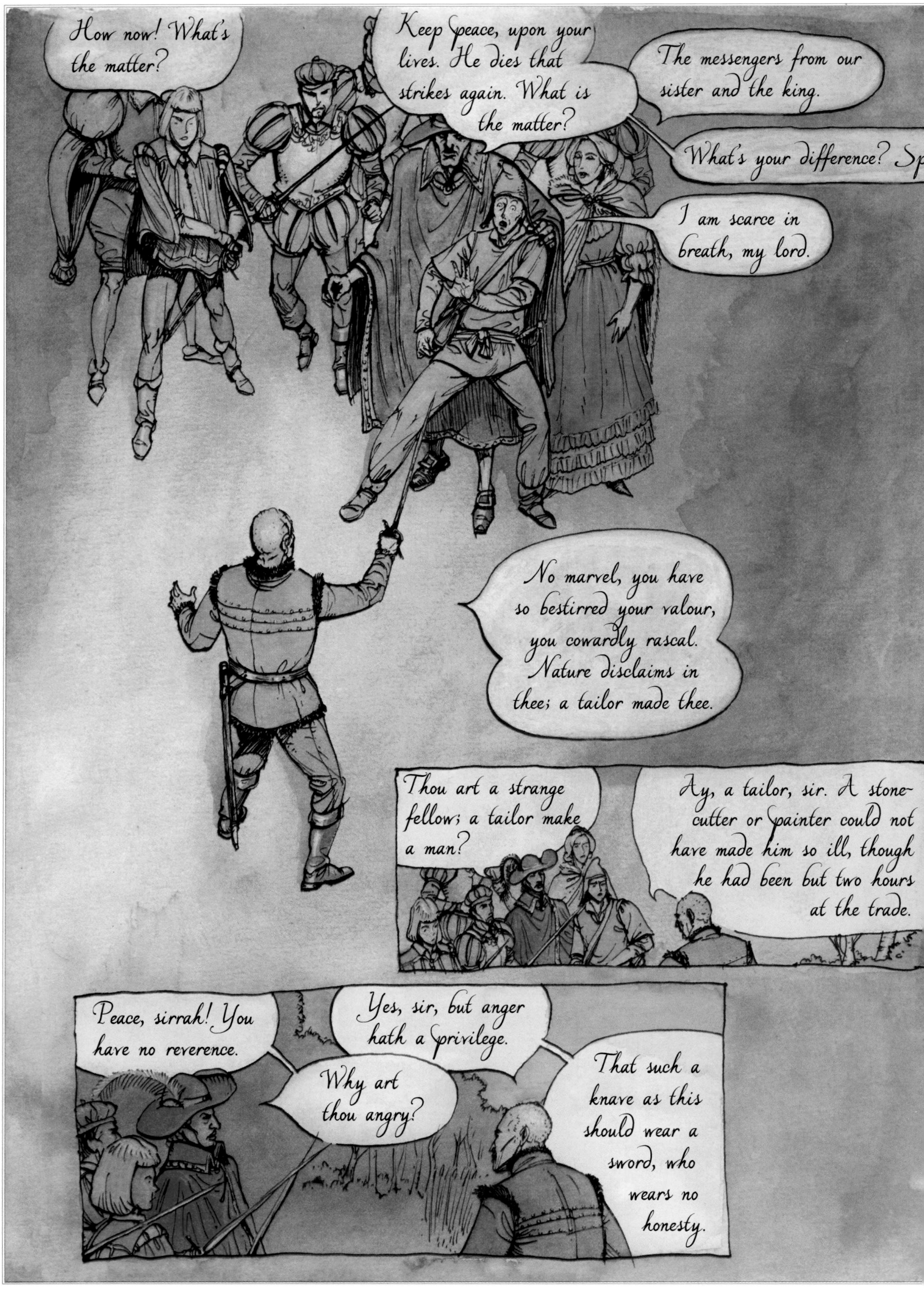
How now! What's the matter?
Keep peace, upon your lives. He dies that strikes again. What is the matter?
The messengers from our sister and the king.
What's your difference? Sp
I am scarce in breath, my lord.
No marvel, you have so bestirred your valour, you cowardly rascal. Nature disclaims in thee; a tailor made thee.
Thou art a strange fellow; a tailor make a man?
Ay, a tailor, sir. A stone-cutter or painter could not have made him so ill, though he had been but two hours at the trade.
Peace, sirrah! You have no reverence.
Yes, sir, but anger hath a privilege.
Why art thou angry?
That such a knave as this should wear a sword, who wears no honesty.

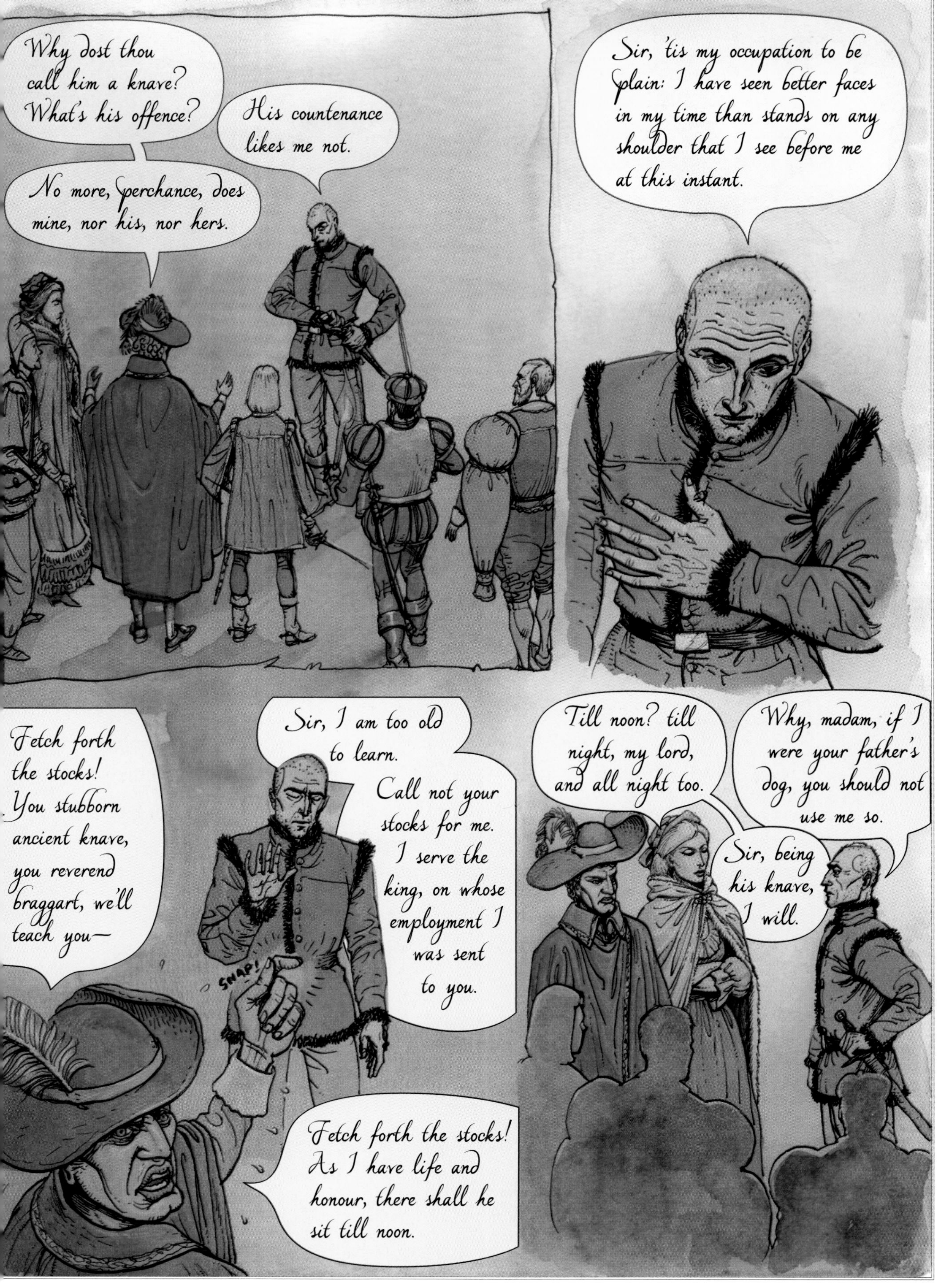

Why dost thou call him a knave? What's his offence?
His countenance likes me not.
No more, perchance, does mine, nor his, nor hers.
Sir, 'tis my occupation to be plain: I have seen better faces in my time than stands on any shoulder that I see before me at this instant.
Fetch forth the stocks! You stubborn ancient knave, you reverend braggart, we'll teach you—
Sir, I am too old to learn.
Call not your stocks for me. I serve the king, on whose employment I was sent to you.
SNAP!
Fetch forth the stocks! As I have life and honour, there shall he sit till noon.
Till noon? till night, my lord, and all night too.
Why, madam, if I were your father's dog, you should not use me so.
Sir, being his knave, I will.

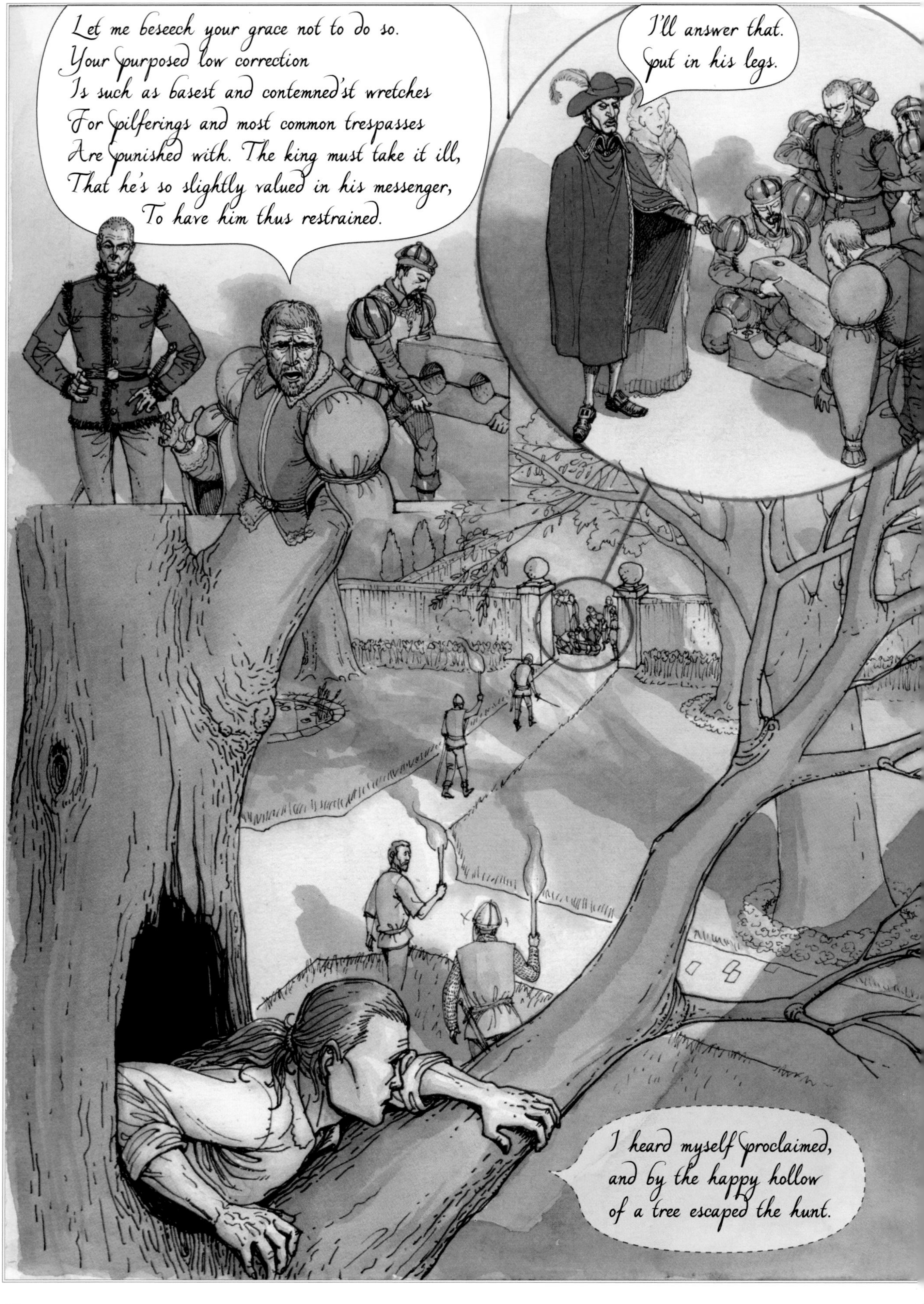
Let me beseech your grace not to do so.
Your purposed low correction
Is such as basest and contemned'st wretches
For pilferings and most common trespasses
Are punished with. The king must take it ill,
That he's so slightly valued in his messenger,
To have him thus restrained.
I'll answer that.
Put in his legs.
I heard myself proclaimed,
and by the happy hollow
of a tree escaped the hunt.

No sport is free, no place
That guard and most unusual vigilance
Does not attend my capture.

Whiles I may 'scape
I will preserve myself, and am bethought
To take the basest and most poorest shape
That ever penury, in contempt of man,
Brought near to beast.

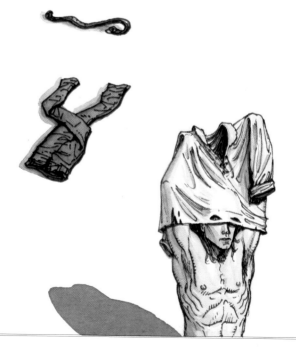

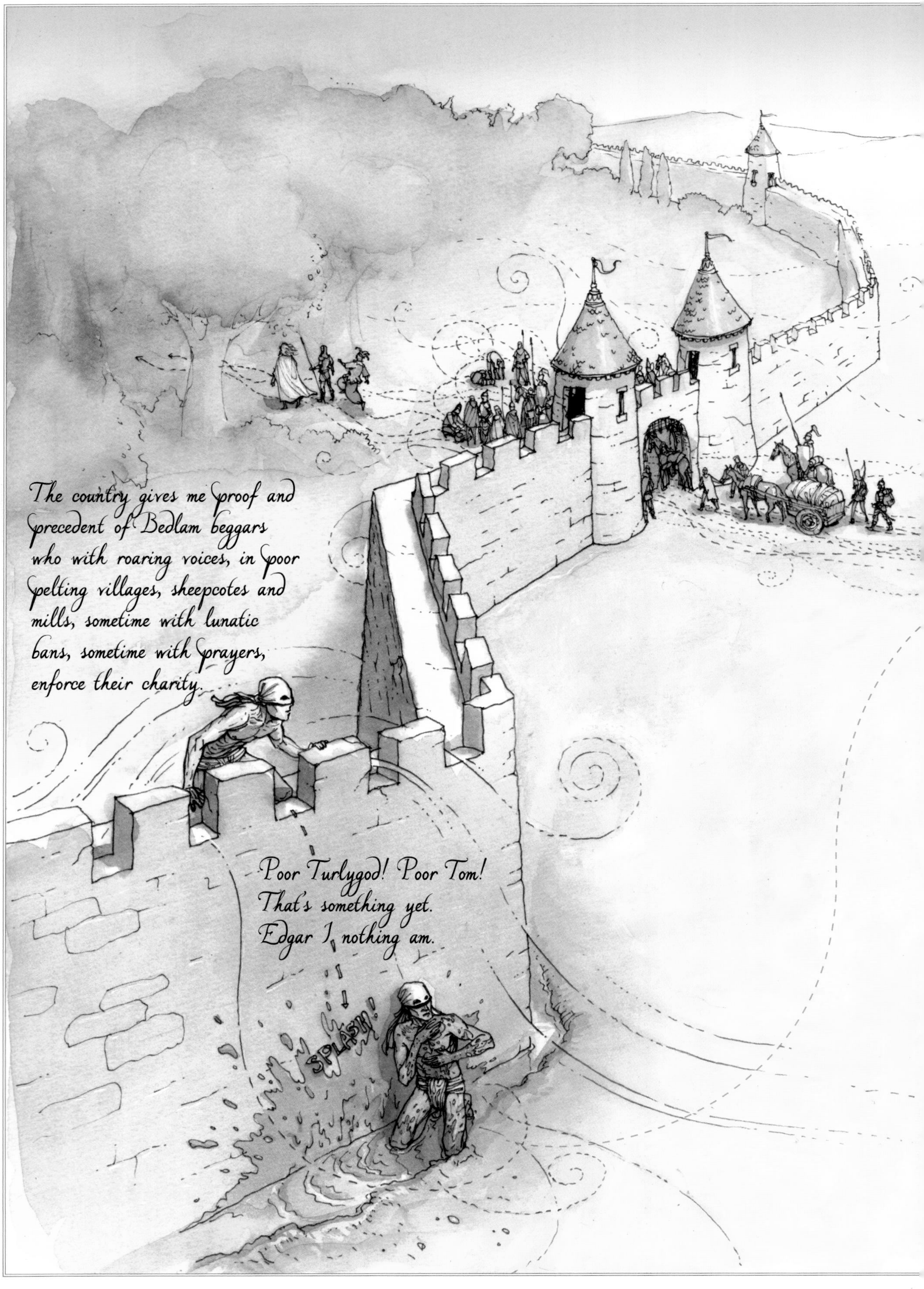
The country gives me proof and precedent of Bedlam beggars who with roaring voices, in poor pelting villages, sheepcotes and mills, sometime with lunatic bans, sometime with prayers, enforce their charity.
Poor Turlygod! Poor Tom! That's something yet. Edgar I nothing am.
SPLASH!

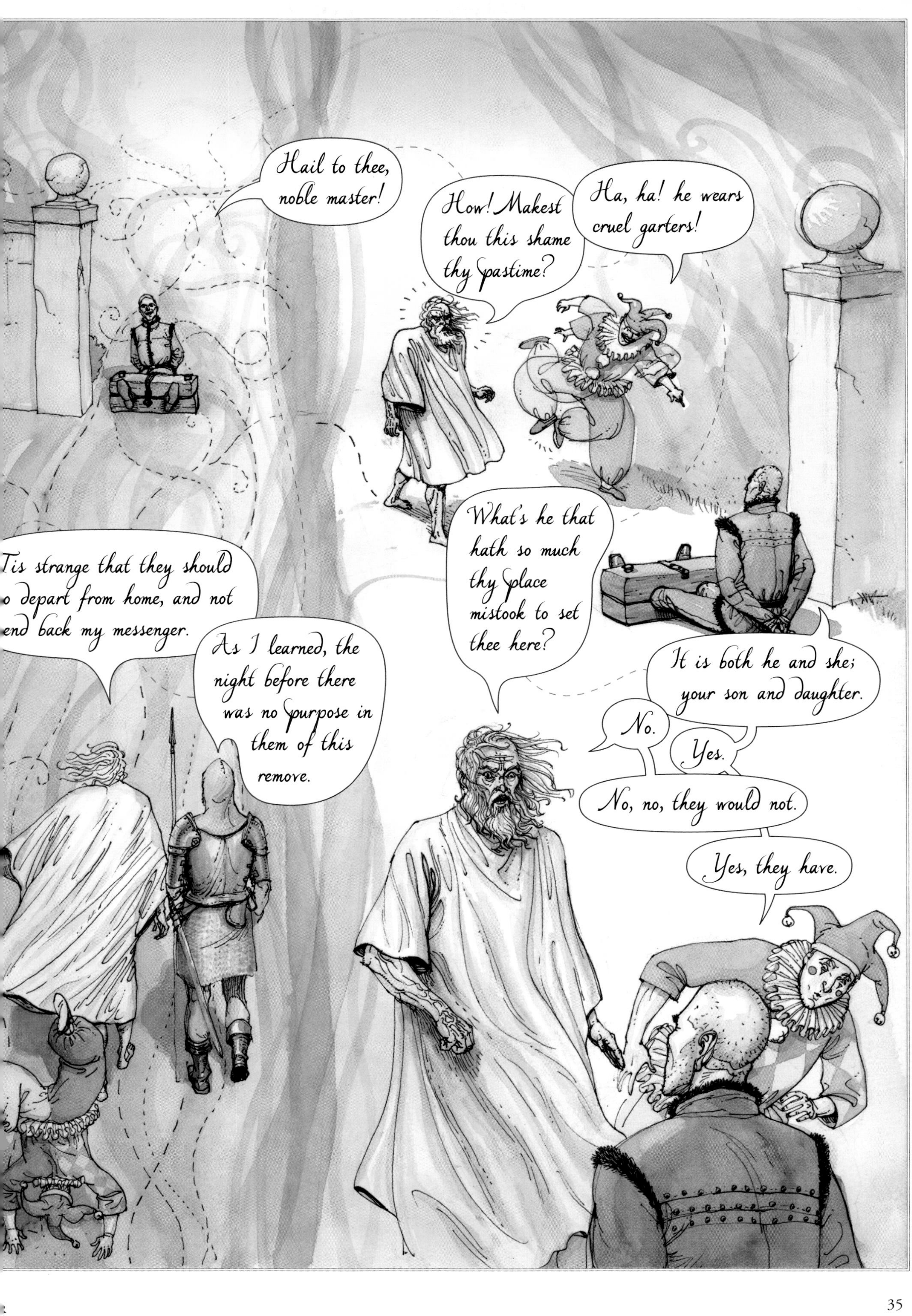
Hail to thee, noble master!
How! Makest thou this shame thy pastime?
Ha, ha! he wears cruel garters!
What's he that hath so much thy place mistook to set thee here?
Tis strange that they should o depart from home, and not end back my messenger.
As I learned, the night before there was no purpose in them of this remove.
It is both he and she; your son and daughter.
No.
Yes.
No, no, they would not.
Yes, they have.

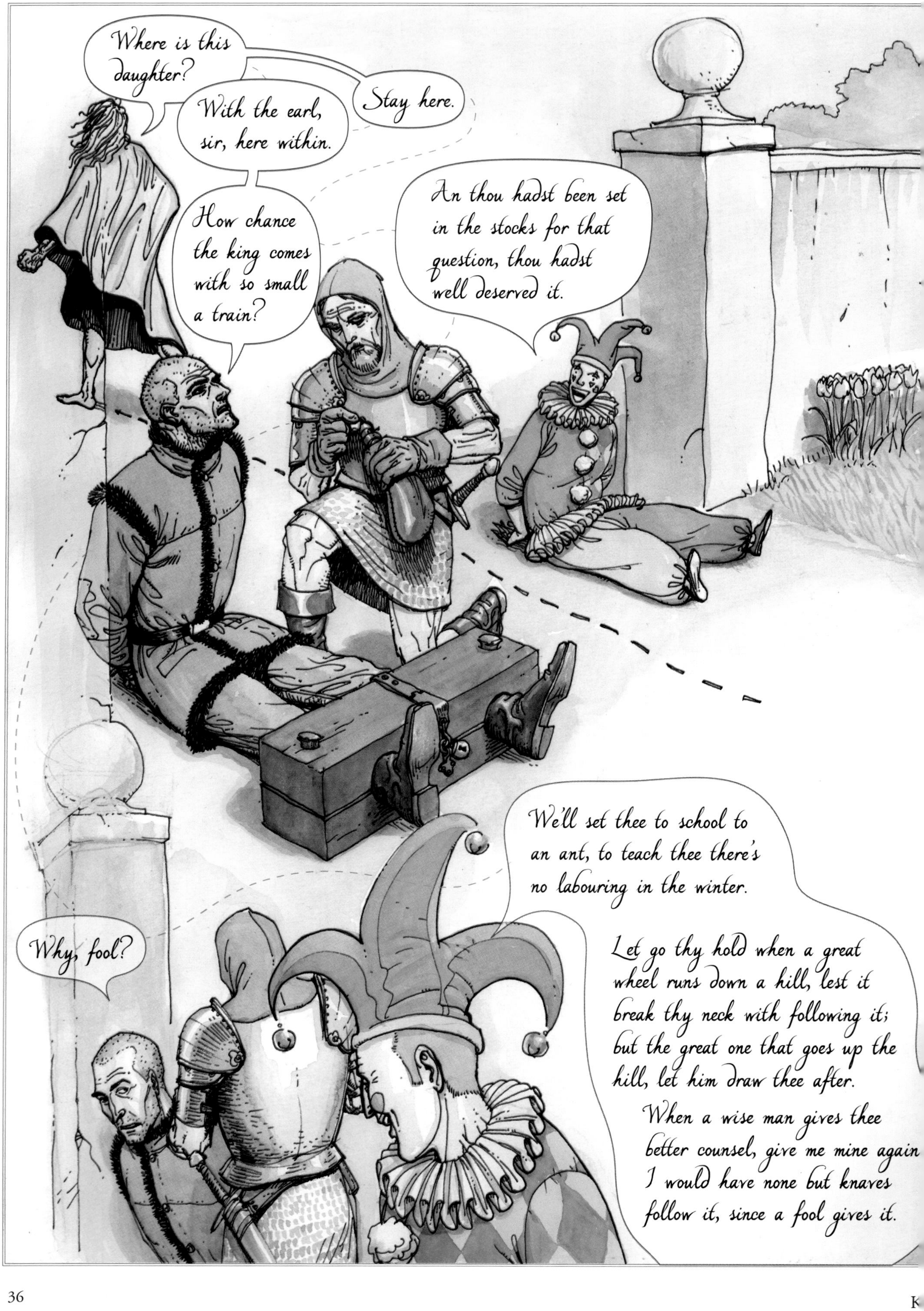
Where is this daughter?
With the earl, sir, here within.
Stay here.
How chance the king comes with so small a train?
An thou hadst been set in the stocks for that question, thou hadst well deserved it.
Why, fool?
We'll set thee to school to an ant, to teach thee there's no labouring in the winter.
Let go thy hold when a great wheel runs down a hill, lest it break thy neck with following it; but the great one that goes up the hill, let him draw thee after.
When a wise man gives thee better counsel, give me mine again
I would have none but knaves follow it, since a fool gives it.

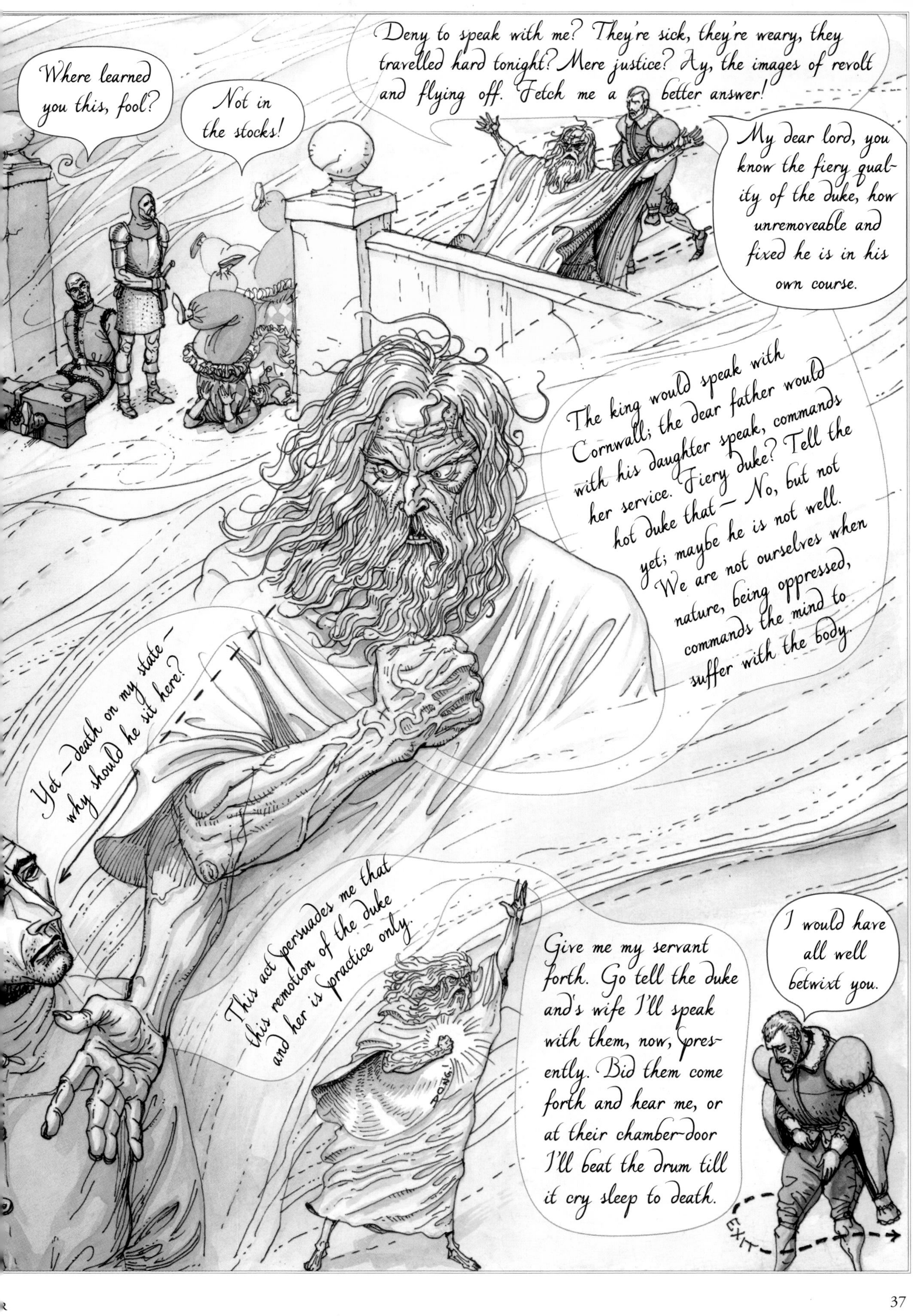
Where learned you this, fool?
Not in the stocks!
Deny to speak with me? They're sick, they're weary, they travelled hard tonight? Mere justice? Ay, the images of revolt and flying off. Fetch me a better answer!
My dear lord, you know the fiery quality of the duke, how unremoveable and fixed he is in his own course.
The king would speak with Cornwall; the dear father would with his daughter speak, commands her service. Fiery duke? Tell the hot duke that— No, but not yet; maybe he is not well. We are not ourselves when nature, being oppressed, commands the mind to suffer with the body.
Yet—death on my state— why should he sit here?
This act persuades me that this remotion of the duke and her is practice only.
Give me my servant forth. Go tell the duke and's wife I'll speak with them, now, presently. Bid them come forth and hear me, or at their chamber-door I'll beat the drum till it cry sleep to death.
I would have all well betwixt you.
EXIT

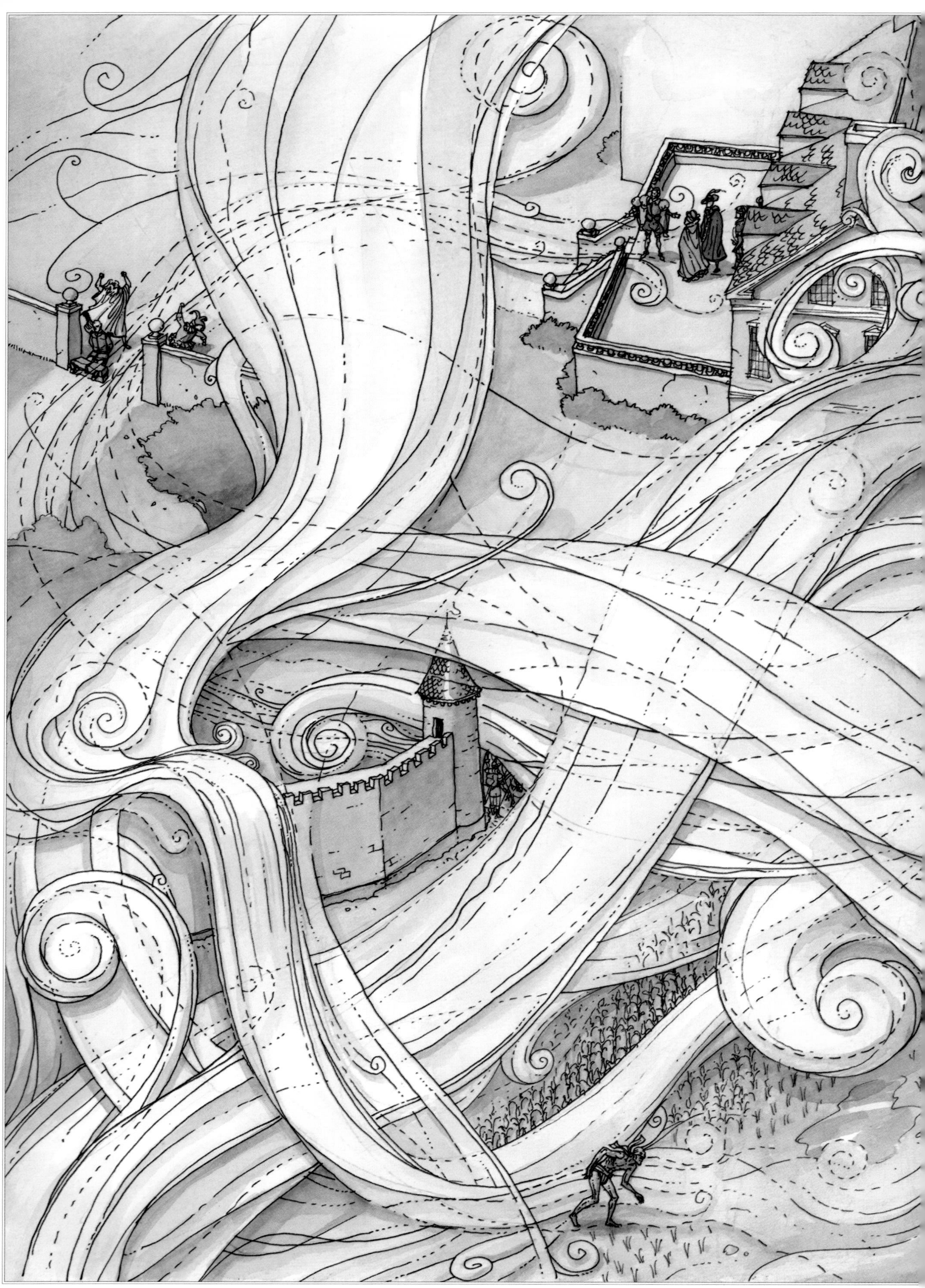

K

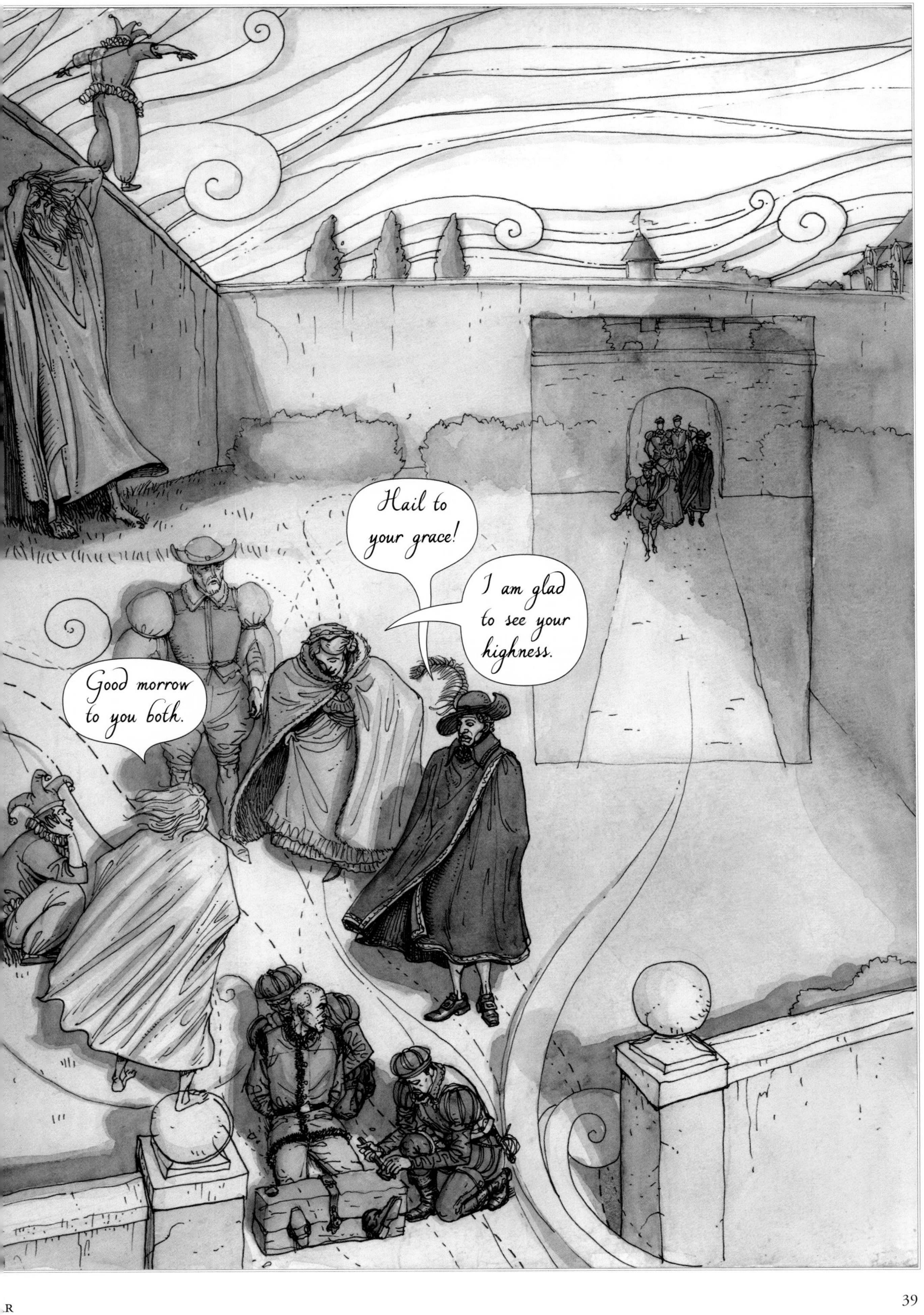
Hail to your grace!
I am glad to see your highness.
Good morrow to you both.

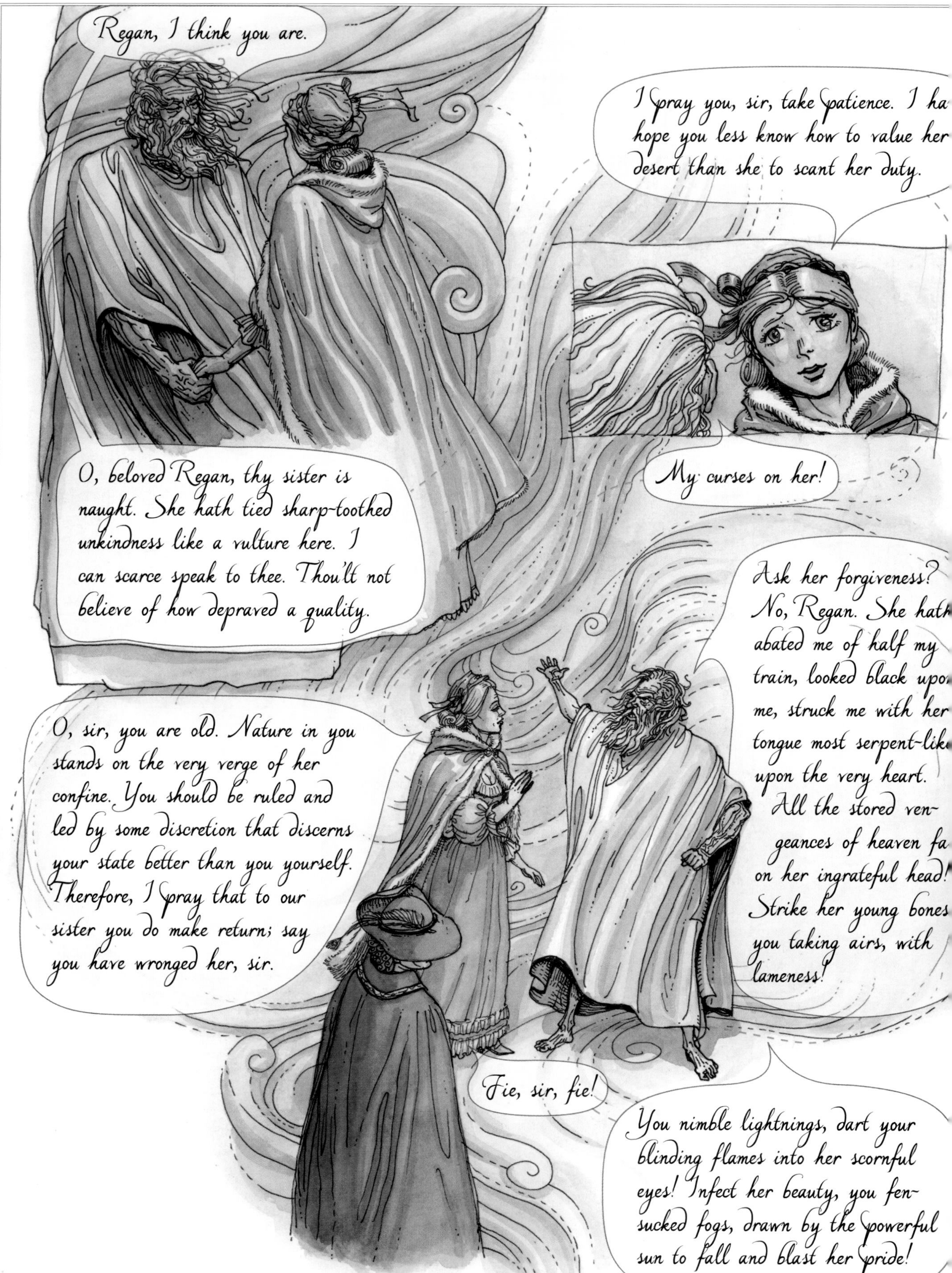
Regan, I think you are.
O, beloved Regan, thy sister is naught. She hath tied sharp-toothed unkindness like a vulture here. I can scarce speak to thee. Thou'lt not believe of how depraved a quality.
I pray you, sir, take patience. I ha
hope you less know how to value her desert than she to scant her duty.
My curses on her!
O, sir, you are old. Nature in you stands on the very verge of her confine. You should be ruled and led by some discretion that discerns your state better than you yourself. Therefore, I pray that to our sister you do make return; say you have wronged her, sir.
Ask her forgiveness? No, Regan. She hat
abated me of half my train, looked black upo
me, struck me with her tongue most serpent-lik
upon the very heart. All the stored ven-geances of heaven fa
on her ingrateful head! Strike her young bones you taking airs, with lameness!
Fie, sir, fie!
You nimble lightnings, dart your blinding flames into her scornful eyes! Infect her beauty, you fen-sucked fogs, drawn by the powerful sun to fall and blast her pride!

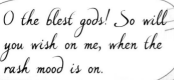
O the blest gods! So will you wish on me, when the rash mood is on.

No, Regan, thou shalt never have my curse. Thy tender-hefted nature shall not give thee o'er to harshness. Her eyes are fierce, but thine do comfort and not burn. 'Tis not in thee to grudge my pleasures, to cut off my train, to bandy hasty words, to scant my sizes, and in conclusion to oppose the bolt against my coming in.

Thou better knowest the offices of nature, bond of childhood...

Good sir, to the purpose.

Who put my man in the stocks?

What trumpet's that?

I know't, my sister's.

Is your lady come?

Out, varlet, from my sight!

THWOK!

What means your grace?

This is a slave whose easy borrowed pride dwells in the fickle grace of her he follows.

Who struck my servant? Regan, I have good hope thou didst not know on't.

Who comes here? O heavens, if you do love old men, if you sweet sway allow obedience, if yourselves are old, make it your cause; send down, and take my part!

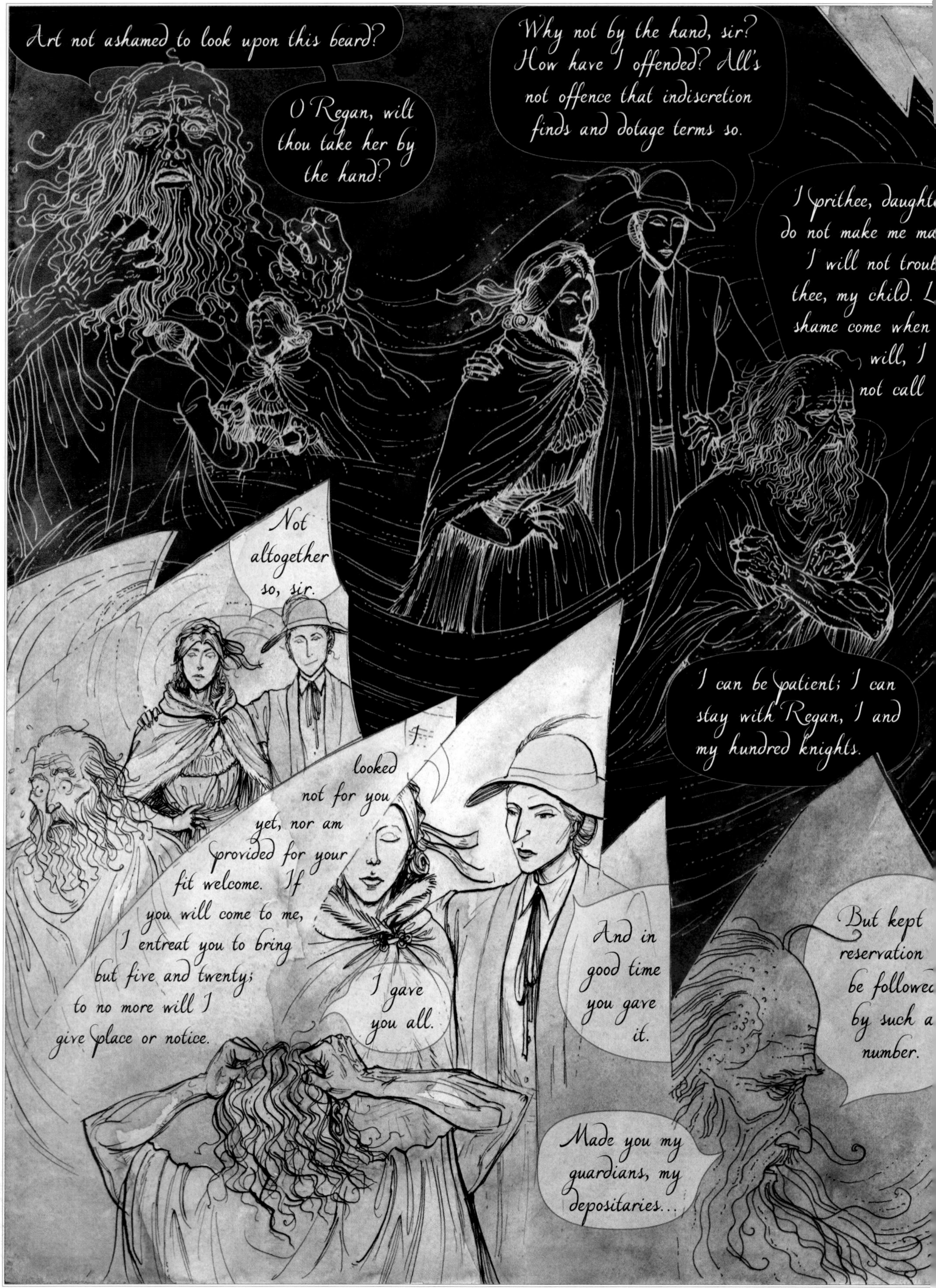
Art not ashamed to look upon this beard?
O Regan, wilt thou take her by the hand?
Why not by the hand, sir? How have I offended? All's not offence that indiscretion finds and dotage terms so.
I prithee, daught do not make me ma I will not trou thee, my child. L shame come when will, I not call
Not altogether so, sir.
I can be patient; I can stay with Regan, I and my hundred knights.
I looked not for you yet, nor am provided for your fit welcome. If you will come to me, I entreat you to bring but five and twenty; to no more will I give place or notice.
I gave you all.
And in good time you gave it.
But kept reservation be followe by such a number.
Made you my guardians, my depositaries...

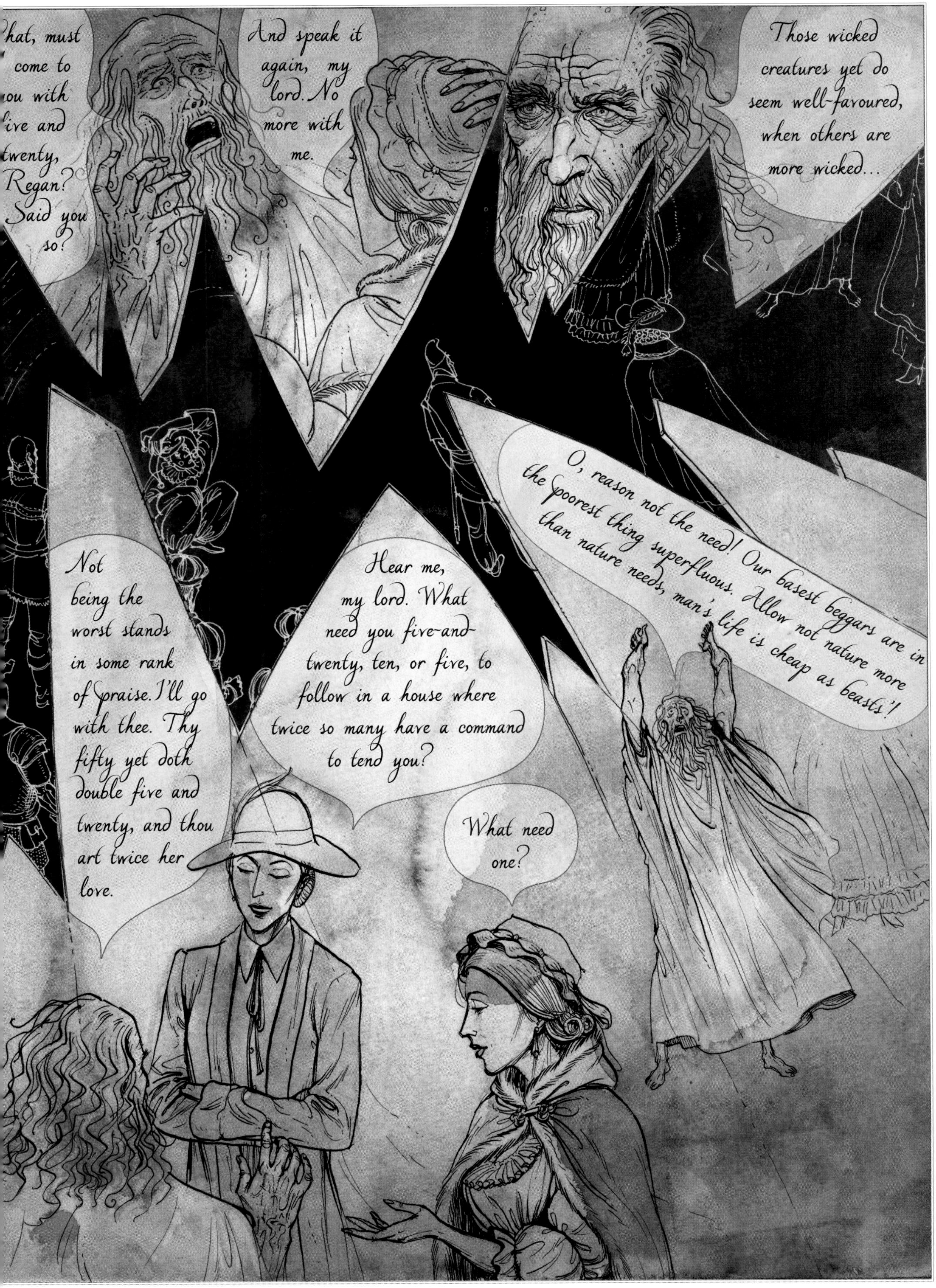
hat, must come to ou with ive and twenty, Regan? Said you so?
And speak it again, my lord. No more with me.
Those wicked creatures yet do seem well-favoured, when others are more wicked...
Not being the worst stands in some rank of praise. I'll go with thee. Thy fifty yet doth double five and twenty, and thou art twice her love.
Hear me, my lord. What need you five-and-twenty, ten, or five, to follow in a house where twice so many have a command to tend you?
What need one?
O, reason not the need! Our basest beggars are in the poorest thing superfluous. Allow not nature more than nature needs, man's life is cheap as beasts'!

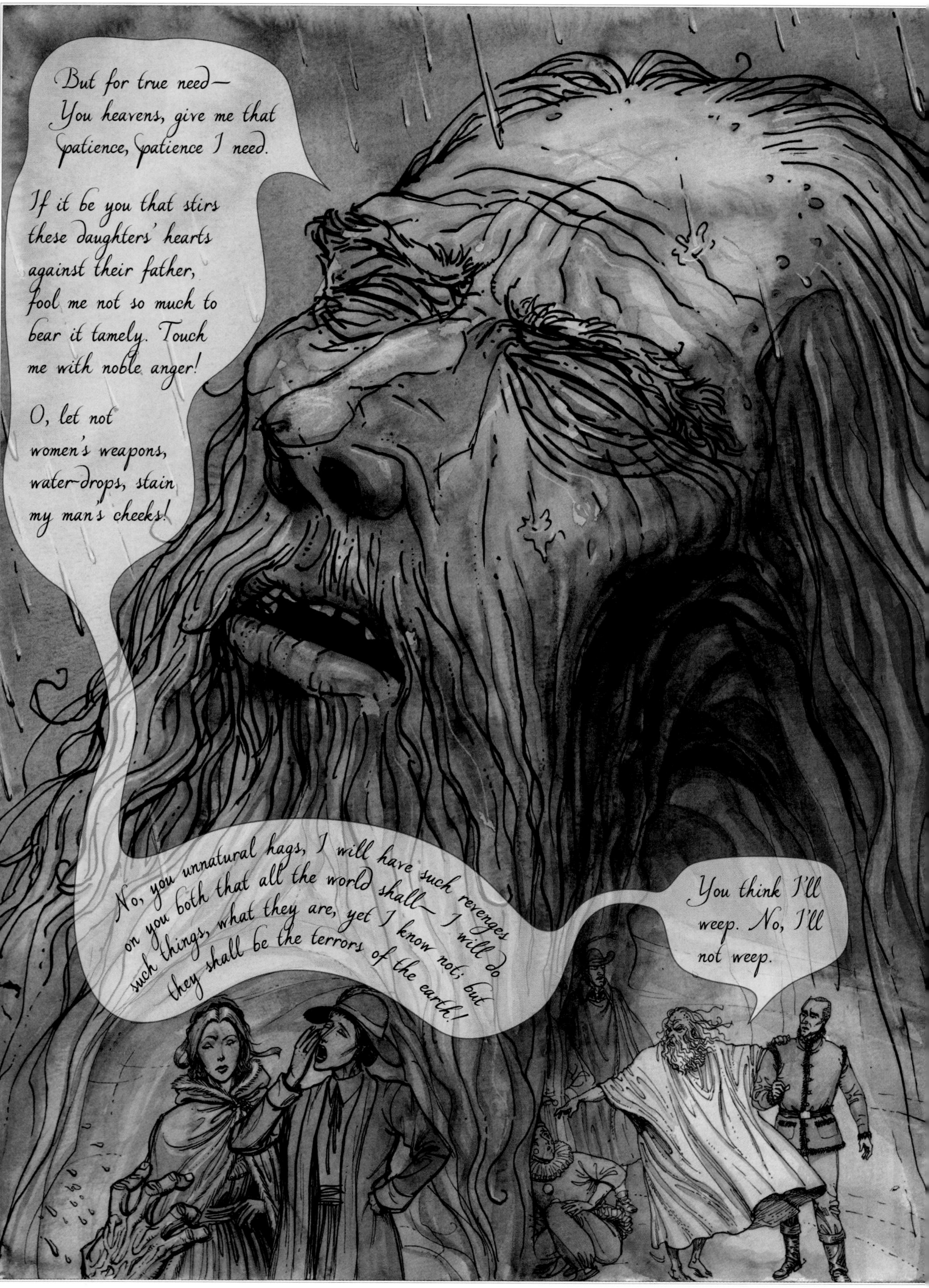
But for true need— You heavens, give me that patience, patience I need.
If it be you that stirs these daughters' hearts against their father, fool me not so much to bear it tamely. Touch me with noble anger!
O, let not women's weapons, water-drops, stain my man's cheeks!
No, you unnatural hags, I will have such revenges on you both that all the world shall— I will do such things, what they are, yet I know not; but they shall be the terrors of the earth!
You think I'll weep. No, I'll not weep.

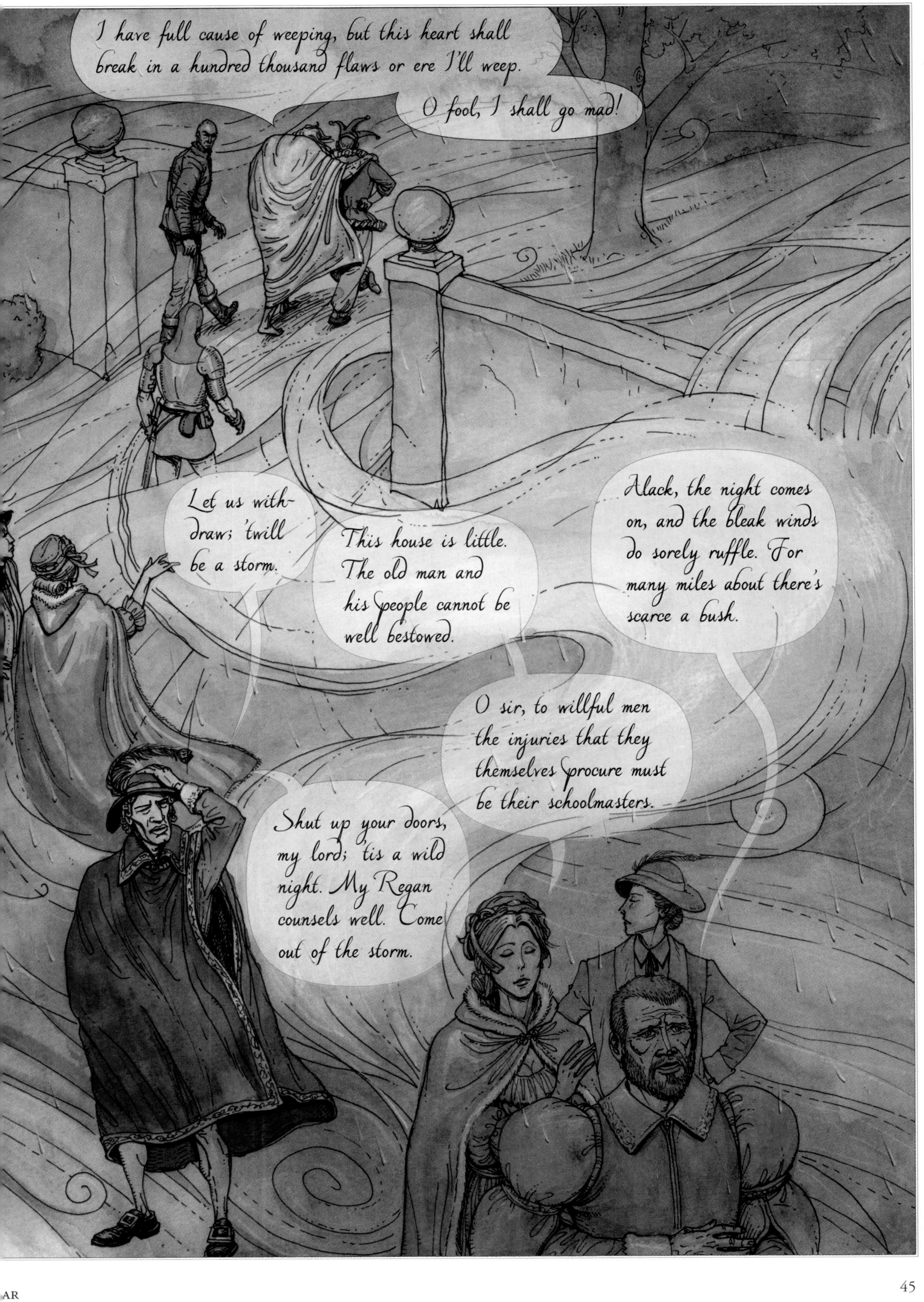

I have full cause of weeping, but this heart shall break in a hundred thousand flaws or ere I'll weep.
O fool, I shall go mad!
Let us withdraw; 'twill be a storm.
This house is little. The old man and his people cannot be well bestowed.
Alack, the night comes on, and the bleak winds do sorely ruffle. For many miles about there's scarce a bush.
O sir, to willful men the injuries that they themselves procure must be their schoolmasters.
Shut up your doors, my lord; 'tis a wild night. My Regan counsels well. Come out of the storm.

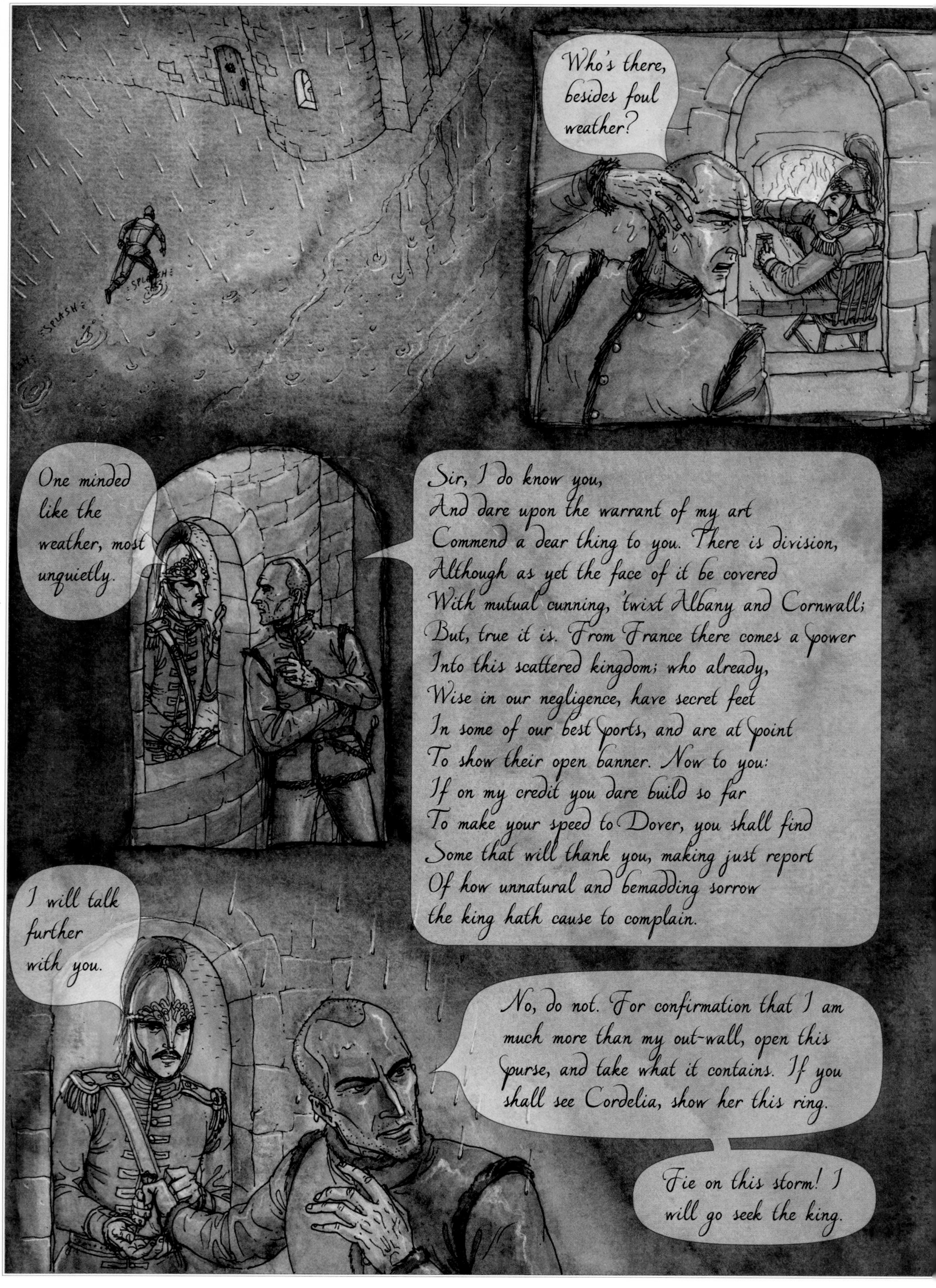
SPLASH
SPLASH
SPLASH
Who's there, besides foul weather?
One minded like the weather, most unquietly.
Sir, I do know you,
And dare upon the warrant of my art
Commend a dear thing to you. There is division,
Although as yet the face of it be covered
With mutual cunning, 'twixt Albany and Cornwall;
But, true it is. From France there comes a power
Into this scattered kingdom; who already,
Wise in our negligence, have secret feet
In some of our best ports, and are at point
To show their open banner. Now to you:
If on my credit you dare build so far
To make your speed to Dover, you shall find
Some that will thank you, making just report
Of how unnatural and bemadding sorrow
the king hath cause to complain.
I will talk further with you.
No, do not. For confirmation that I am much more than my out-wall, open this purse, and take what it contains. If you shall see Cordelia, show her this ring.
Fie on this storm! I will go seek the king.

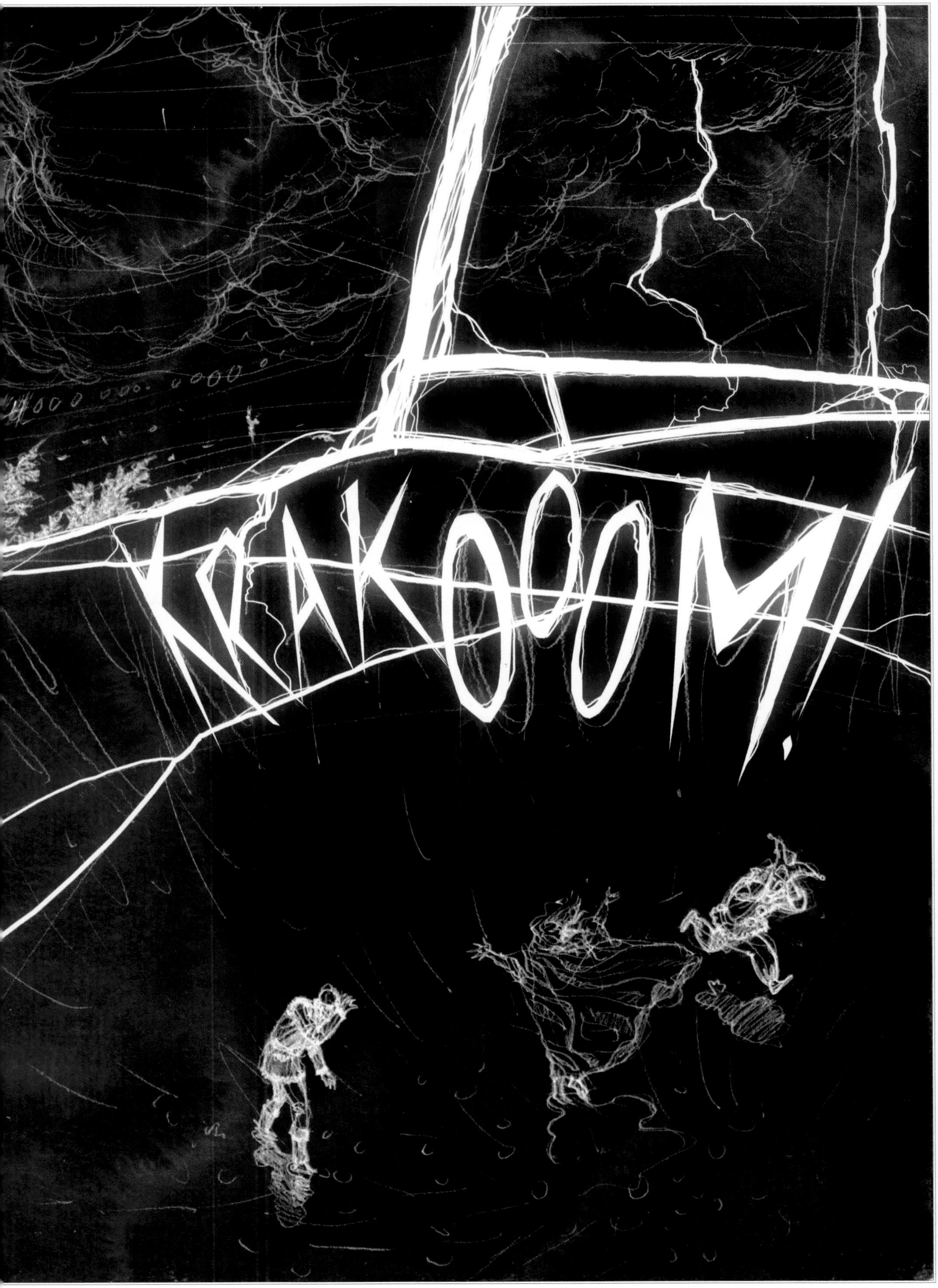
KRAKOOOM!

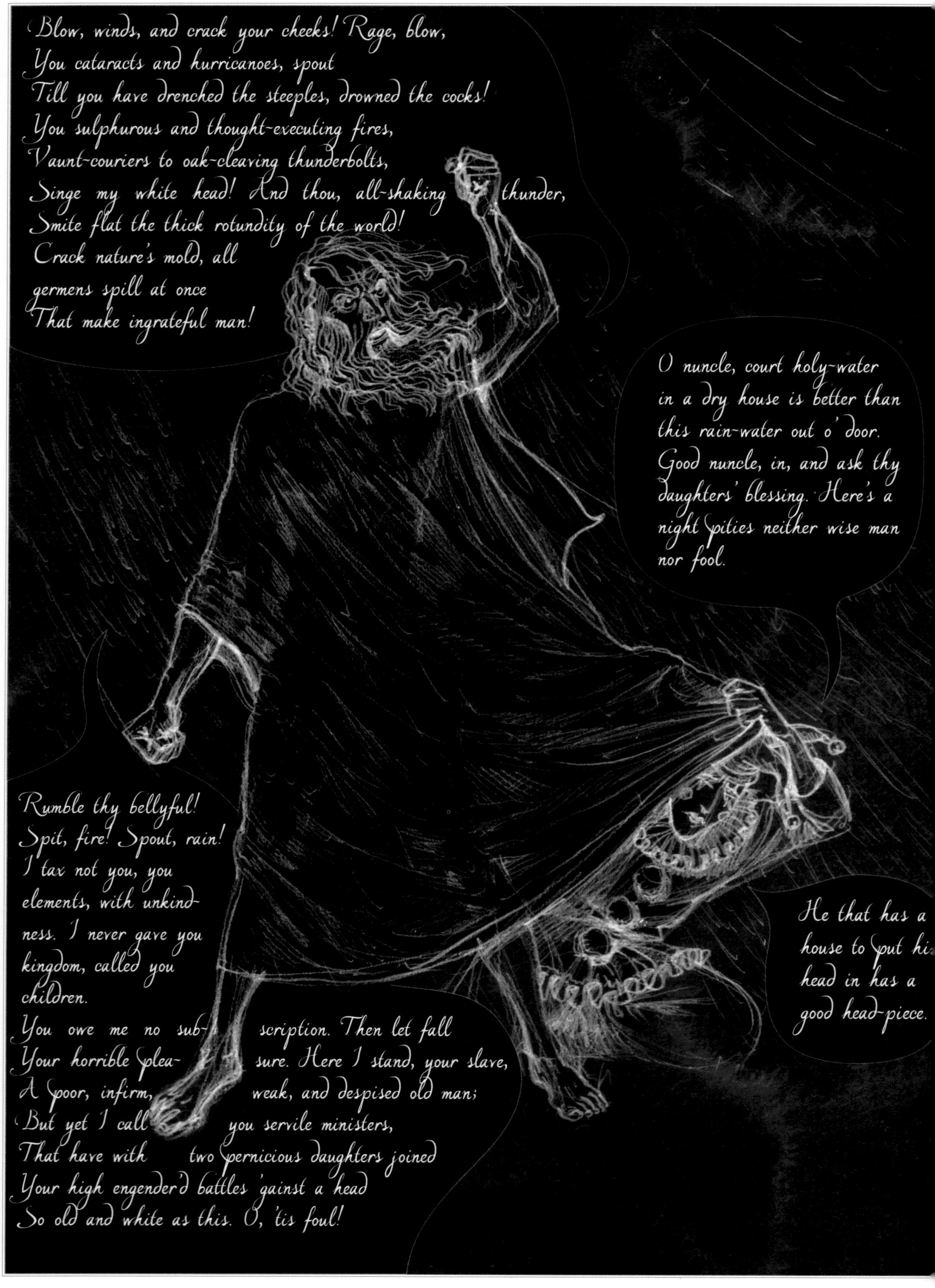
Blow, winds, and crack your cheeks! Rage, blow,
You cataracts and hurricanoes, spout
Till you have drenched the steeples, drowned the cocks!
You sulphurous and thought-executing fires,
Vaunt-couriers to oak-cleaving thunderbolts,
Singe my white head! And thou, all-shaking thunder,
Smite flat the thick rotundity of the world!
Crack nature's mold, all
germens spill at once
That make ingrateful man!
O nuncle, court holy-water
in a dry house is better than
this rain-water out o' door.
Good nuncle, in, and ask thy
daughters' blessing. Here's a
night pities neither wise man
nor fool.
Rumble thy bellyful!
Spit, fire! Spout, rain!
I tax not you, you
elements, with unkind-
ness. I never gave you
kingdom, called you
children.
You owe me no sub- scription. Then let fall
Your horrible plea- sure. Here I stand, your slave,
A poor, infirm, weak, and despised old man;
But yet I call you servile ministers,
That have with two pernicious daughters joined
Your high engender'd battles 'gainst a head
So old and white as this. O, 'tis foul!
He that has a
house to put hi
head in has a
good head-piece.

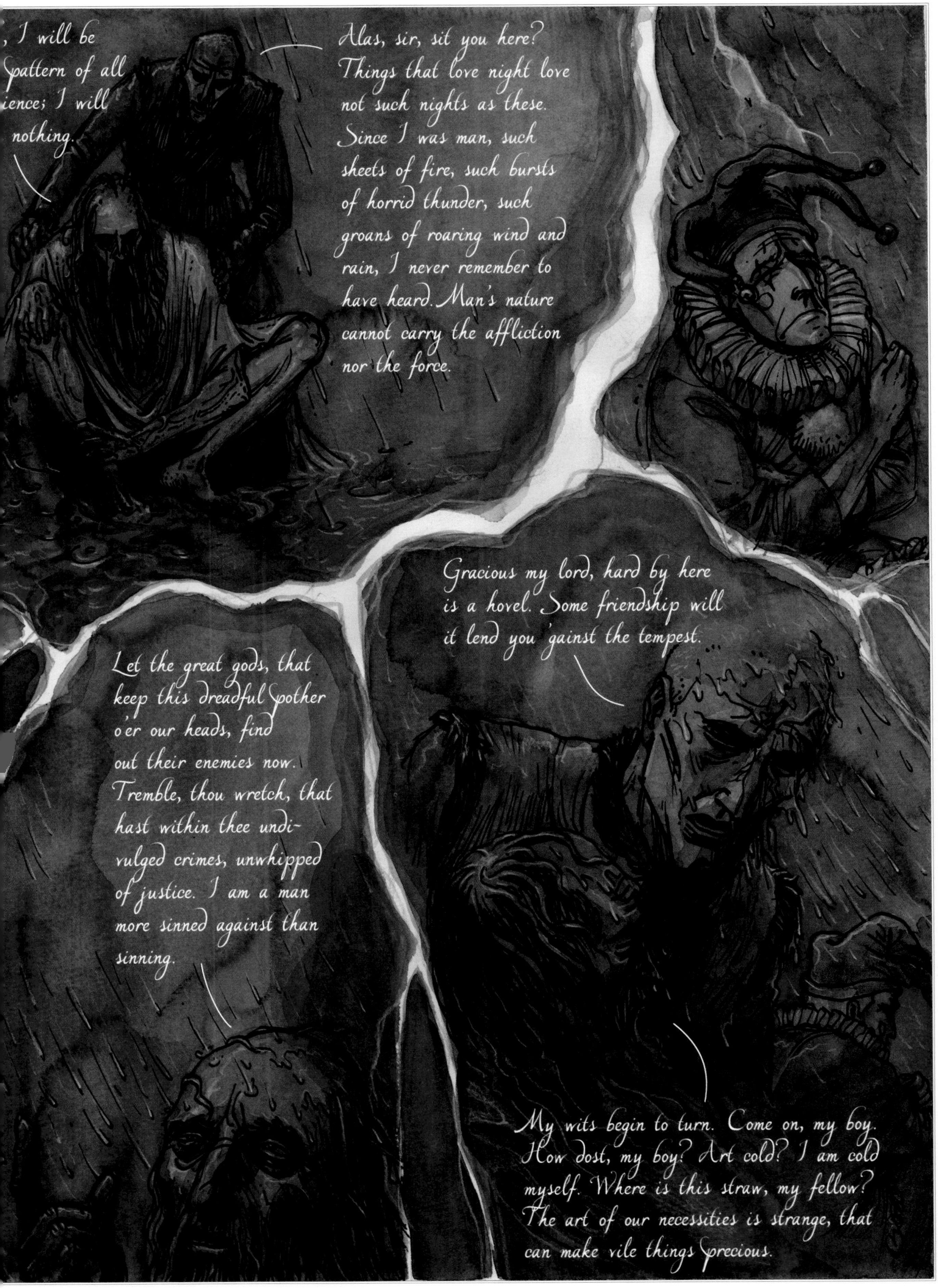
, I will be pattern of all ience; I will nothing.
Alas, sir, sit you here? Things that love night love not such nights as these. Since I was man, such sheets of fire, such bursts of horrid thunder, such groans of roaring wind and rain, I never remember to have heard. Man's nature cannot carry the affliction nor the force.
Gracious my lord, hard by here is a hovel. Some friendship will it lend you 'gainst the tempest.
Let the great gods, that keep this dreadful pother o'er our heads, find out their enemies now. Tremble, thou wretch, that hast within thee undivulged crimes, unwhipped of justice. I am a man more sinned against than sinning.
My wits begin to turn. Come on, my boy. How dost, my boy? Art cold? I am cold myself. Where is this straw, my fellow? The art of our necessities is strange, that can make vile things precious.

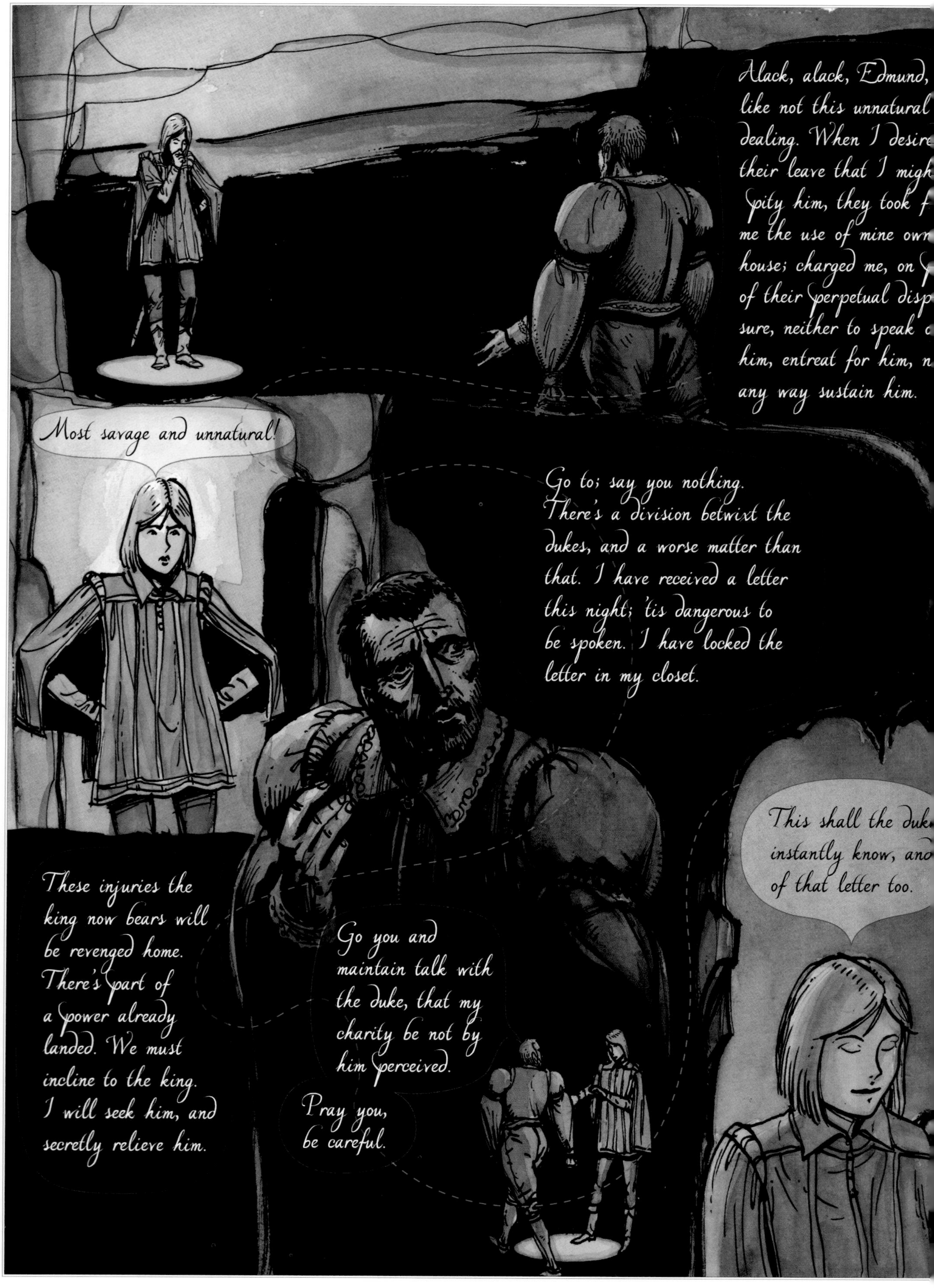
Alack, alack, Edmund, I like not this unnatural dealing. When I desire their leave that I migh pity him, they took f me the use of mine own house; charged me, on of their perpetual disp sure, neither to speak him, entreat for him, n any way sustain him.
Most savage and unnatural!
Go to; say you nothing. There's a division betwixt the dukes, and a worse matter than that. I have received a letter this night; 'tis dangerous to be spoken. I have locked the letter in my closet.
These injuries the king now bears will be revenged home. There's part of a power already landed. We must incline to the king. I will seek him, and secretly relieve him.
Go you and maintain talk with the duke, that my charity be not by him perceived.
Pray you, be careful.
This shall the duk instantly know, and of that letter too.

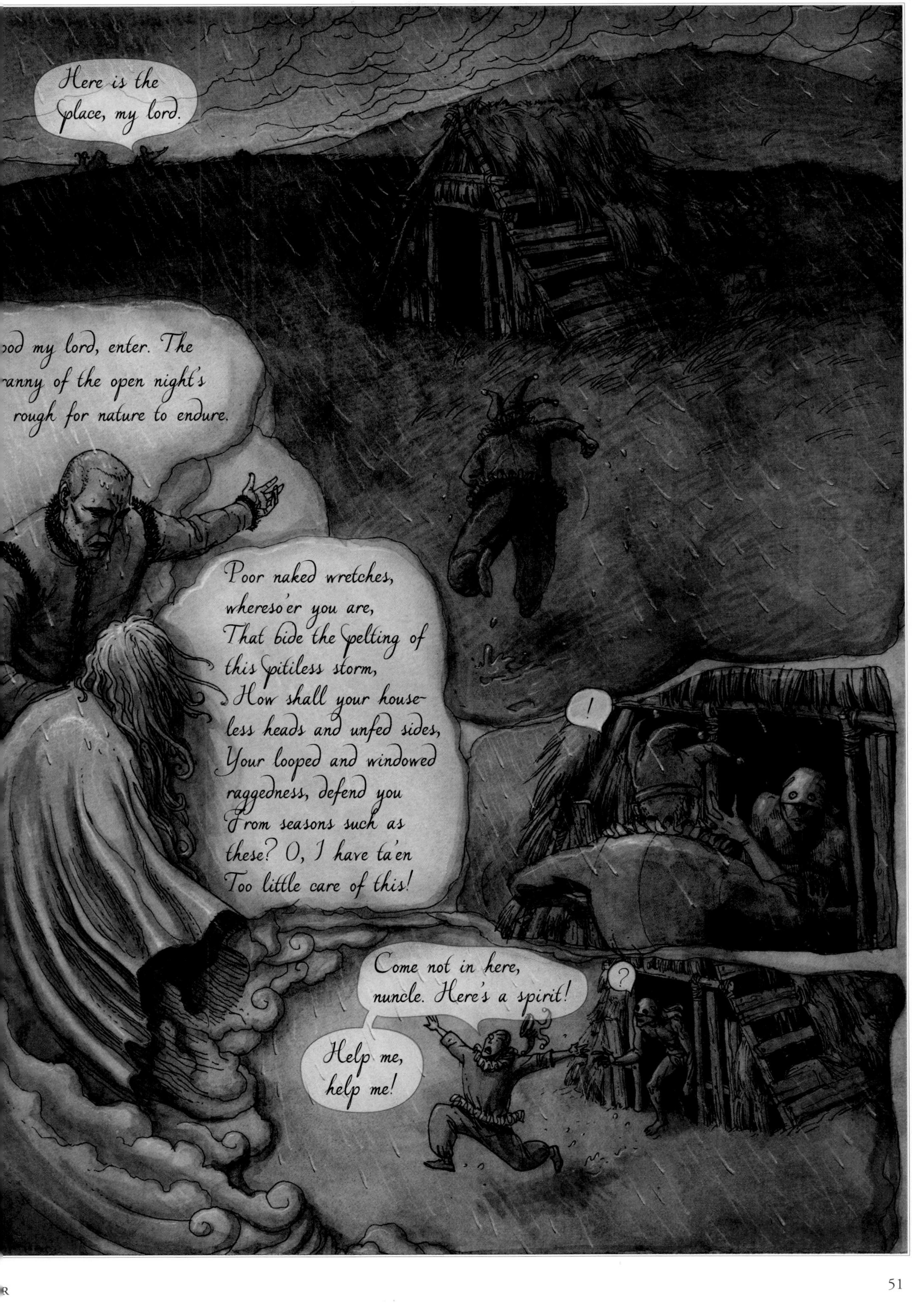
Here is the place, my lord.
ood my lord, enter. The ranny of the open night's rough for nature to endure.
Poor naked wretches, whereso'er you are, That bide the pelting of this pitiless storm, How shall your houseless heads and unfed sides, Your looped and windowed raggedness, defend you From seasons such as these? O, I have ta'en Too little care of this!
!
?
Come not in here, nuncle. Here's a spirit!
Help me, help me!

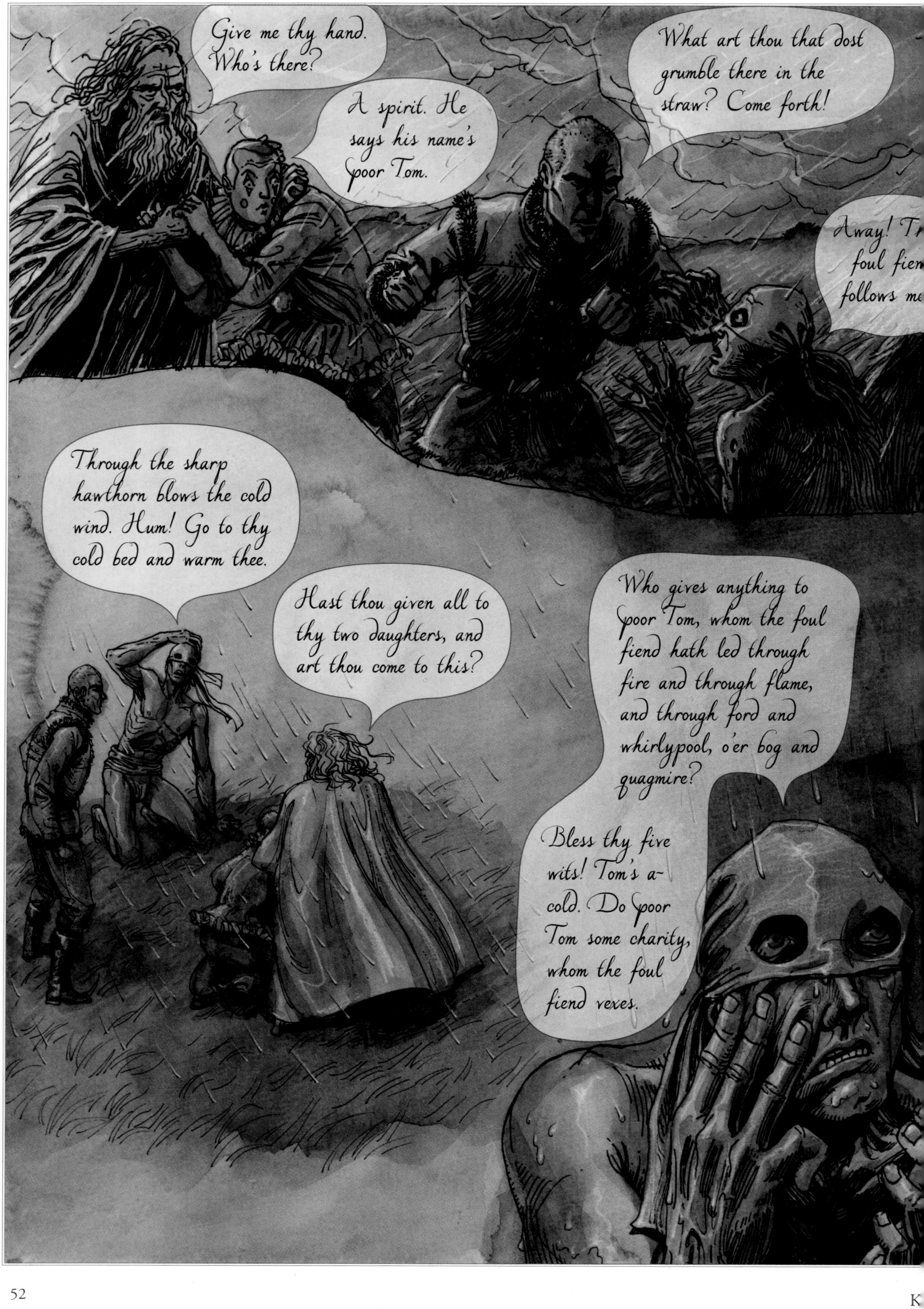
Give me thy hand. Who's there?
A spirit. He says his name's poor Tom.
What art thou that dost grumble there in the straw? Come forth!
Away! Th
foul fien
follows me
Through the sharp hawthorn blows the cold wind. Hum! Go to thy cold bed and warm thee.
Hast thou given all to thy two daughters, and art thou come to this?
Who gives anything to poor Tom, whom the foul fiend hath led through fire and through flame, and through ford and whirlypool, o'er bog and quagmire?
Bless thy five wits! Tom's a-cold. Do poor Tom some charity, whom the foul fiend vexes.

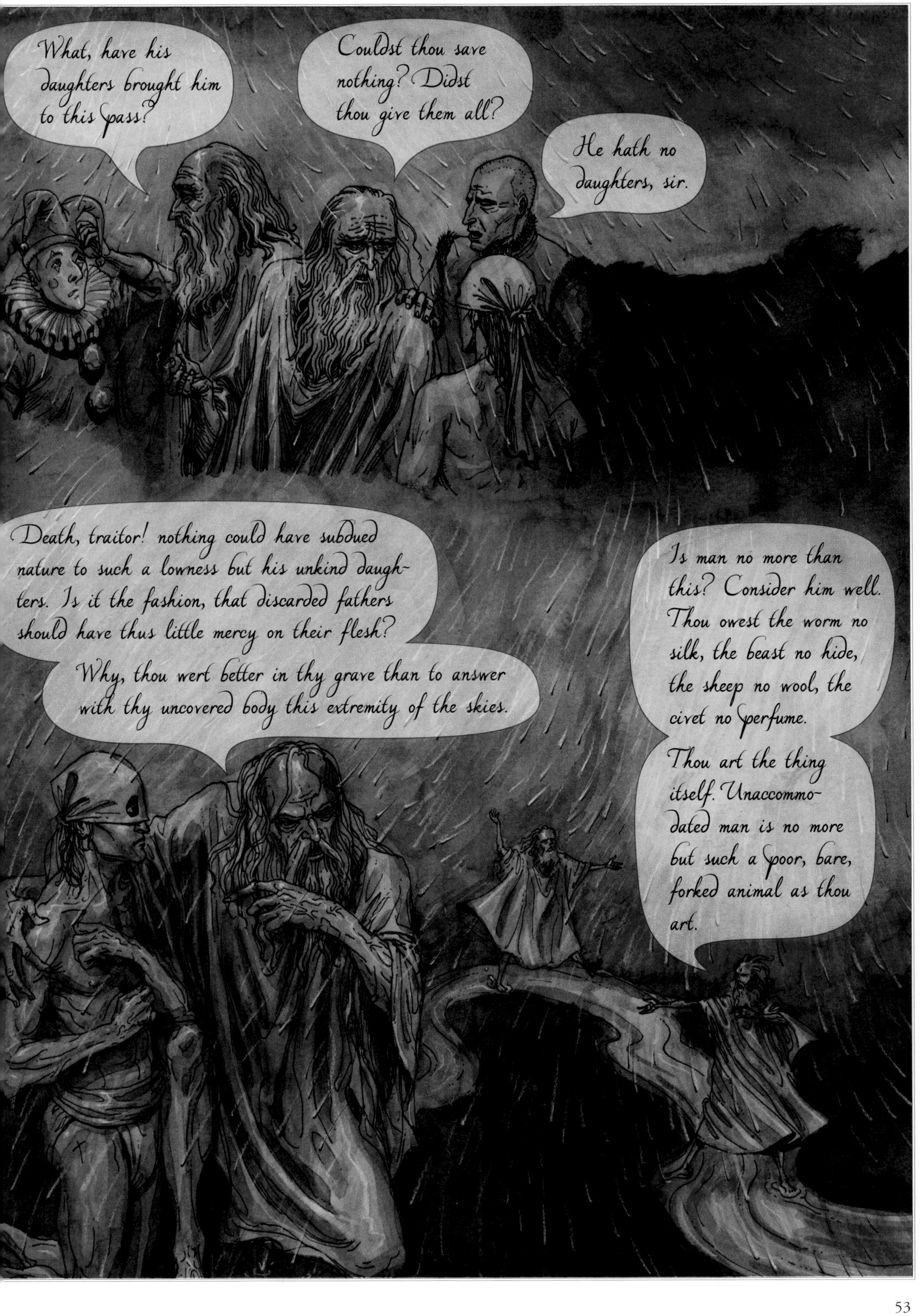
What, have his daughters brought him to this pass?
Couldst thou save nothing? Didst thou give them all?
He hath no daughters, sir.
Death, traitor! nothing could have subdued nature to such a lowness but his unkind daughters. Is it the fashion, that discarded fathers should have thus little mercy on their flesh?
Why, thou wert better in thy grave than to answer with thy uncovered body this extremity of the skies.
Is man no more than this? Consider him well. Thou owest the worm no silk, the beast no hide, the sheep no wool, the civet no perfume.
Thou art the thing itself. Unaccommodated man is no more but such a poor, bare, forked animal as thou art.

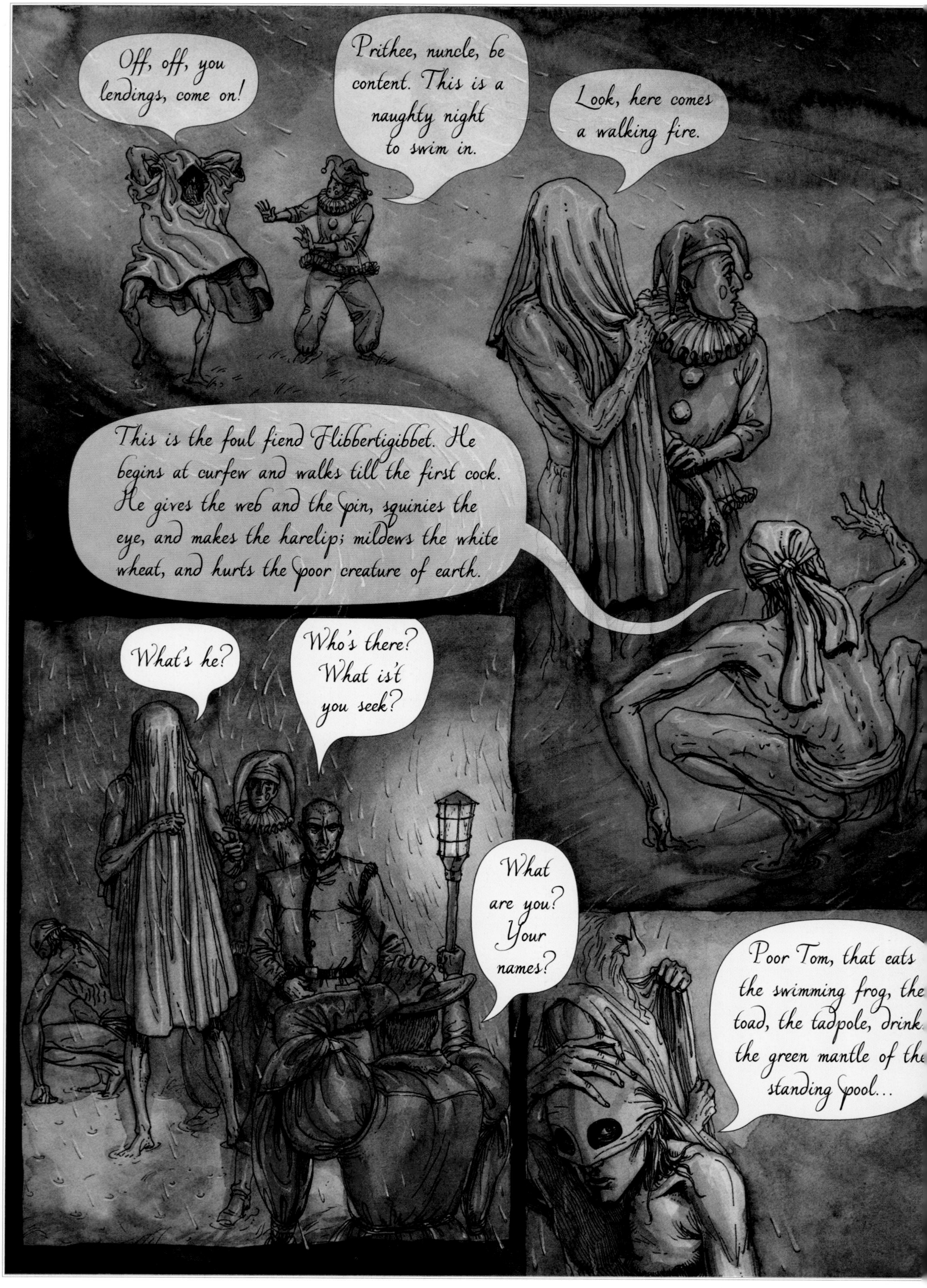
Off, off, you lendings, come on!
Prithee, nuncle, be content. This is a naughty night to swim in.
Look, here comes a walking fire.
This is the foul fiend Flibbertigibbet. He begins at curfew and walks till the first cock. He gives the web and the pin, squinies the eye, and makes the harelip; mildews the white wheat, and hurts the poor creature of earth.
What's he?
Who's there? What is't you seek?
What are you? Your names?
Poor Tom, that eats the swimming frog, the toad, the tadpole, drink the green mantle of the standing pool...

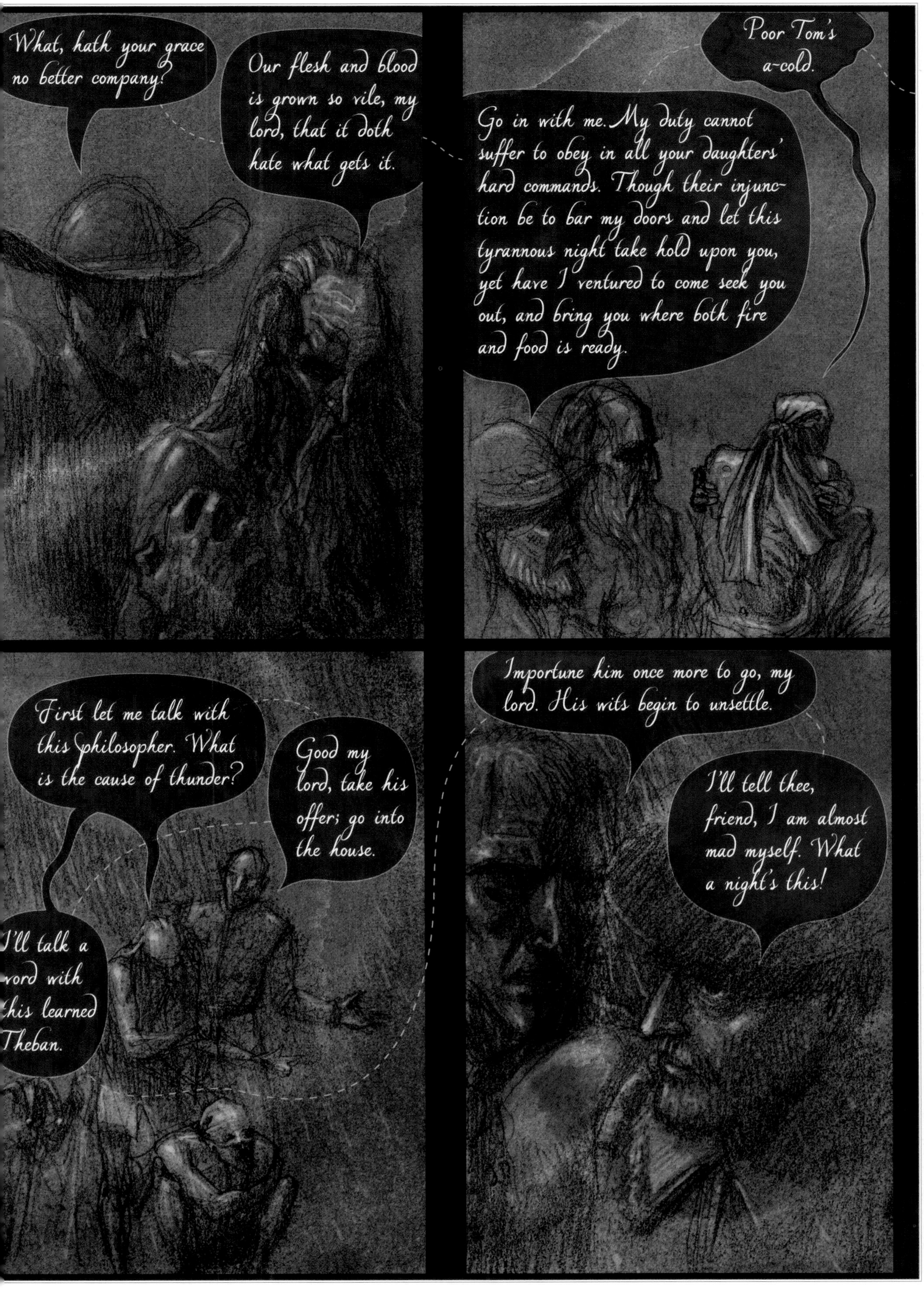
What, hath your grace no better company?
Our flesh and blood is grown so vile, my lord, that it doth hate what gets it.
Poor Tom's a-cold.
Go in with me. My duty cannot suffer to obey in all your daughters' hard commands. Though their injunction be to bar my doors and let this tyrannous night take hold upon you, yet have I ventured to come seek you out, and bring you where both fire and food is ready.
First let me talk with this philosopher. What is the cause of thunder?
Good my lord, take his offer; go into the house.
I'll talk a word with this learned Theban.
Importune him once more to go, my lord. His wits begin to unsettle.
I'll tell thee, friend, I am almost mad myself. What a night's this!

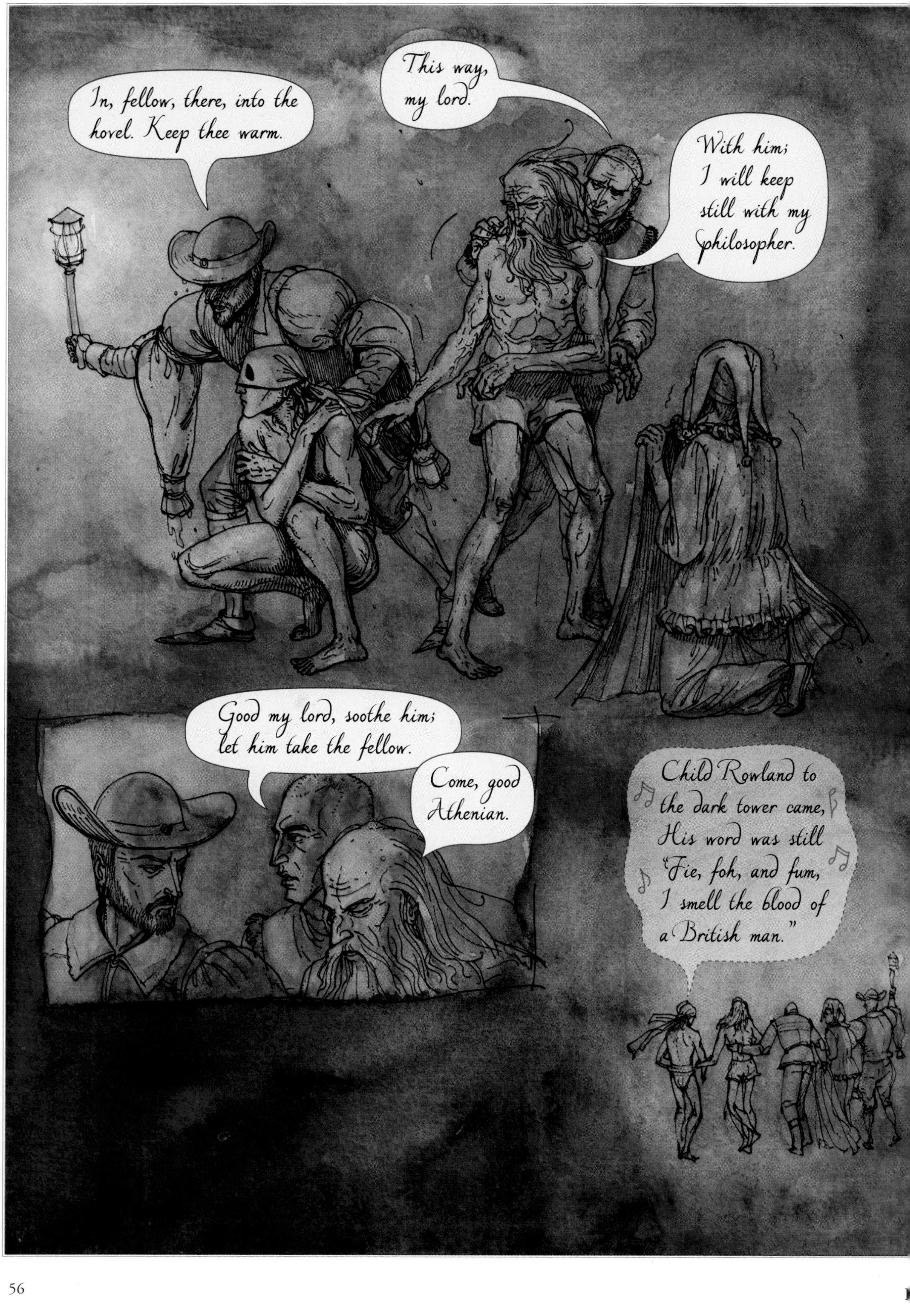

In, fellow, there, into the hovel. Keep thee warm.
This way, my lord.
With him; I will keep still with my philosopher.
Good my lord, soothe him; let him take the fellow.
Come, good Athenian.
Child Rowland to the dark tower came, His word was still "Fie, foh, and fum, I smell the blood of a British man."

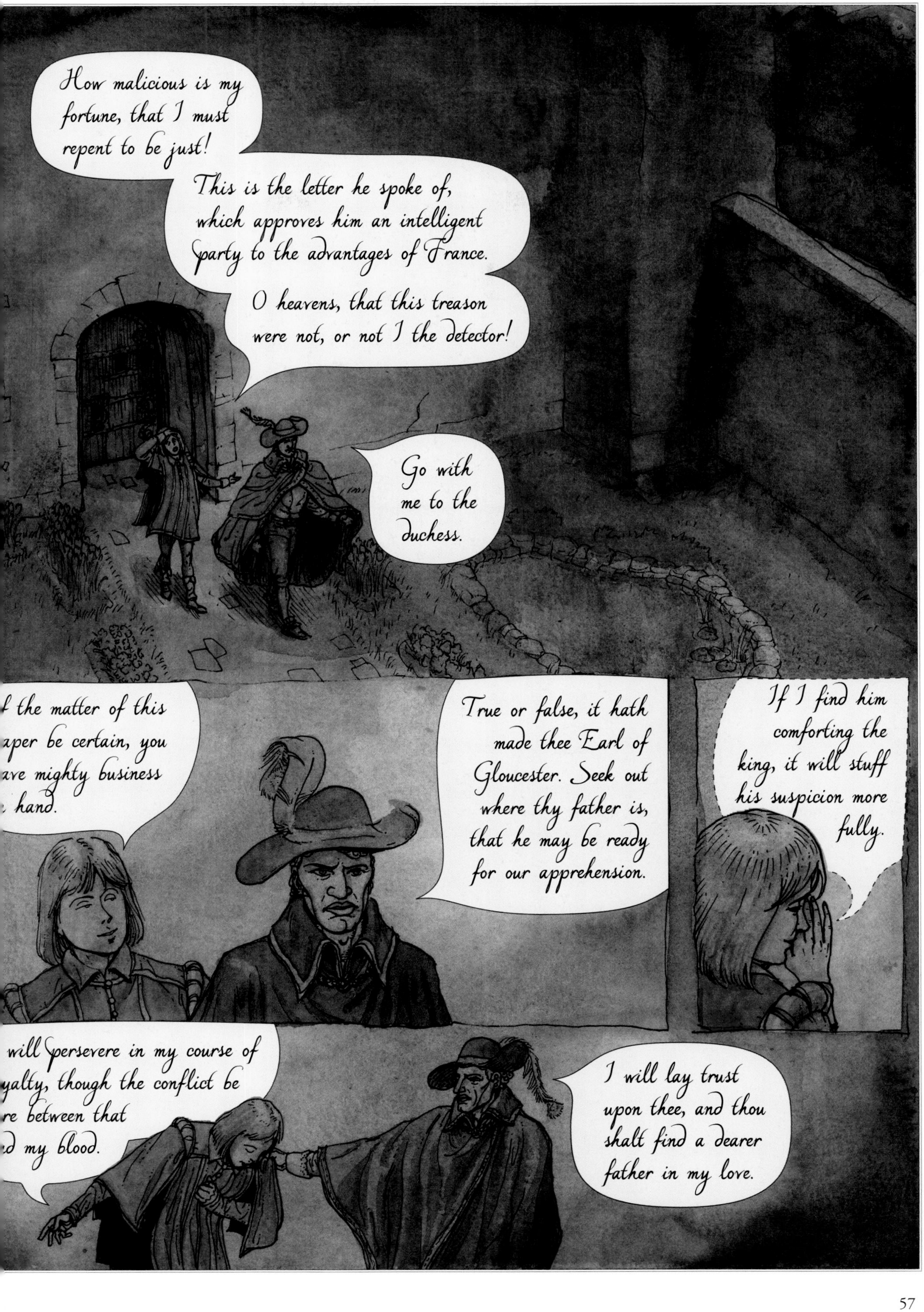
How malicious is my fortune, that I must repent to be just!
This is the letter he spoke of, which approves him an intelligent party to the advantages of France.
O heavens, that this treason were not, or not I the detector!
Go with me to the duchess.
f the matter of this aper be certain, you ave mighty business hand.
True or false, it hath made thee Earl of Gloucester. Seek out where thy father is, that he may be ready for our apprehension.
If I find him comforting the king, it will stuff his suspicion more fully.
will persevere in my course of yalty, though the conflict be re between that d my blood.
I will lay trust upon thee, and thou shalt find a dearer father in my love.

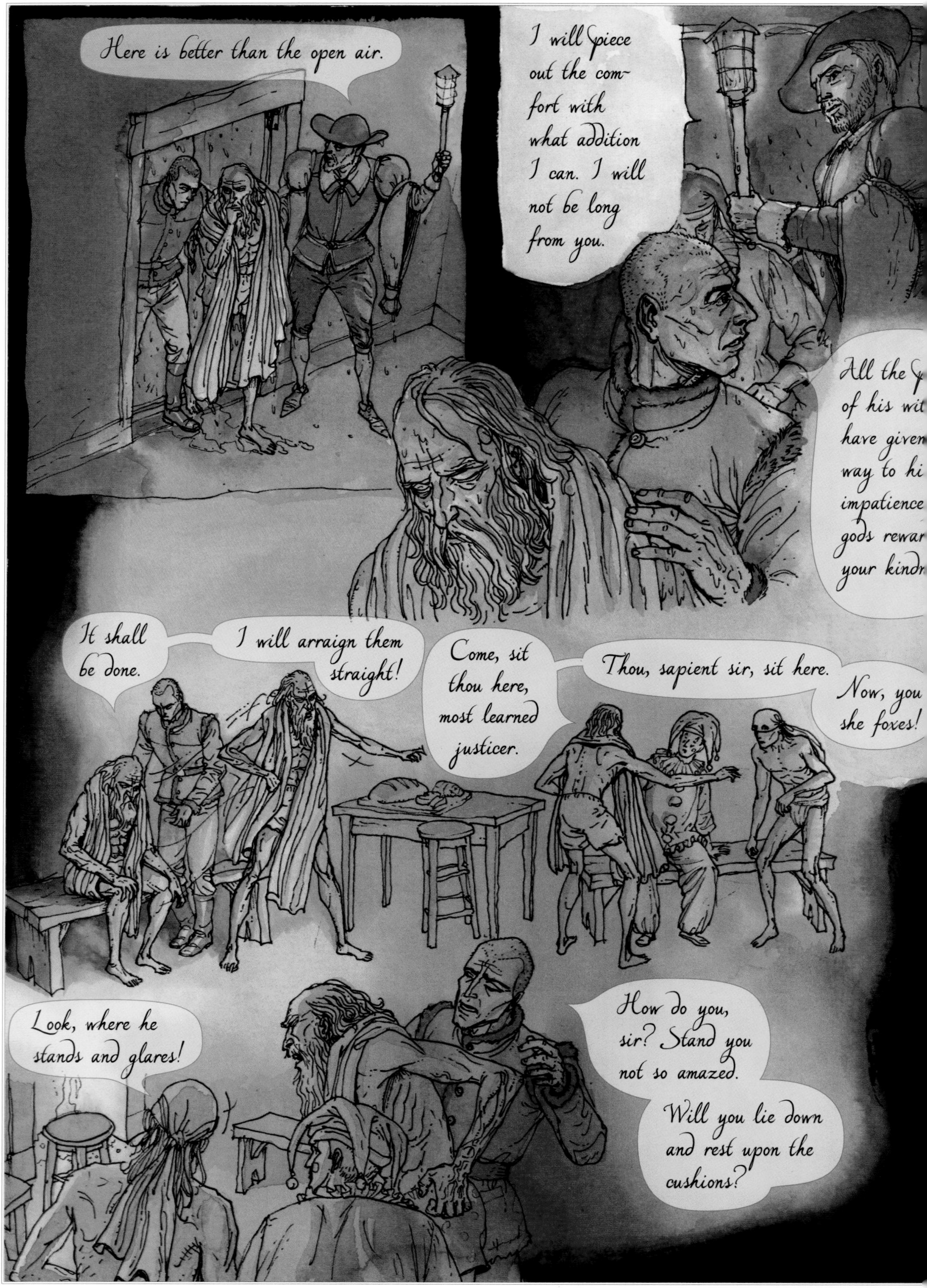
Here is better than the open air.
I will piece out the comfort with what addition I can. I will not be long from you.
All the of his wit have given way to hi impatience gods rewar your kindn
It shall be done.
I will arraign them straight!
Come, sit thou here, most learned justicer.
Thou, sapient sir, sit here.
Now, you she foxes!
Look, where he stands and glares!
How do you, sir? Stand you not so amazed.
Will you lie down and rest upon the cushions?

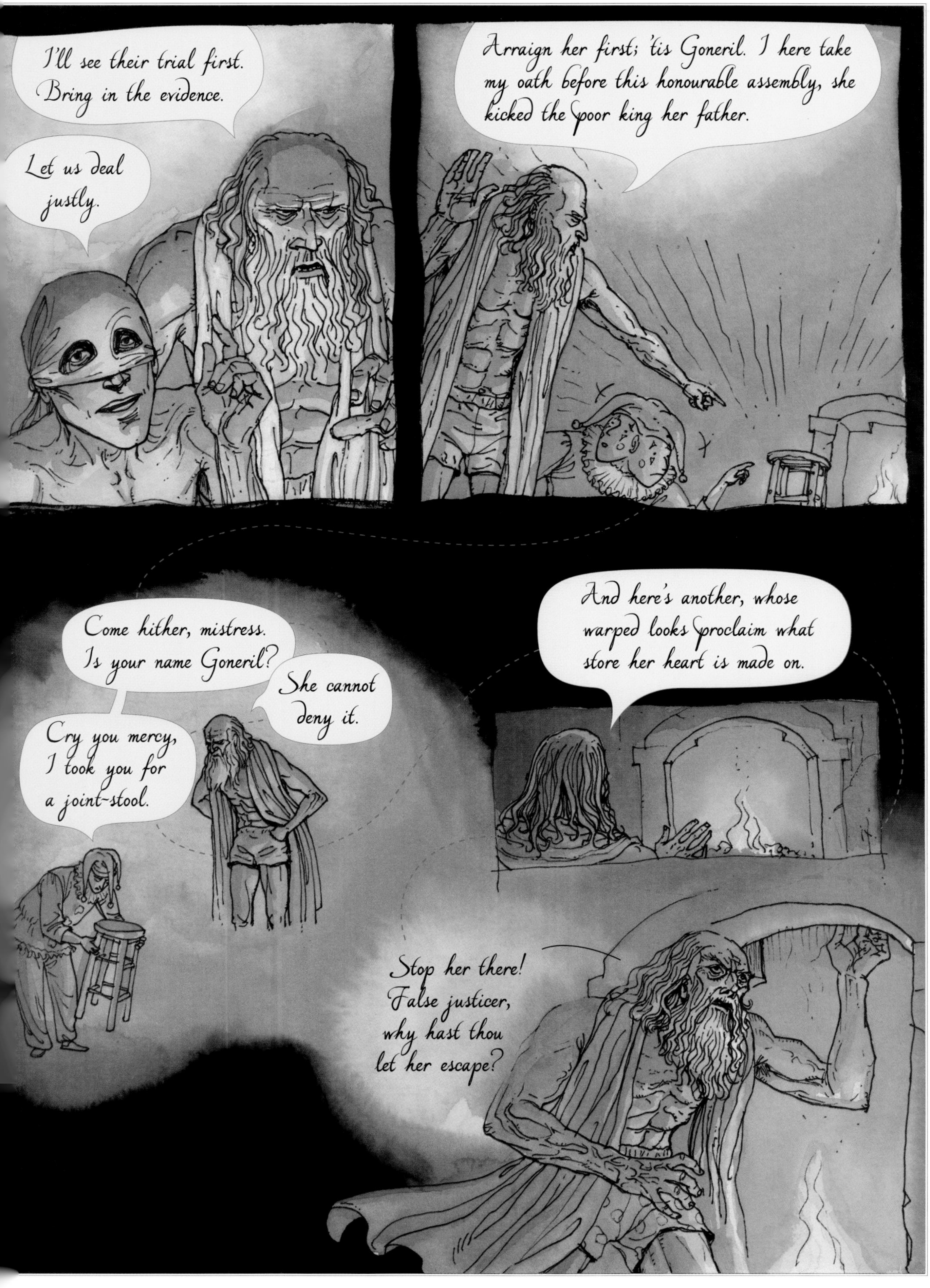
I'll see their trial first. Bring in the evidence.
Let us deal justly.
Arraign her first; 'tis Goneril. I here take my oath before this honourable assembly, she kicked the poor king her father.
Come hither, mistress. Is your name Goneril?
She cannot deny it.
Cry you mercy, I took you for a joint-stool.
And here's another, whose warped looks proclaim what store her heart is made on.
Stop her there! False justicer, why hast thou let her escape?

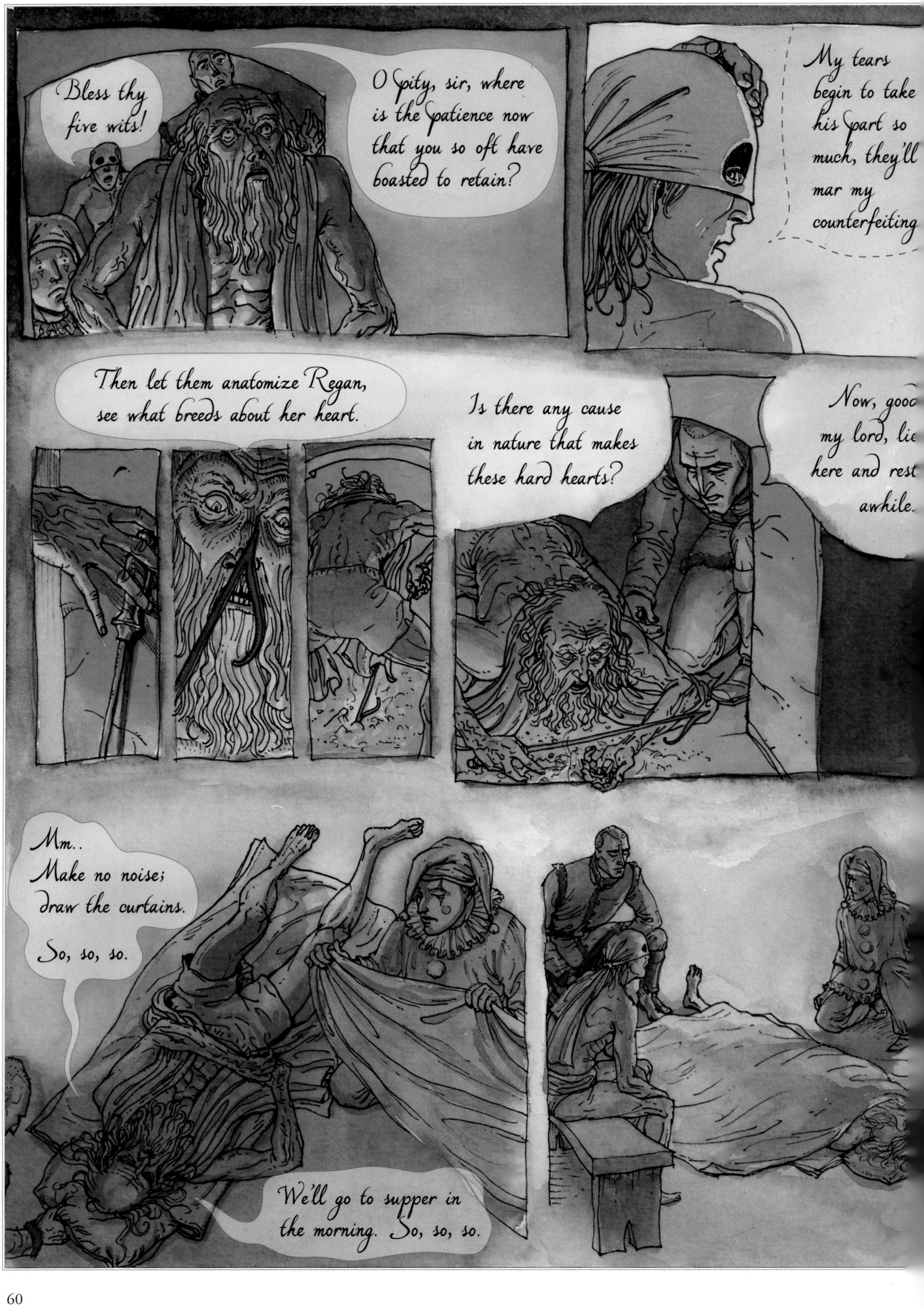
Bless thy five wits!
O pity, sir, where is the patience now that you so oft have boasted to retain?
My tears begin to take his part so much, they'll mar my counterfeiting
Then let them anatomize Regan, see what breeds about her heart.
Is there any cause in nature that makes these hard hearts?
Now, good my lord, lie here and rest awhile.
Mm.. Make no noise; draw the curtains.
So, so, so.
We'll go to supper in the morning. So, so, so.

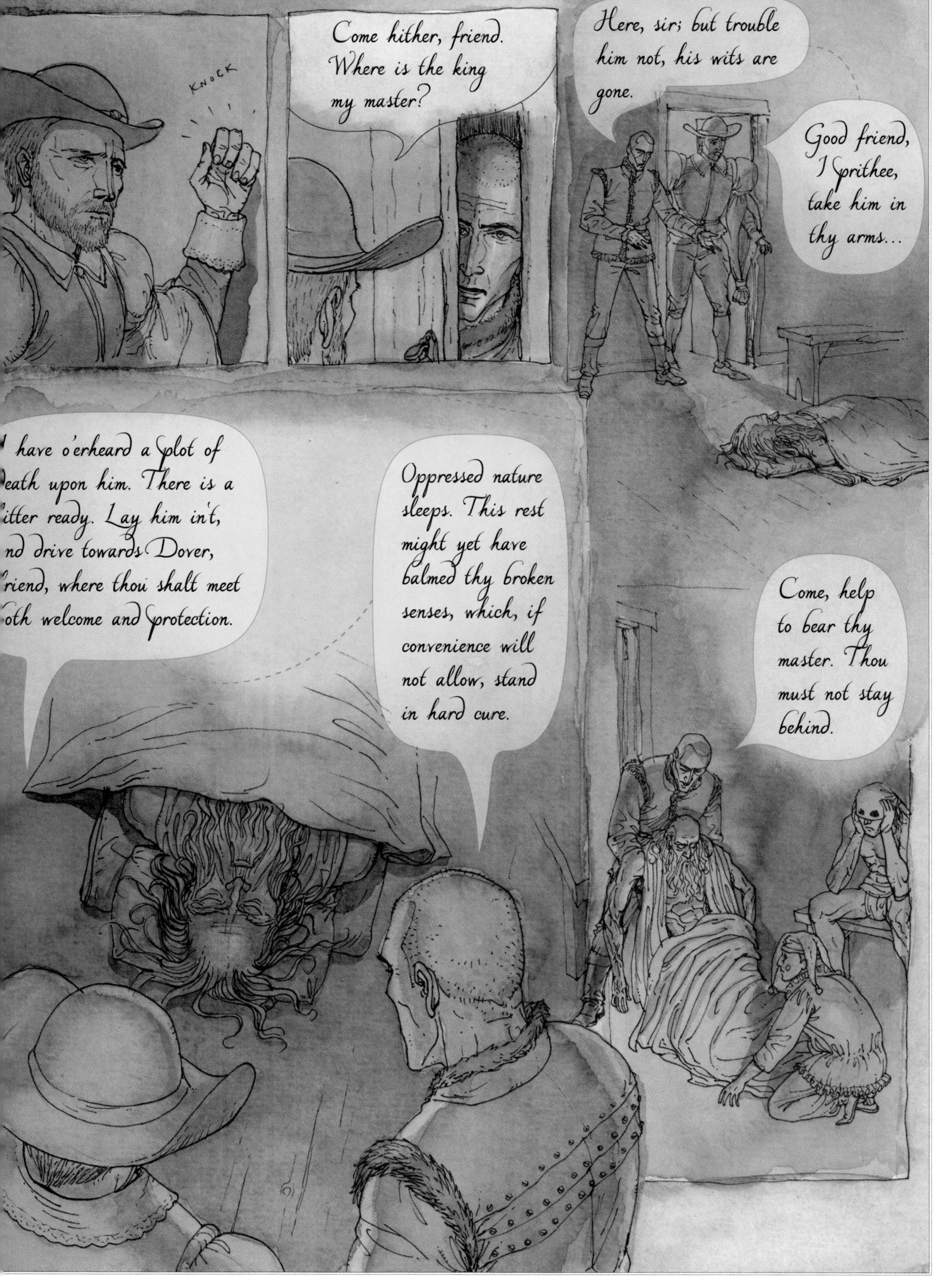
KNOCK
Come hither, friend. Where is the king my master?
Here, sir; but trouble him not, his wits are gone.
Good friend, I prithee, take him in thy arms...
have o'erheard a plot of eath upon him. There is a itter ready. Lay him in't, nd drive towards Dover, riend, where thou shalt meet oth welcome and protection.
Oppressed nature sleeps. This rest might yet have balmed thy broken senses, which, if convenience will not allow, stand in hard cure.
Come, help to bear thy master. Thou must not stay behind.

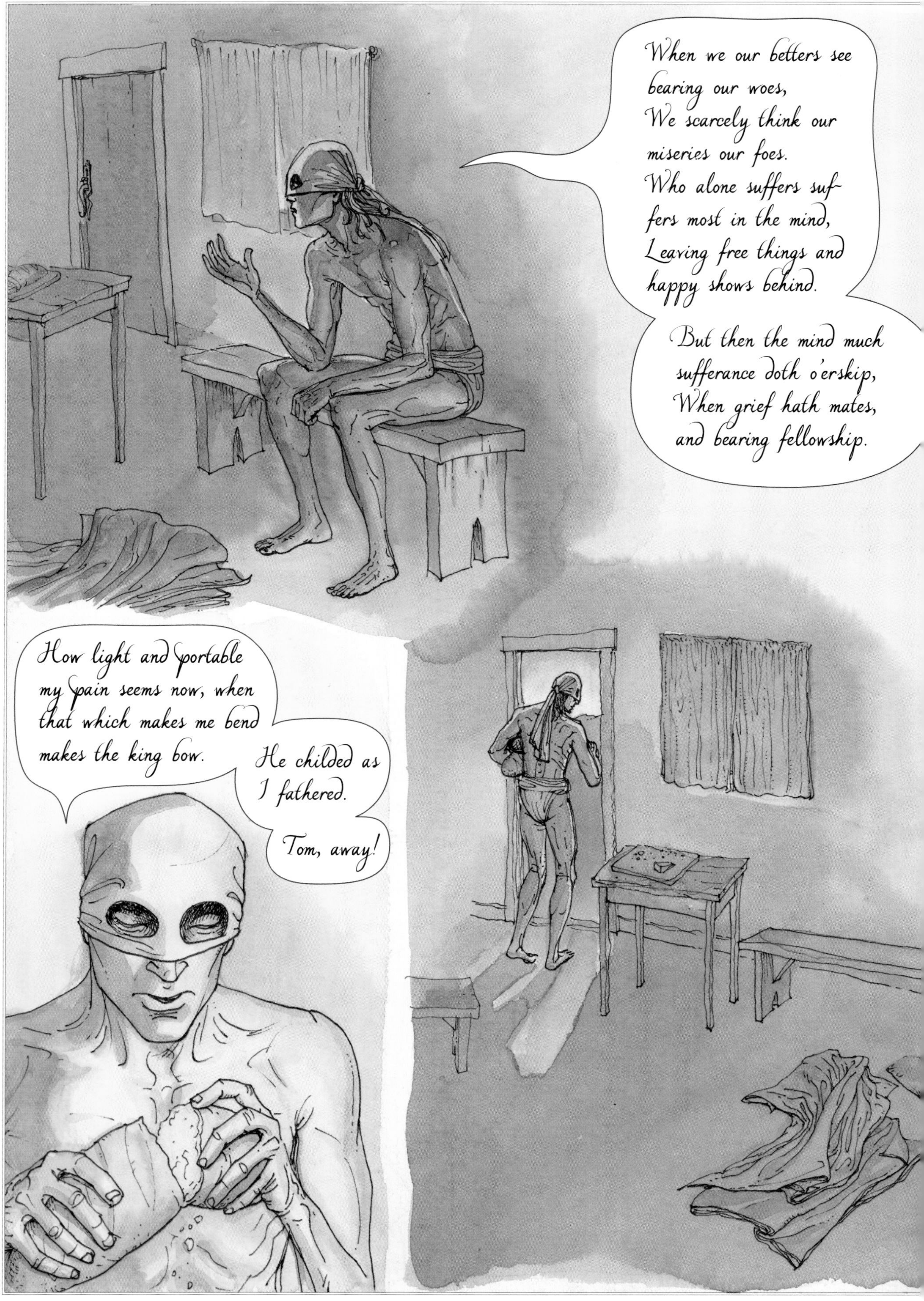
When we our betters see bearing our woes, We scarcely think our miseries our foes. Who alone suffers suffers most in the mind, Leaving free things and happy shows behind.
But then the mind much sufferance doth o'erskip, When grief hath mates, and bearing fellowship.
How light and portable my pain seems now, when that which makes me bend makes the king bow.
He childed as I fathered.
Tom, away!

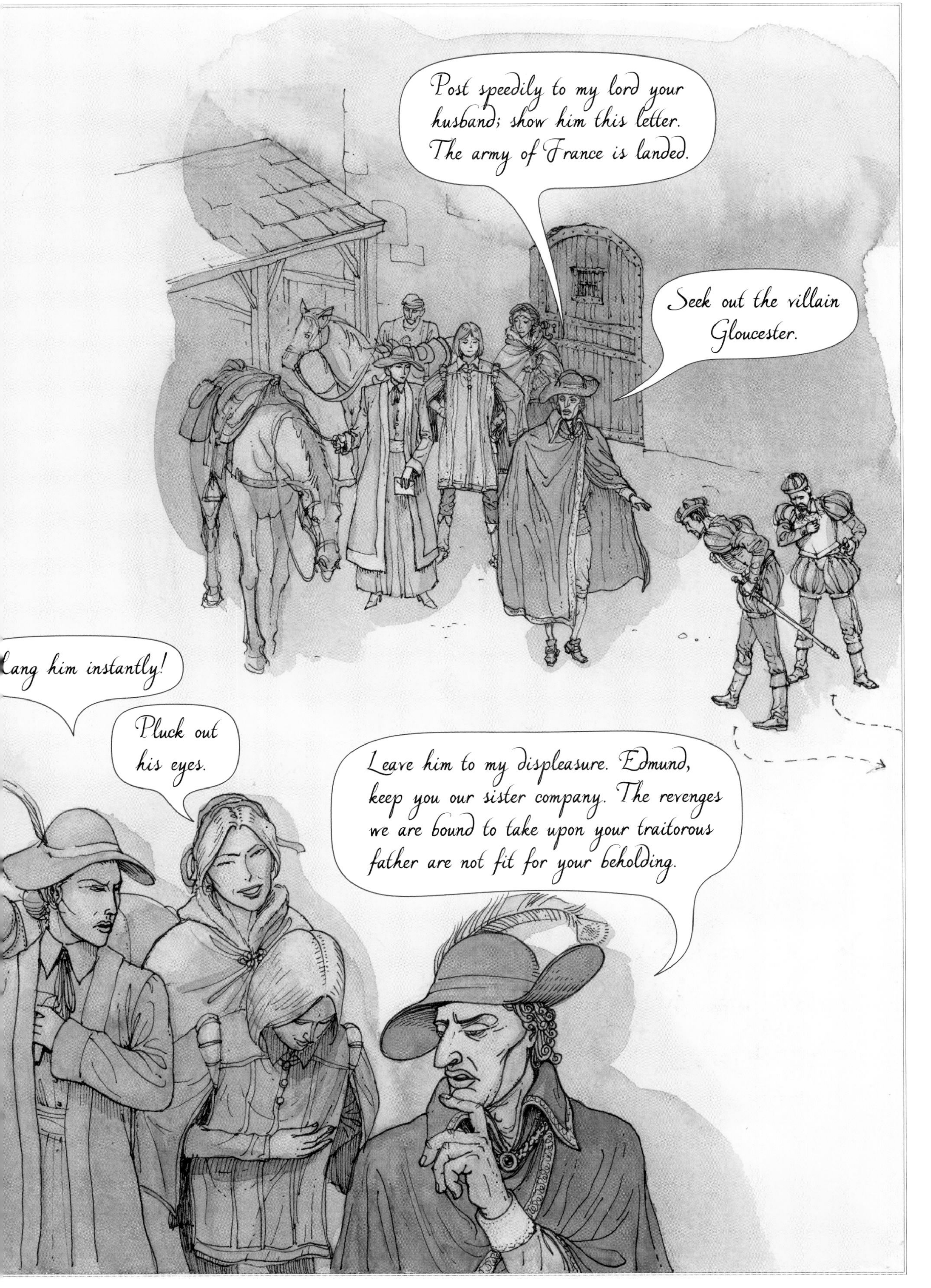
Post speedily to my lord your husband; show him this letter. The army of France is landed.
Seek out the villain Gloucester.
Hang him instantly!
Pluck out his eyes.
Leave him to my displeasure. Edmund, keep you our sister company. The revenges we are bound to take upon your traitorous father are not fit for your beholding.

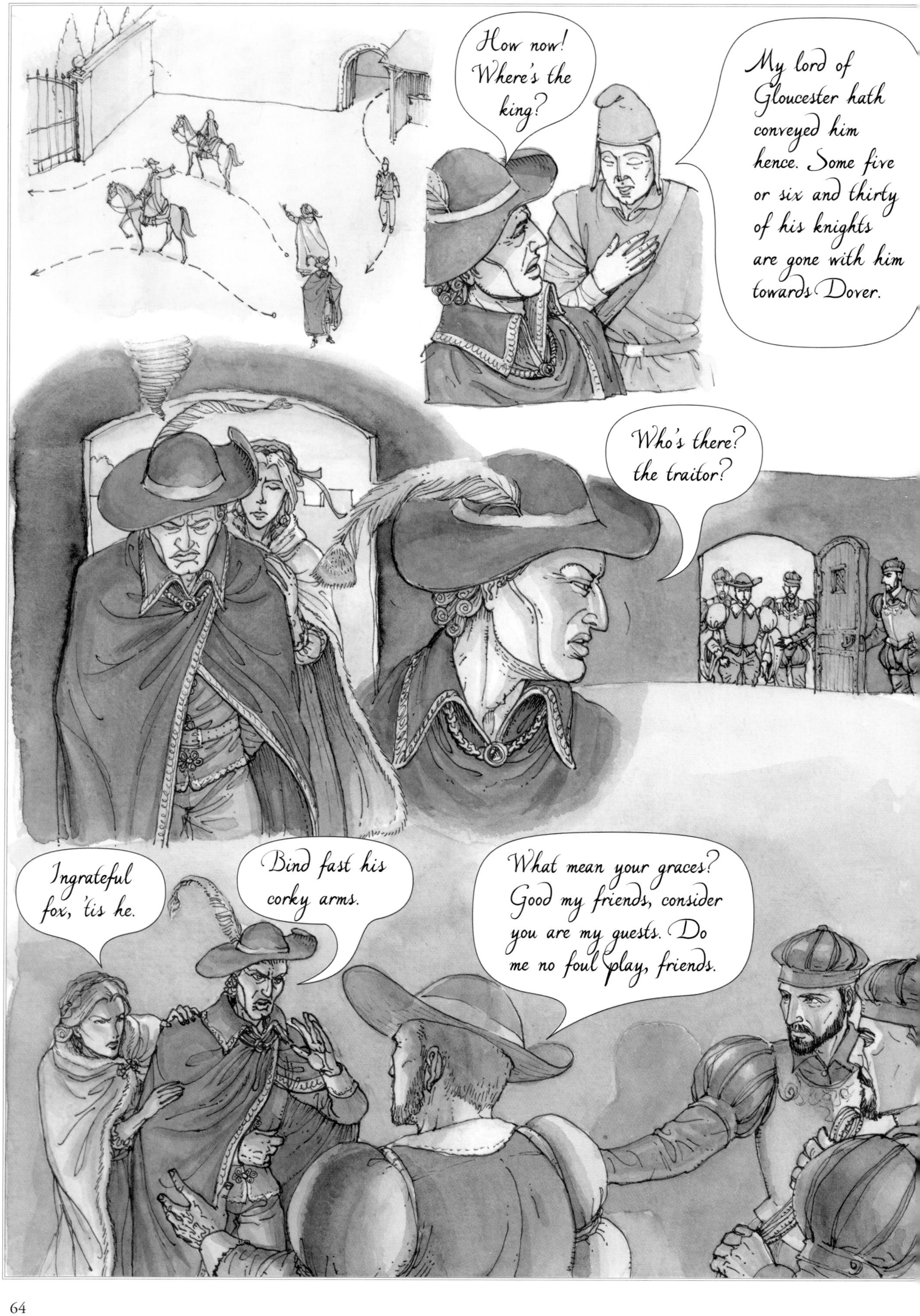
How now! Where's the king?
My lord of Gloucester hath conveyed him hence. Some five or six and thirty of his knights are gone with him towards Dover.
Who's there? the traitor?
Ingrateful fox, 'tis he.
Bind fast his corky arms.
What mean your graces? Good my friends, consider you are my guests. Do me no foul play, friends.

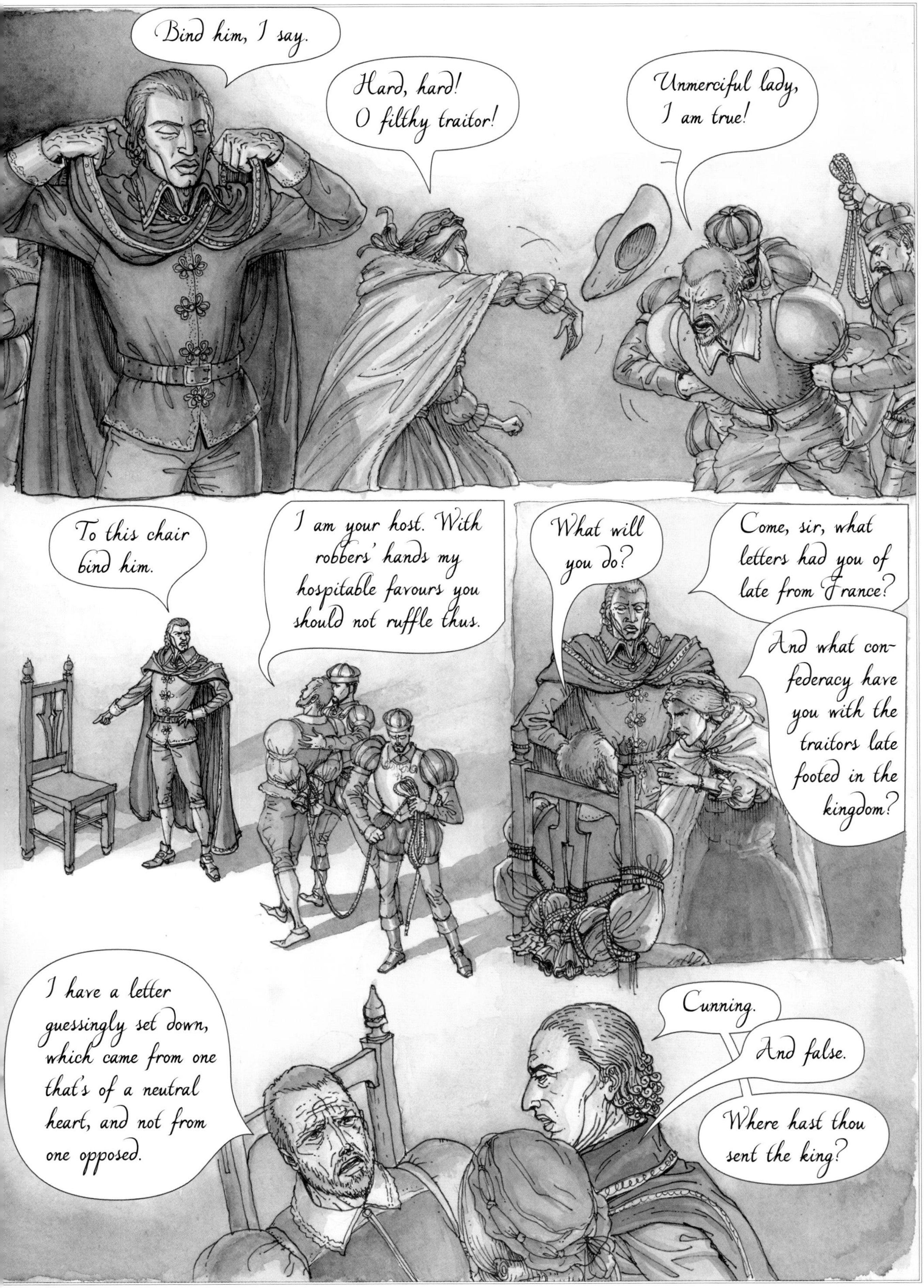
Bind him, I say.
Hard, hard! O filthy traitor!
Unmerciful lady, I am true!
To this chair bind him.
I am your host. With robbers' hands my hospitable favours you should not ruffle thus.
What will you do?
Come, sir, what letters had you of late from France?
And what confederacy have you with the traitors late footed in the kingdom?
I have a letter guessingly set down, which came from one that's of a neutral heart, and not from one opposed.
Cunning.
And false.
Where hast thou sent the king?

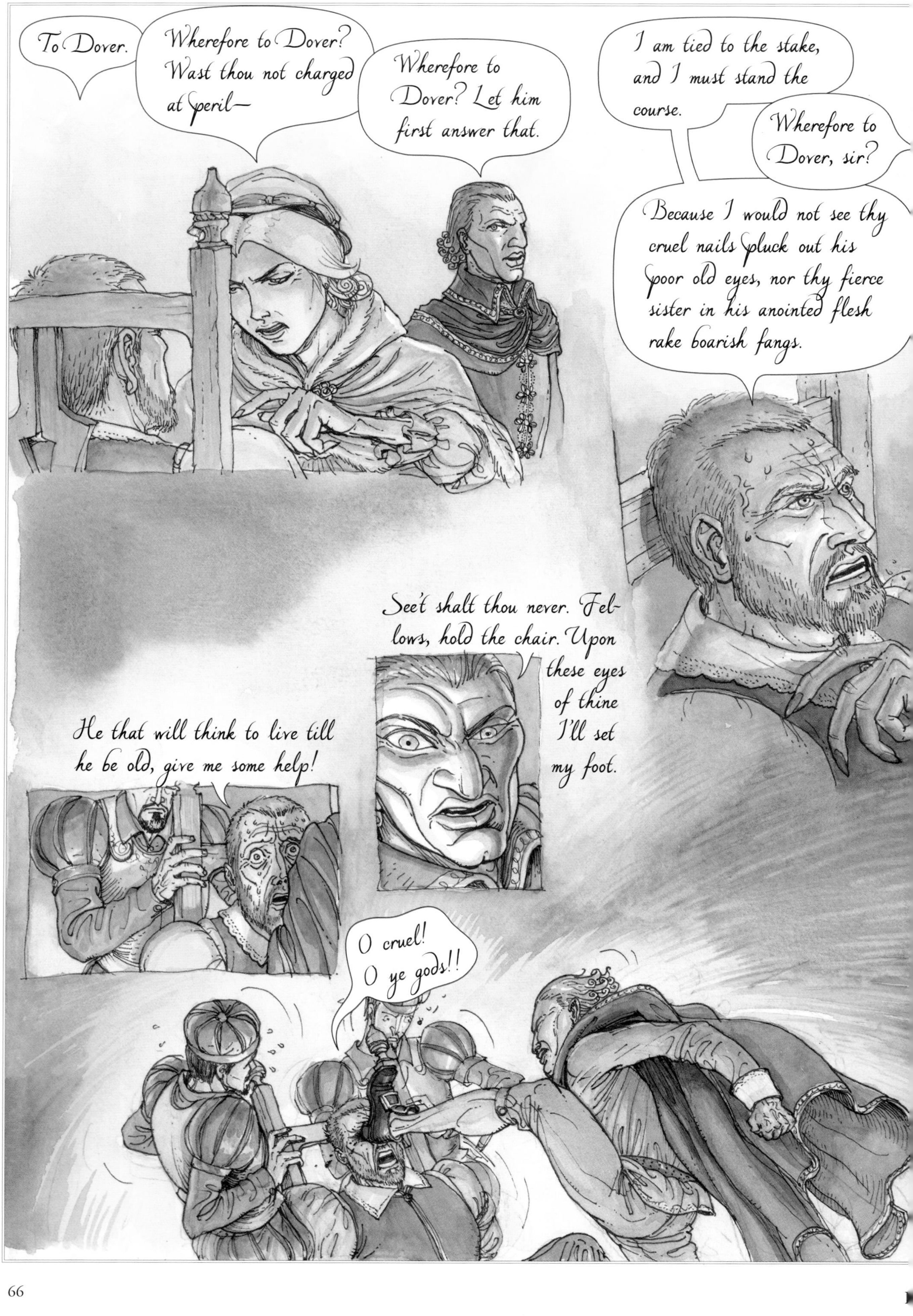
To Dover.
Wherefore to Dover? Wast thou not charged at peril—
Wherefore to Dover? Let him first answer that.
I am tied to the stake, and I must stand the course.
Wherefore to Dover, sir?
Because I would not see thy cruel nails pluck out his poor old eyes, nor thy fierce sister in his anointed flesh rake boarish fangs.
See't shalt thou never. Fellows, hold the chair. Upon these eyes of thine I'll set my foot.
He that will think to live till he be old, give me some help!
O cruel! O ye gods!!

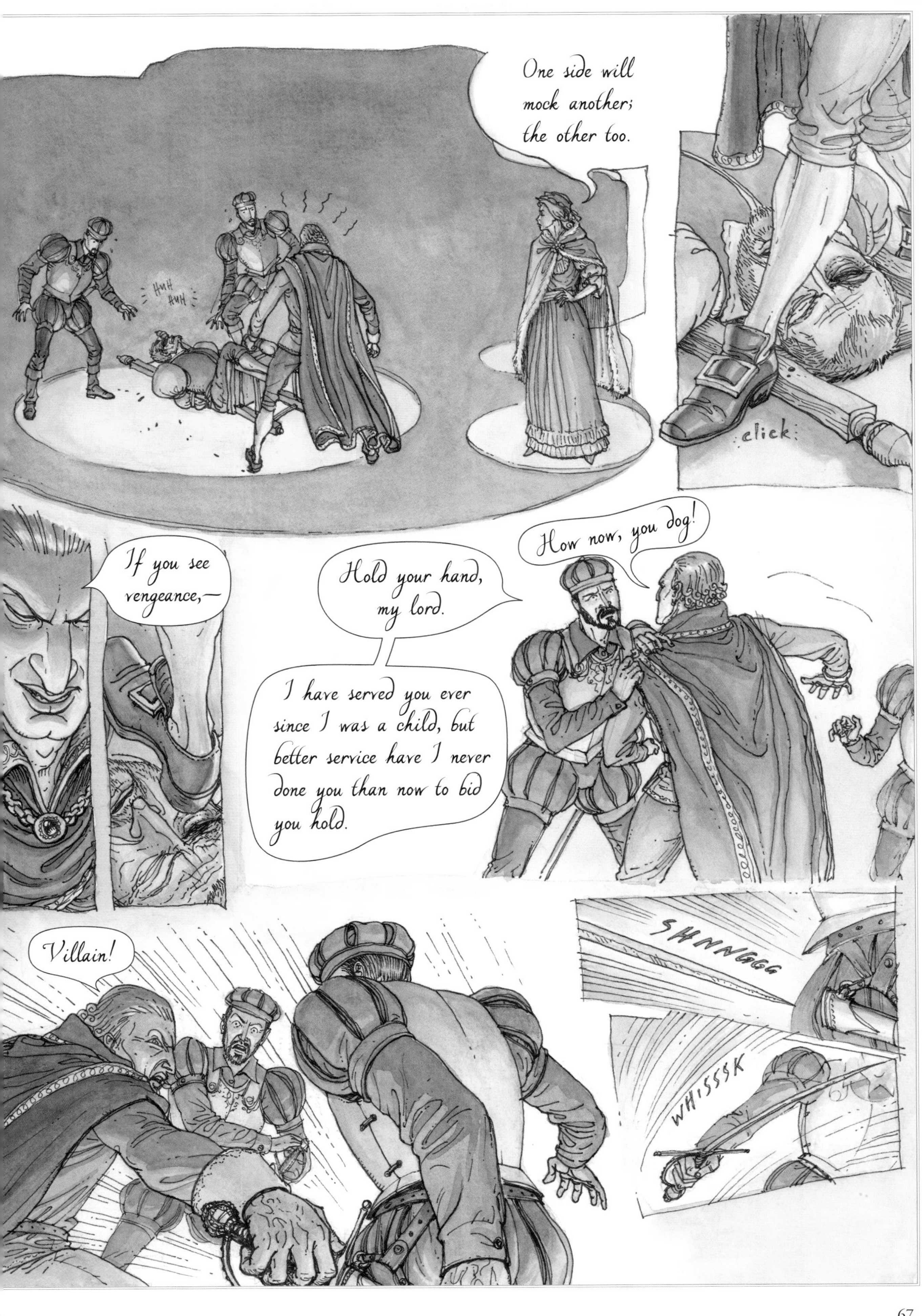
HUH
HUH
One side will mock another; the other too.
click
If you see vengeance,—
Hold your hand, my lord.
I have served you ever since I was a child, but better service have I never done you than now to bid you hold.
How now, you dog!
Villain!
SHNNGGG
WHISSSK

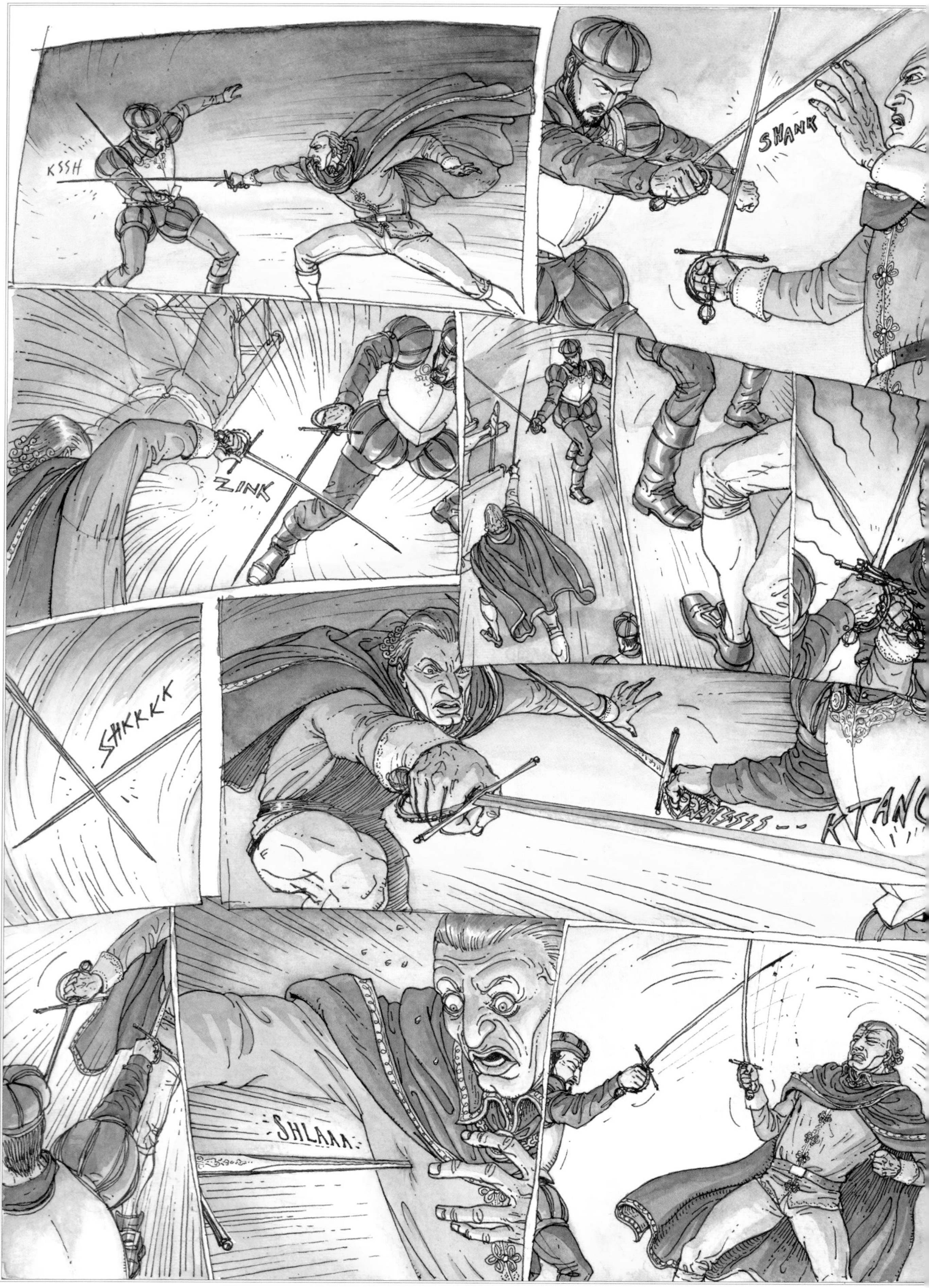
KSSH
SHANK
ZINK
SHKKKK
WHSSSSS--
KTAN
SHLAAA

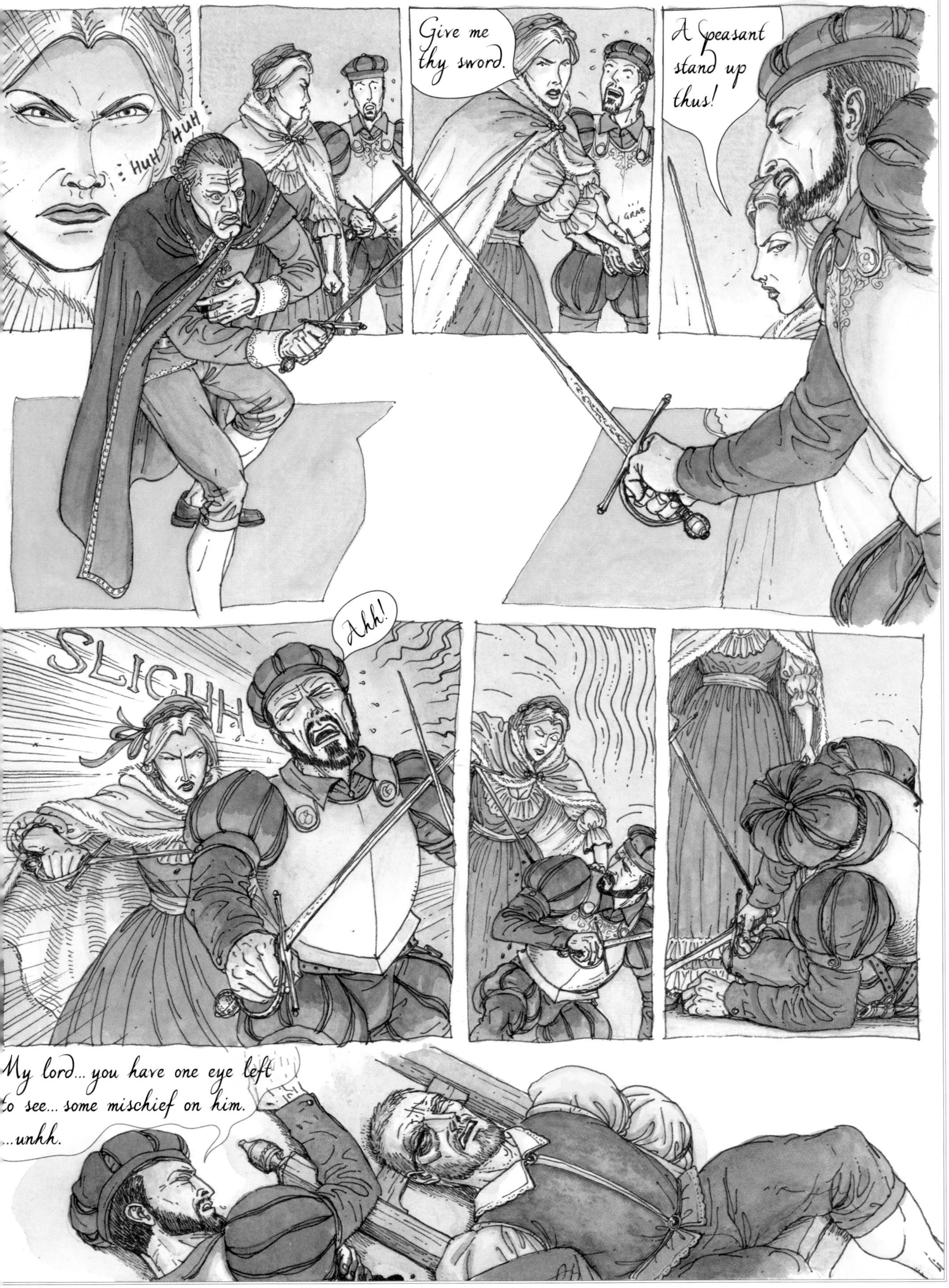
HUH
HUH
HUH
Give me thy sword.
GRAB
A peasant stand up thus!
SLICHH
Ahh!
My lord... you have one eye left to see... some mischief on him.
...unhh.

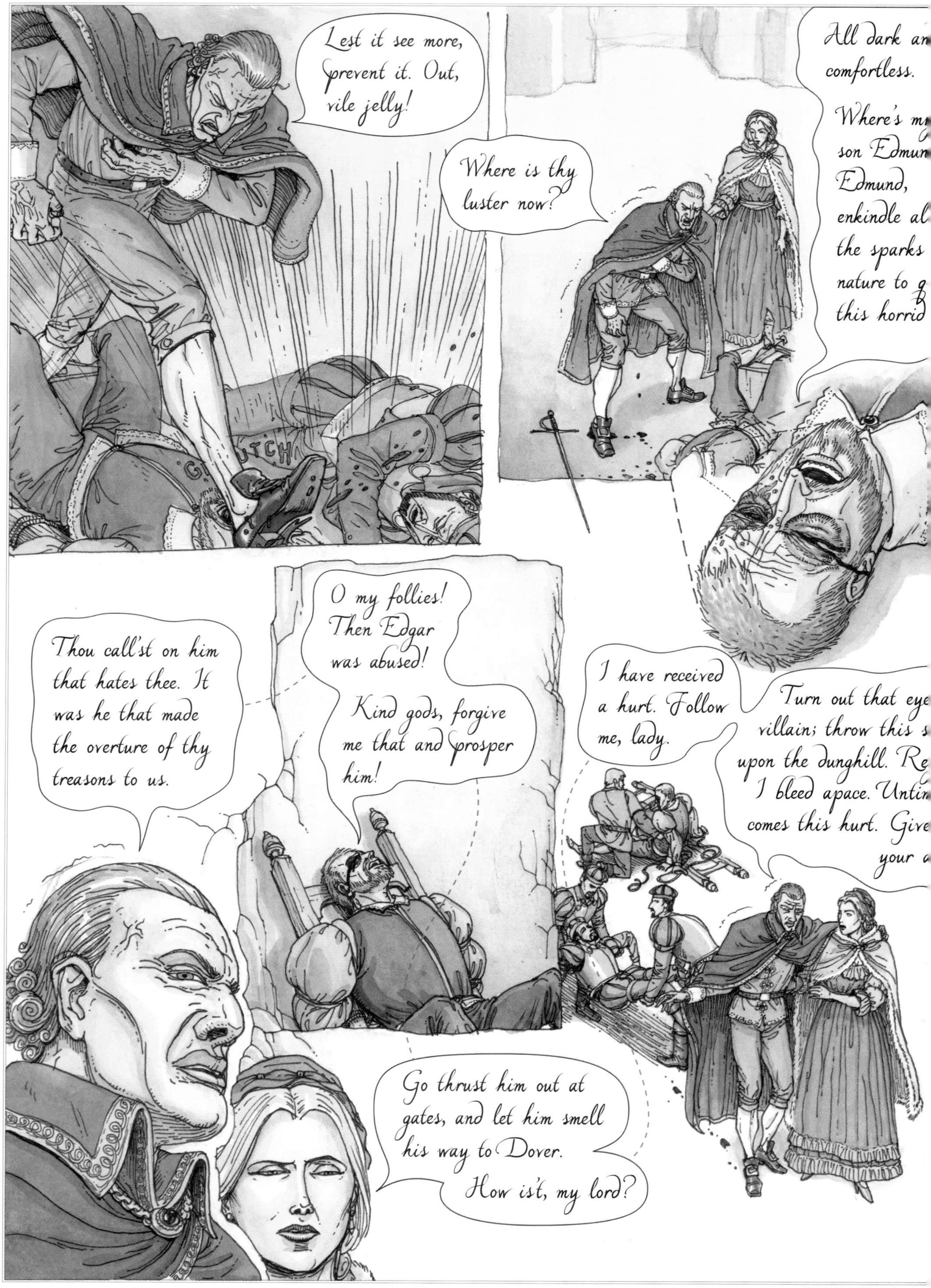
Lest it see more, prevent it. Out, vile jelly!
Where is thy luster now?
All dark an comfortless.
Where's m son Edmun Edmund, enkindle al the sparks nature to this horrid
Thou call'st on him that hates thee. It was he that made the overture of thy treasons to us.
O my follies! Then Edgar was abused!
Kind gods, forgive me that and prosper him!
Go thrust him out at gates, and let him smell his way to Dover.
How is't, my lord?
I have received a hurt. Follow me, lady.
Turn out that eye villain; throw this s upon the dunghill. Re I bleed apace. Untin comes this hurt. Give your

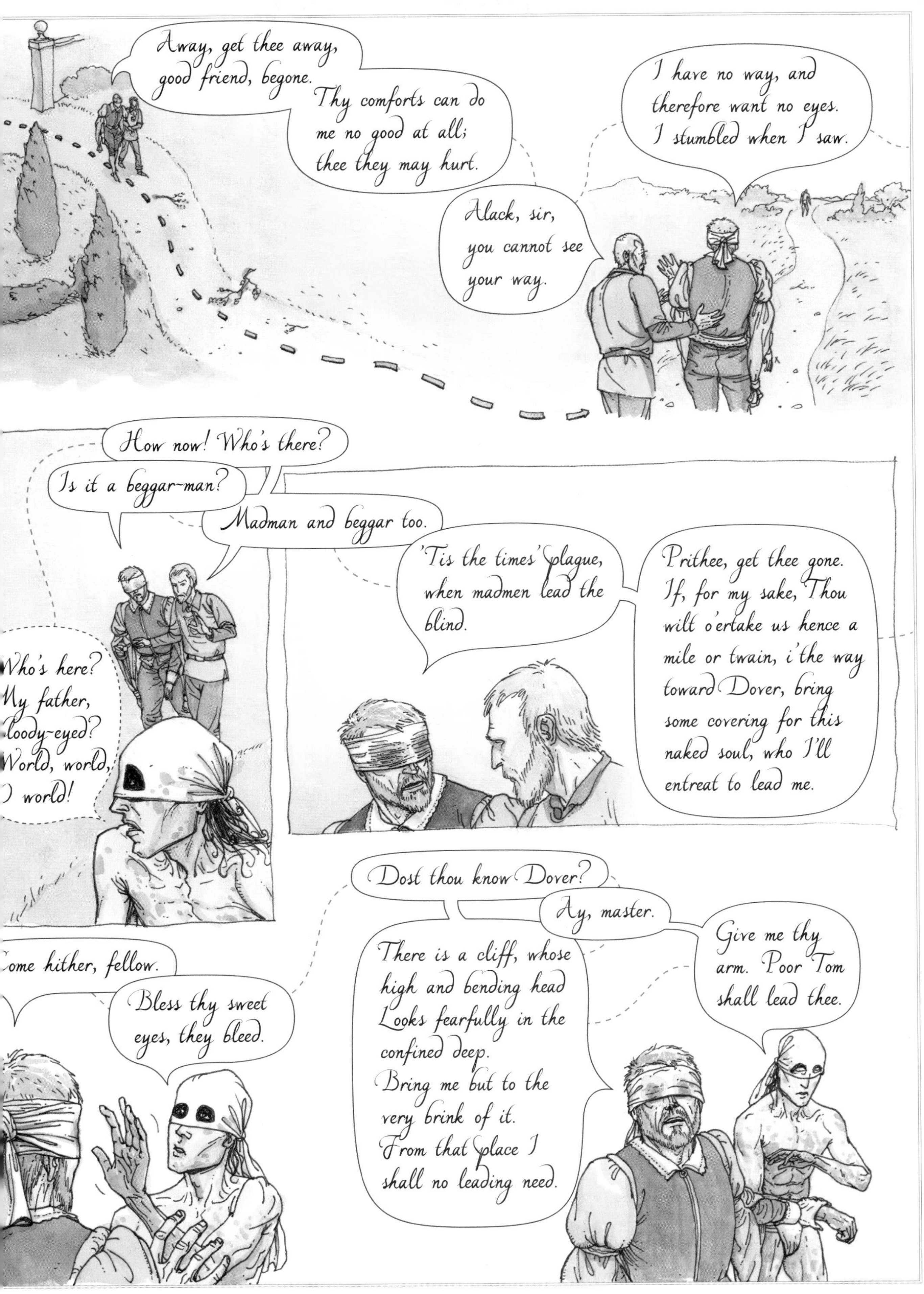

Away, get thee away, good friend, begone.
Thy comforts can do me no good at all; thee they may hurt.
Alack, sir, you cannot see your way.
I have no way, and therefore want no eyes. I stumbled when I saw.
How now! Who's there?
Is it a beggar-man?
Madman and beggar too.
Who's here? My father, bloody-eyed? World, world, O world!
'Tis the times' plague, when madmen lead the blind.
Prithee, get thee gone. If, for my sake, Thou wilt o'ertake us hence a mile or twain, i' the way toward Dover, bring some covering for this naked soul, who I'll entreat to lead me.
Come hither, fellow.
Bless thy sweet eyes, they bleed.
Dost thou know Dover?
Ay, master.
There is a cliff, whose high and bending head Looks fearfully in the confined deep.
Bring me but to the very brink of it.
From that place I shall no leading need.
Give me thy arm. Poor Tom shall lead thee.

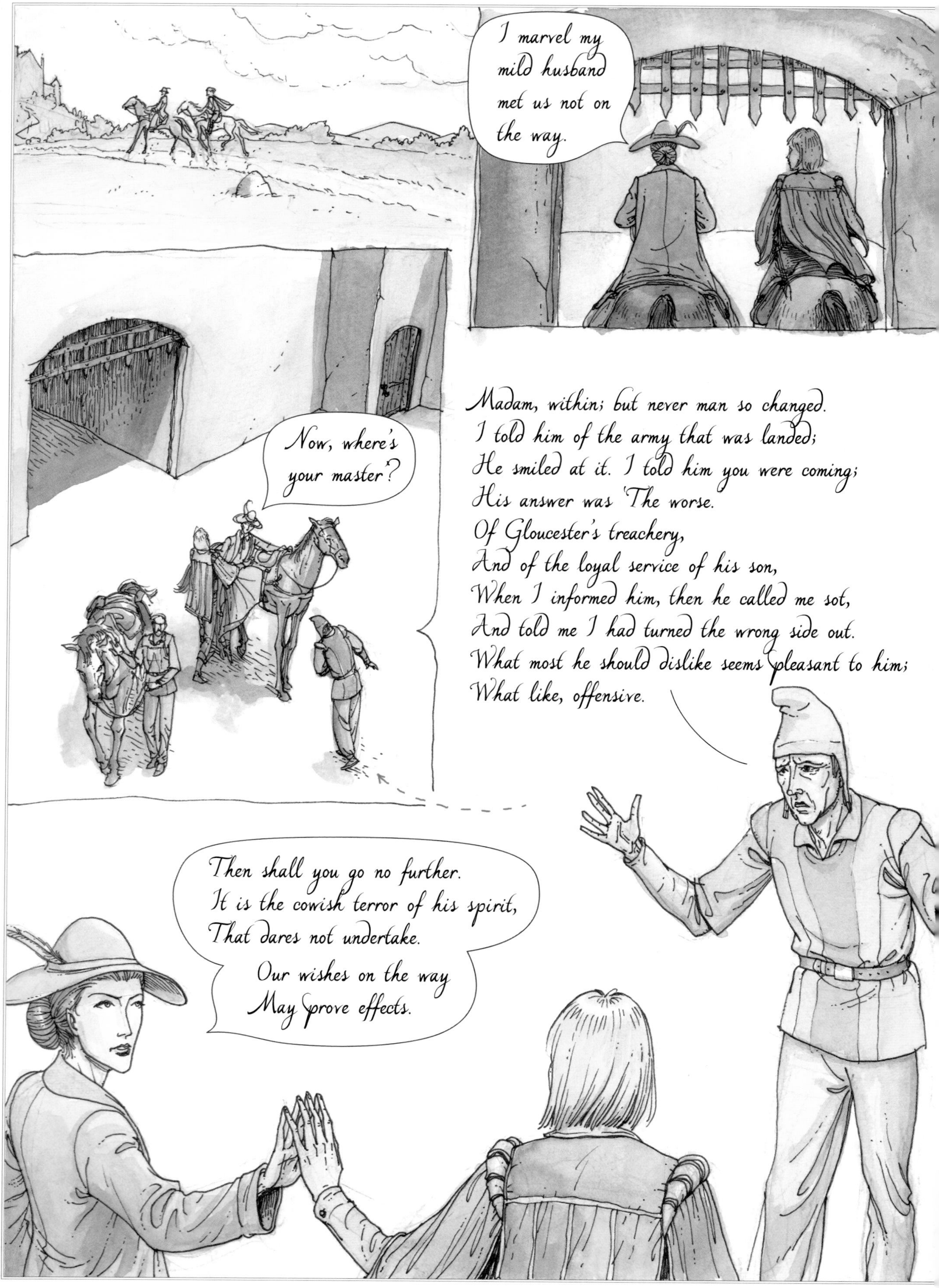
I marvel my mild husband met us not on the way.
Now, where's your master?
Madam, within; but never man so changed.
I told him of the army that was landed;
He smiled at it. I told him you were coming;
His answer was 'The worse.
Of Gloucester's treachery,
And of the loyal service of his son,
When I informed him, then he called me sot,
And told me I had turned the wrong side out.
What most he should dislike seems pleasant to him;
What like, offensive.
Then shall you go no further.
It is the cowish terror of his spirit,
That dares not undertake.
Our wishes on the way
May prove effects.

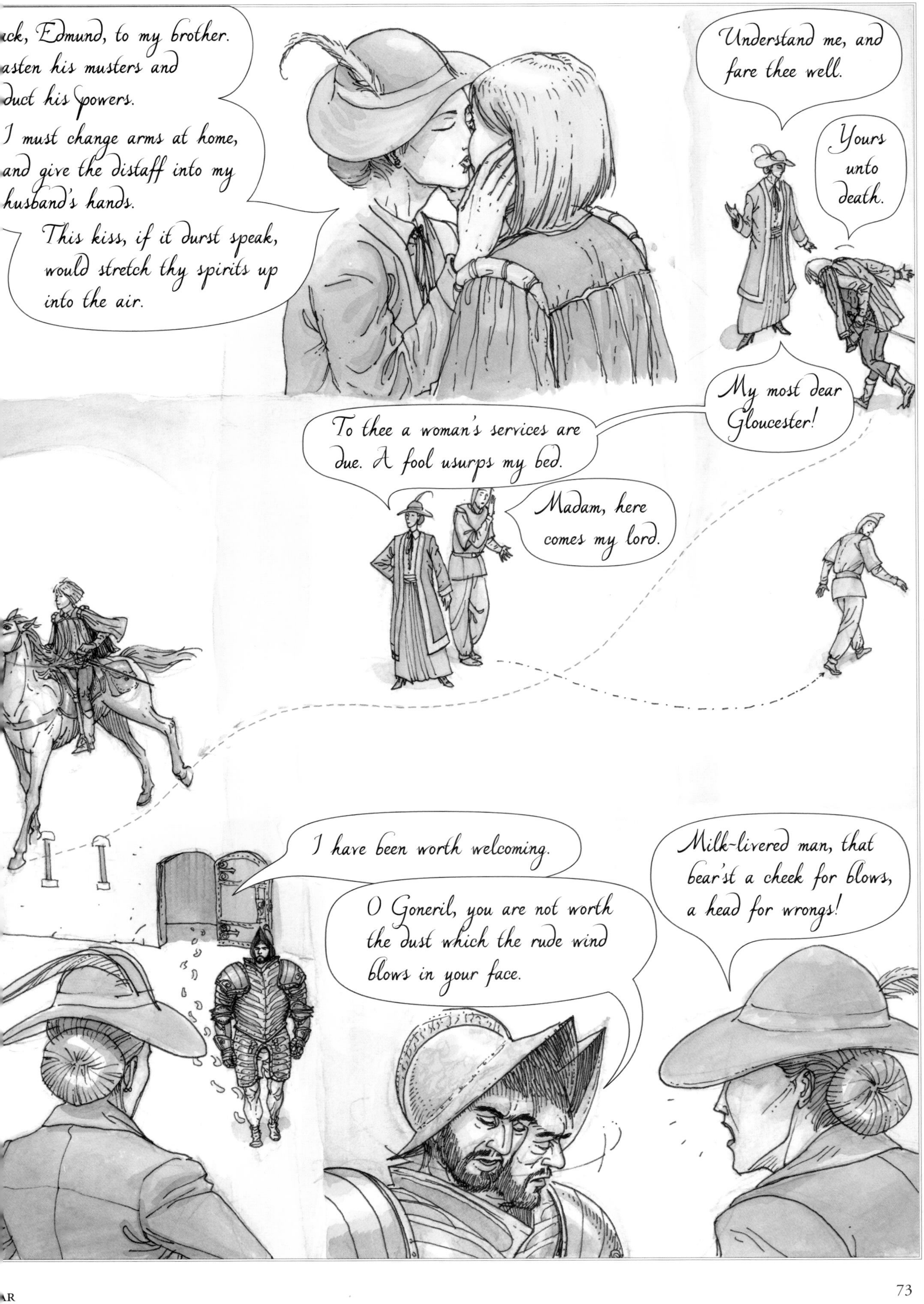
ack, Edmund, to my brother. asten his musters and duct his powers.
I must change arms at home, and give the distaff into my husband's hands.
This kiss, if it durst speak, would stretch thy spirits up into the air.
Understand me, and fare thee well.
Yours unto death.
My most dear Gloucester!
To thee a woman's services are due. A fool usurps my bed.
Madam, here comes my lord.
I have been worth welcoming.
O Goneril, you are not worth the dust which the rude wind blows in your face.
Milk-livered man, that bear'st a cheek for blows, a head for wrongs!

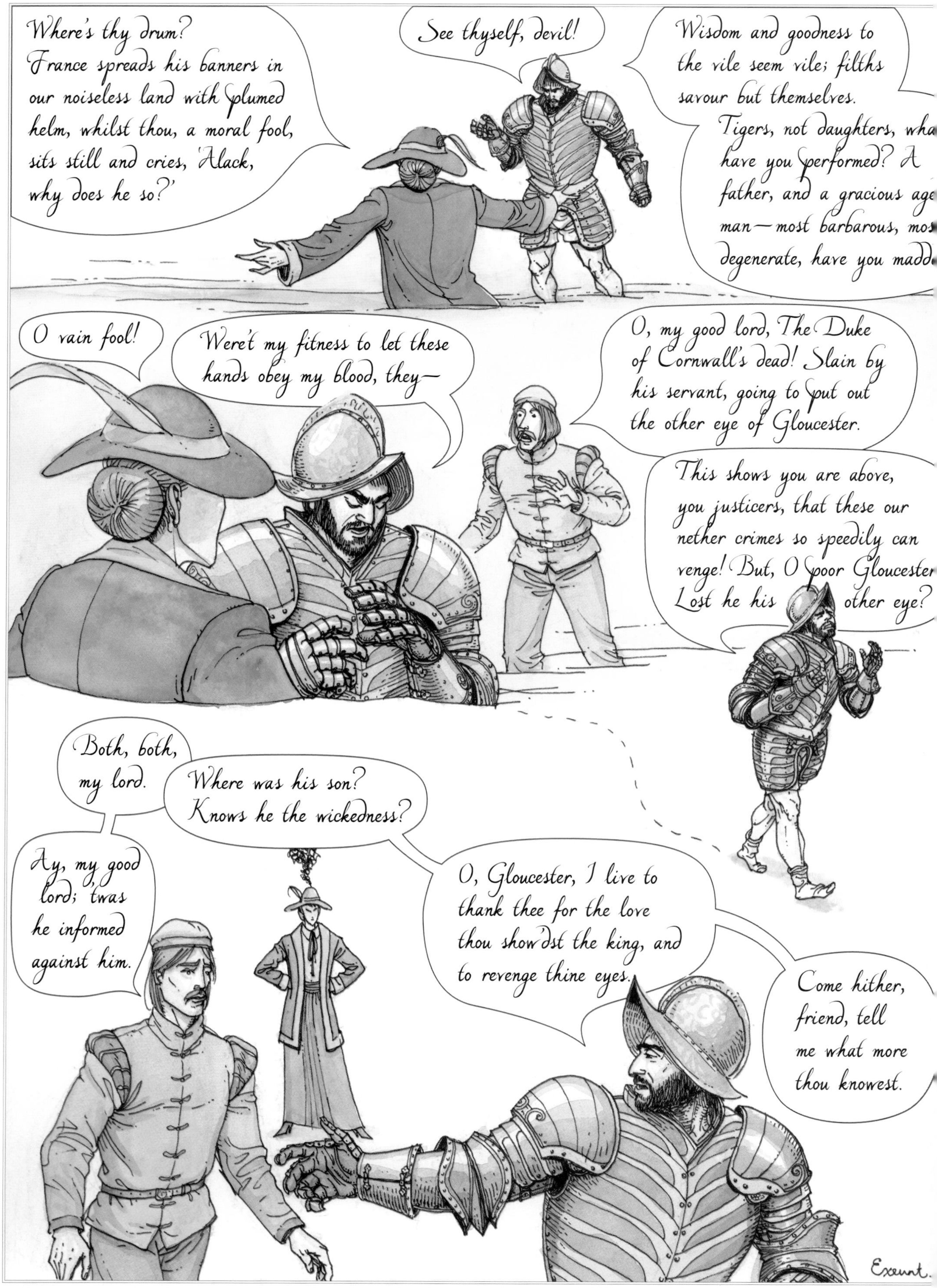

Where's thy drum? France spreads his banners in our noiseless land with plumed helm, whilst thou, a moral fool, sits still and cries, 'Alack, why does he so?'
See thyself, devil!
Wisdom and goodness to the vile seem vile; filths savour but themselves.
Tigers, not daughters, wha have you performed? A father, and a gracious age man—most barbarous, mos degenerate, have you madd
O vain fool!
Were't my fitness to let these hands obey my blood, they—
O, my good lord, The Duke of Cornwall's dead! Slain by his servant, going to put out the other eye of Gloucester.
This shows you are above, you justicers, that these our nether crimes so speedily can venge! But, O poor Gloucester Lost he his other eye?
Both, both, my lord.
Where was his son? Knows he the wickedness?
Ay, my good lord; twas he informed against him.
O, Gloucester, I live to thank thee for the love thou show'dst the king, and to revenge thine eyes.
Come hither, friend, tell me what more thou knowest.
Exeunt.

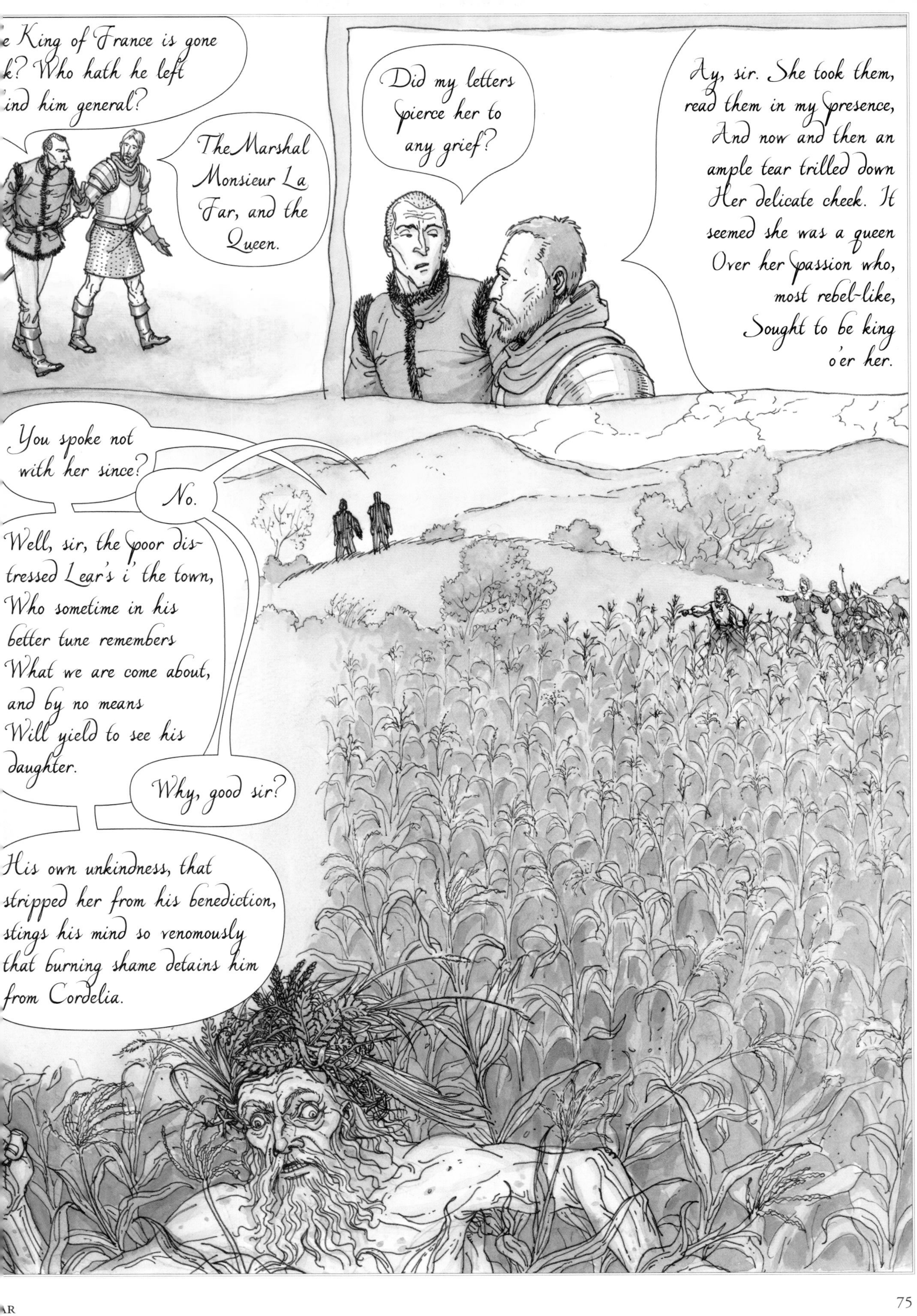

e King of France is gone
k? Who hath he left
ind him general?
The Marshal Monsieur La Far, and the Queen.
Did my letters pierce her to any grief?
Ay, sir. She took them, read them in my presence, And now and then an ample tear trilled down Her delicate cheek. It seemed she was a queen Over her passion who, most rebel-like, Sought to be king o'er her.
You spoke not with her since?
No.
Well, sir, the poor distressed Lear's i' the town, Who sometime in his better tune remembers What we are come about, and by no means Will yield to see his daughter.
Why, good sir?
His own unkindness, that stripped her from his benediction, stings his mind so venomously that burning shame detains him from Cordelia.

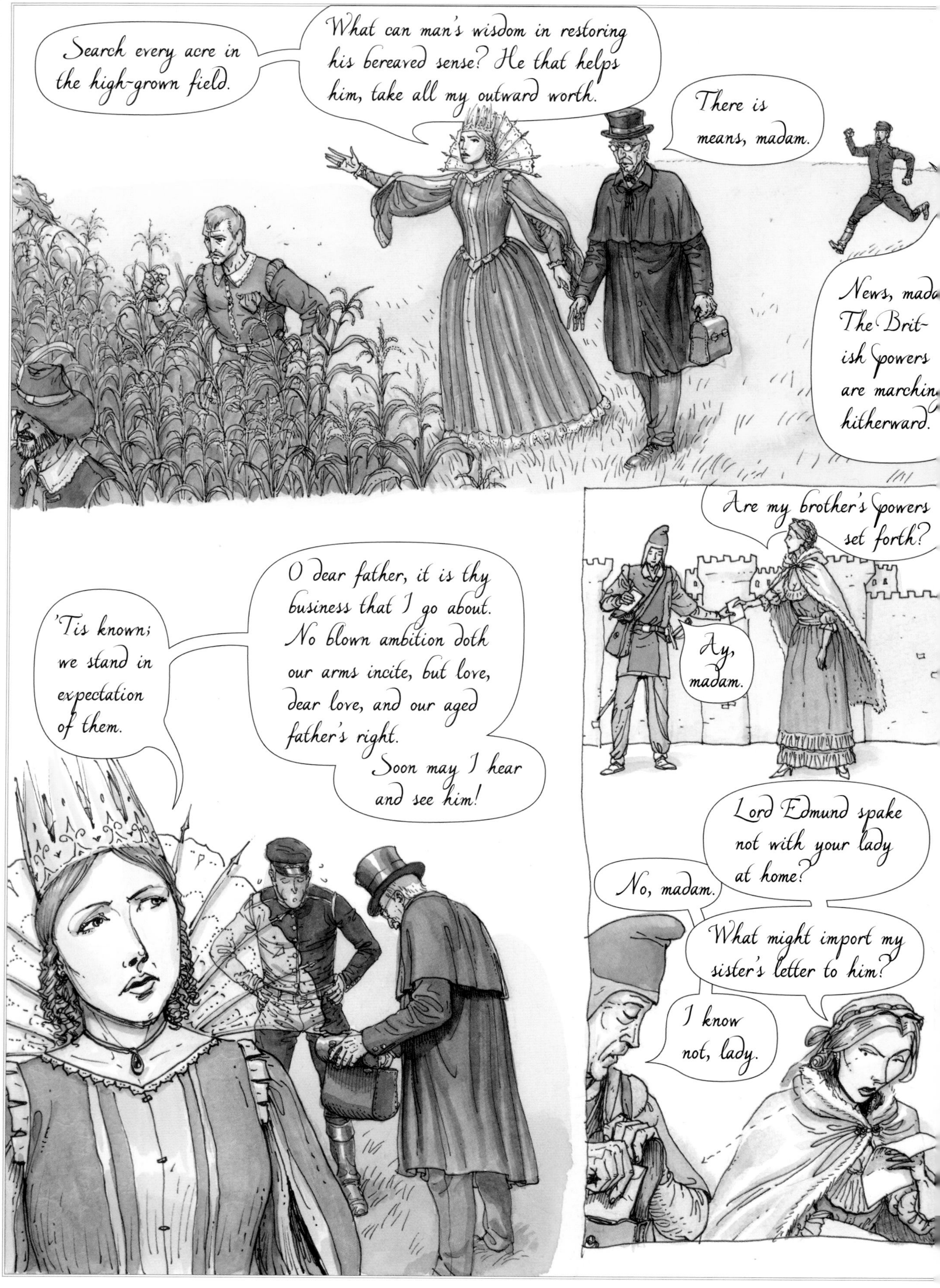
Search every acre in the high-grown field.
What can man's wisdom in restoring his bereaved sense? He that helps him, take all my outward worth.
There is means, madam.
News, mada The Brit-ish powers are marchin hitherward.
'Tis known; we stand in expectation of them.
O dear father, it is thy business that I go about. No blown ambition doth our arms incite, but love, dear love, and our aged father's right.
Soon may I hear and see him!
Are my brother's powers set forth?
Ay, madam.
Lord Edmund spake not with your lady at home?
No, madam.
What might import my sister's letter to him?
I know not, lady.

Kı

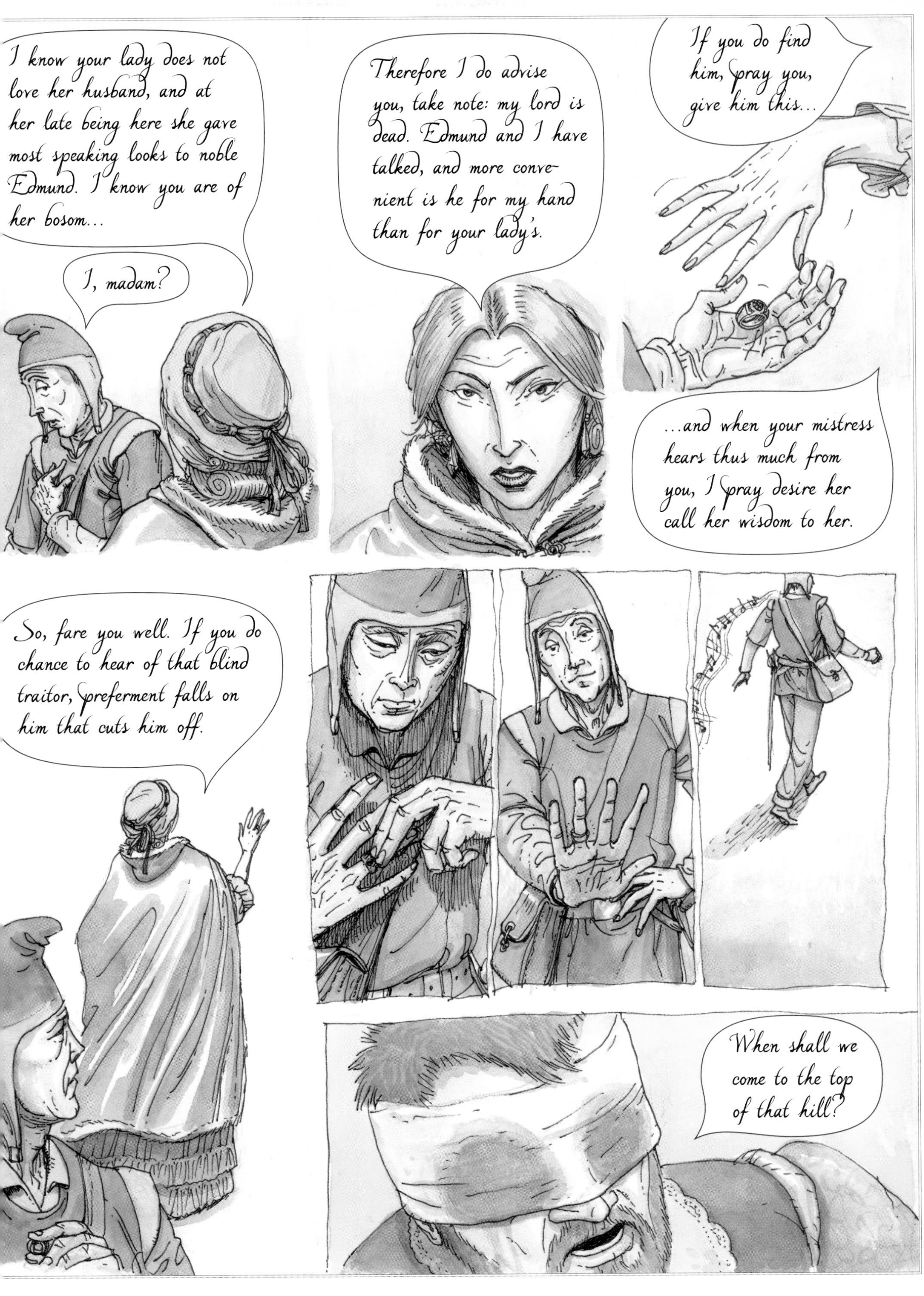

I know your lady does not love her husband, and at her late being here she gave most speaking looks to noble Edmund. I know you are of her bosom...
I, madam?
Therefore I do advise you, take note: my lord is dead. Edmund and I have talked, and more convenient is he for my hand than for your lady's.
If you do find him, pray you, give him this...
...and when your mistress hears thus much from you, I pray desire her call her wisdom to her.
So, fare you well. If you do chance to hear of that blind traitor, preferment falls on him that cuts him off.
When shall we come to the top of that hill?

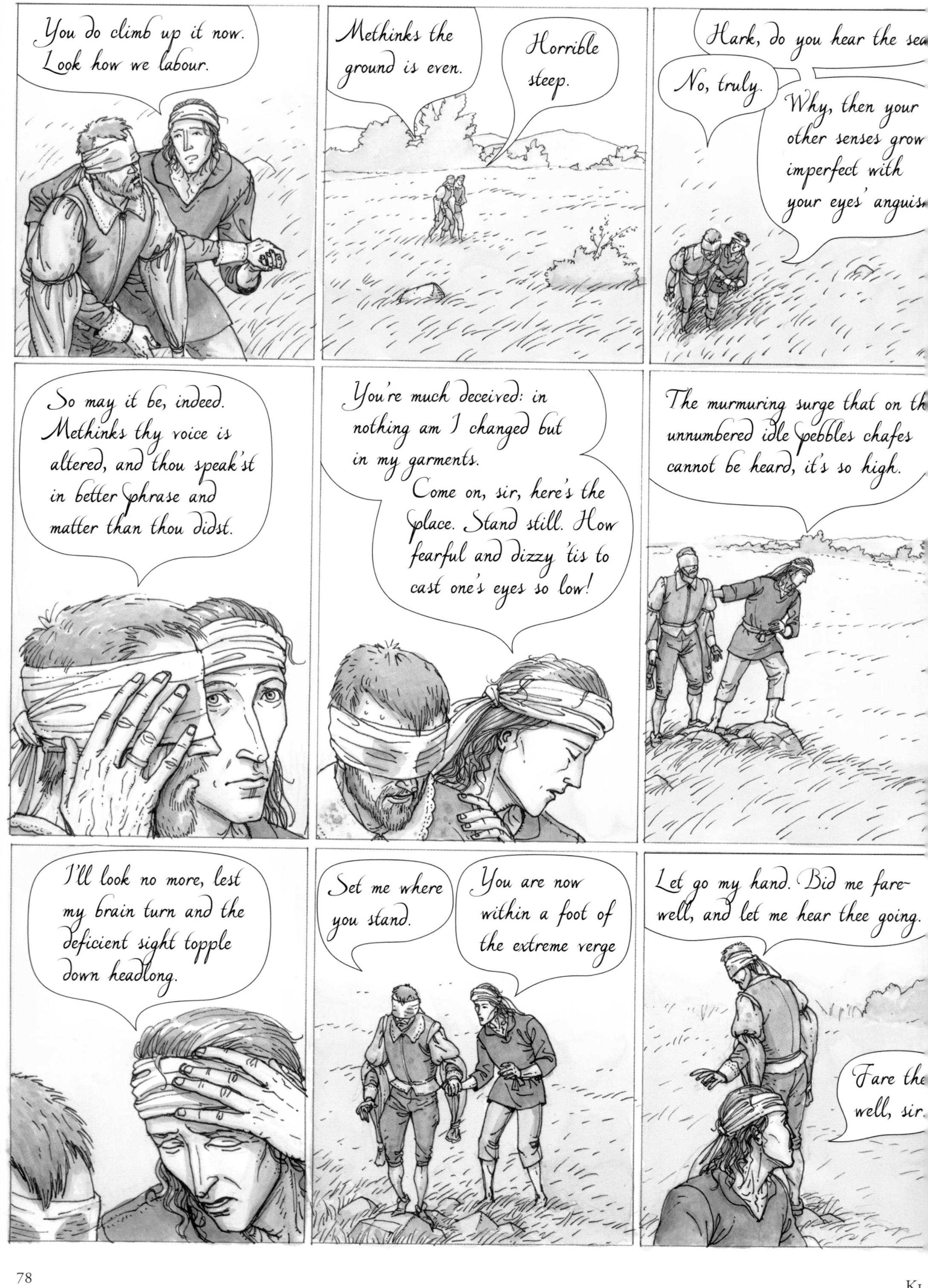
You do climb up it now. Look how we labour.
Methinks the ground is even.
Horrible steep.
Hark, do you hear the sea
No, truly.
Why, then your other senses grow imperfect with your eyes' anguis
So may it be, indeed. Methinks thy voice is altered, and thou speak'st in better phrase and matter than thou didst.
You're much deceived: in nothing am I changed but in my garments.
Come on, sir, here's the place. Stand still. How fearful and dizzy 'tis to cast one's eyes so low!
The murmuring surge that on th unnumbered idle pebbles chafes cannot be heard, it's so high.
I'll look no more, lest my brain turn and the deficient sight topple down headlong.
Set me where you stand.
You are now within a foot of the extreme verge
Let go my hand. Bid me fare-well, and let me hear thee going.
Fare the well, sir.

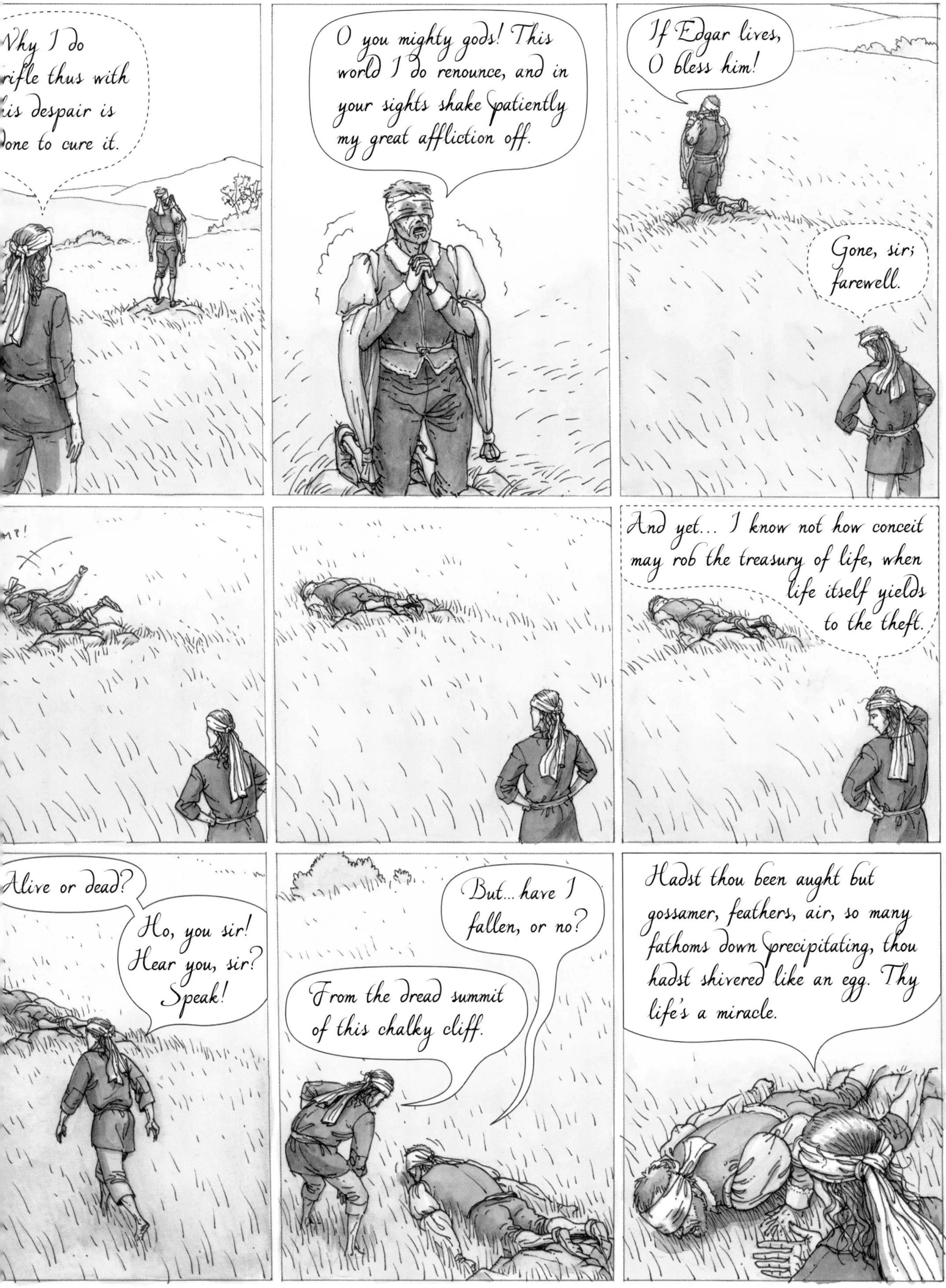

hy I do rifle thus with is despair is one to cure it.
O you mighty gods! This world I do renounce, and in your sights shake patiently my great affliction off.
If Edgar lives, O bless him!
Gone, sir; farewell.
And yet... I know not how conceit may rob the treasury of life, when life itself yields to the theft.
Alive or dead?
Ho, you sir! Hear you, sir? Speak!
But... have I fallen, or no?
From the dread summit of this chalky cliff.
Hadst thou been aught but gossamer, feathers, air, so many fathoms down precipitating, thou hadst shivered like an egg. Thy life's a miracle.

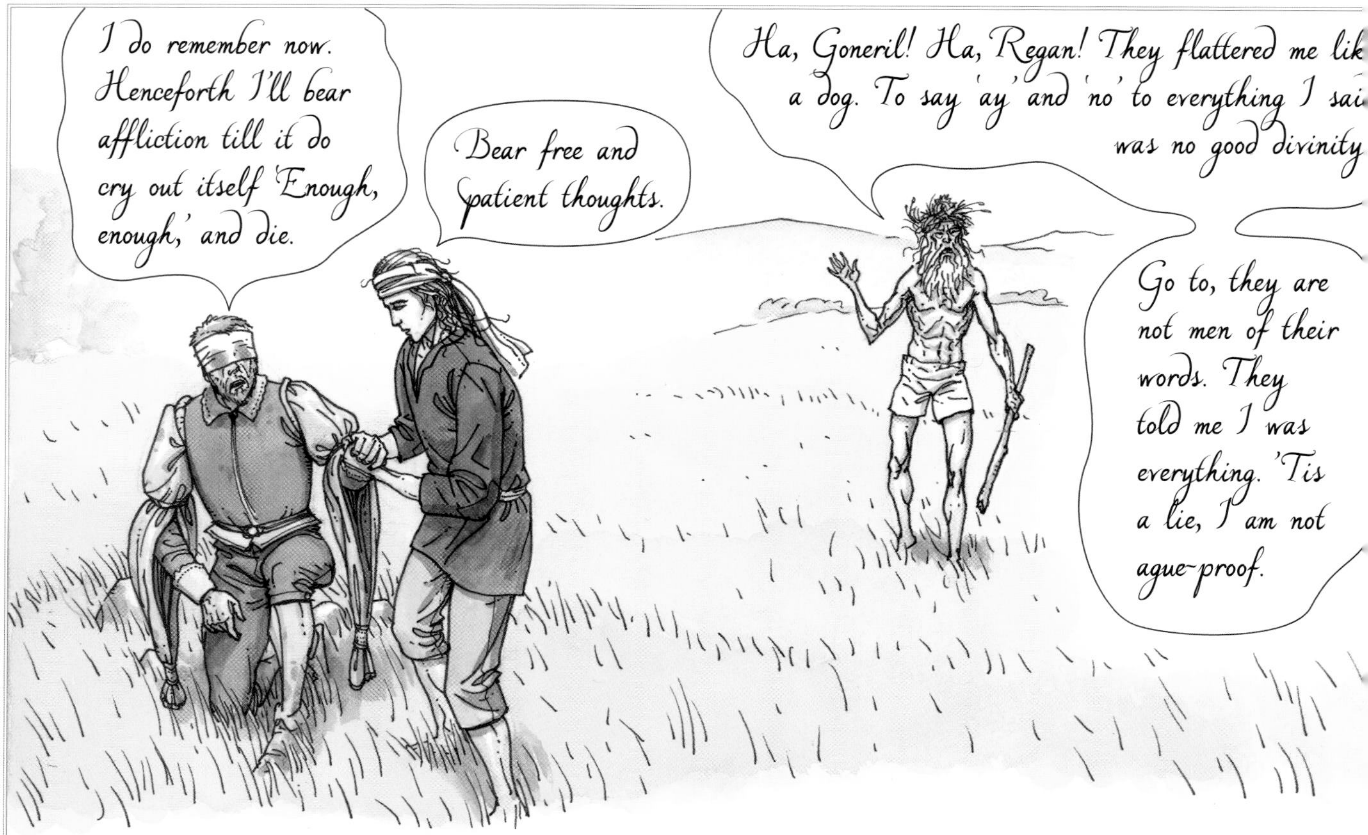
I do remember now. Henceforth I'll bear affliction till it do cry out itself 'Enough, enough,' and die.
Bear free and patient thoughts.
Ha, Goneril! Ha, Regan! They flattered me lik a dog. To say 'ay' and 'no' to everything I sai was no good divinity
Go to, they are not men of their words. They told me I was everything. 'Tis a lie, I am not ague-proof.

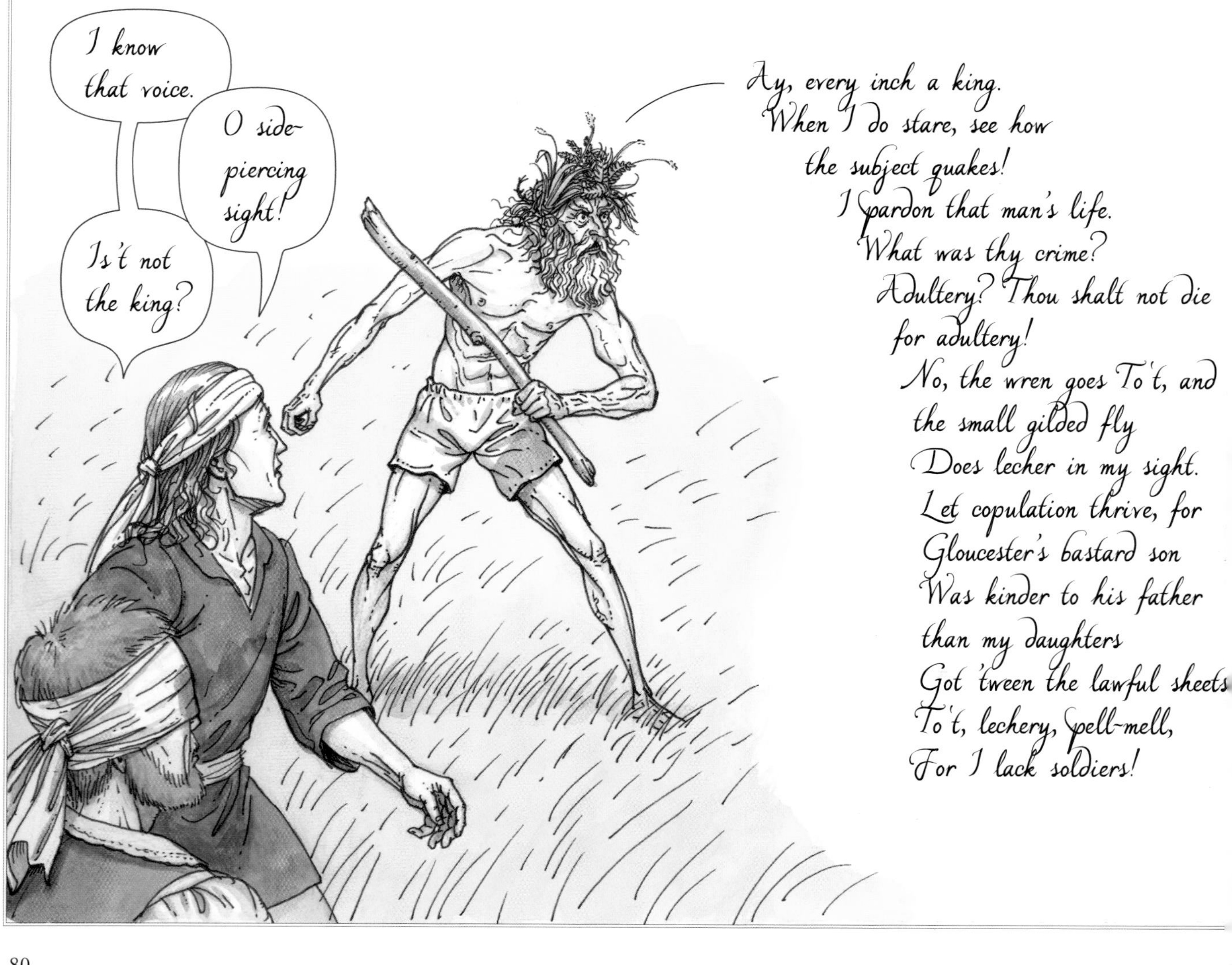
I know that voice.
Is't not the king?
O side-piercing sight!
Ay, every inch a king.
When I do stare, see how the subject quakes!
I pardon that man's life.
What was thy crime?
Adultery? Thou shalt not die for adultery!
No, the wren goes To't, and the small gilded fly
Does lecher in my sight.
Let copulation thrive, for Gloucester's bastard son
Was kinder to his father than my daughters
Got 'tween the lawful sheets
To't, lechery, pell-mell,
For I lack soldiers!

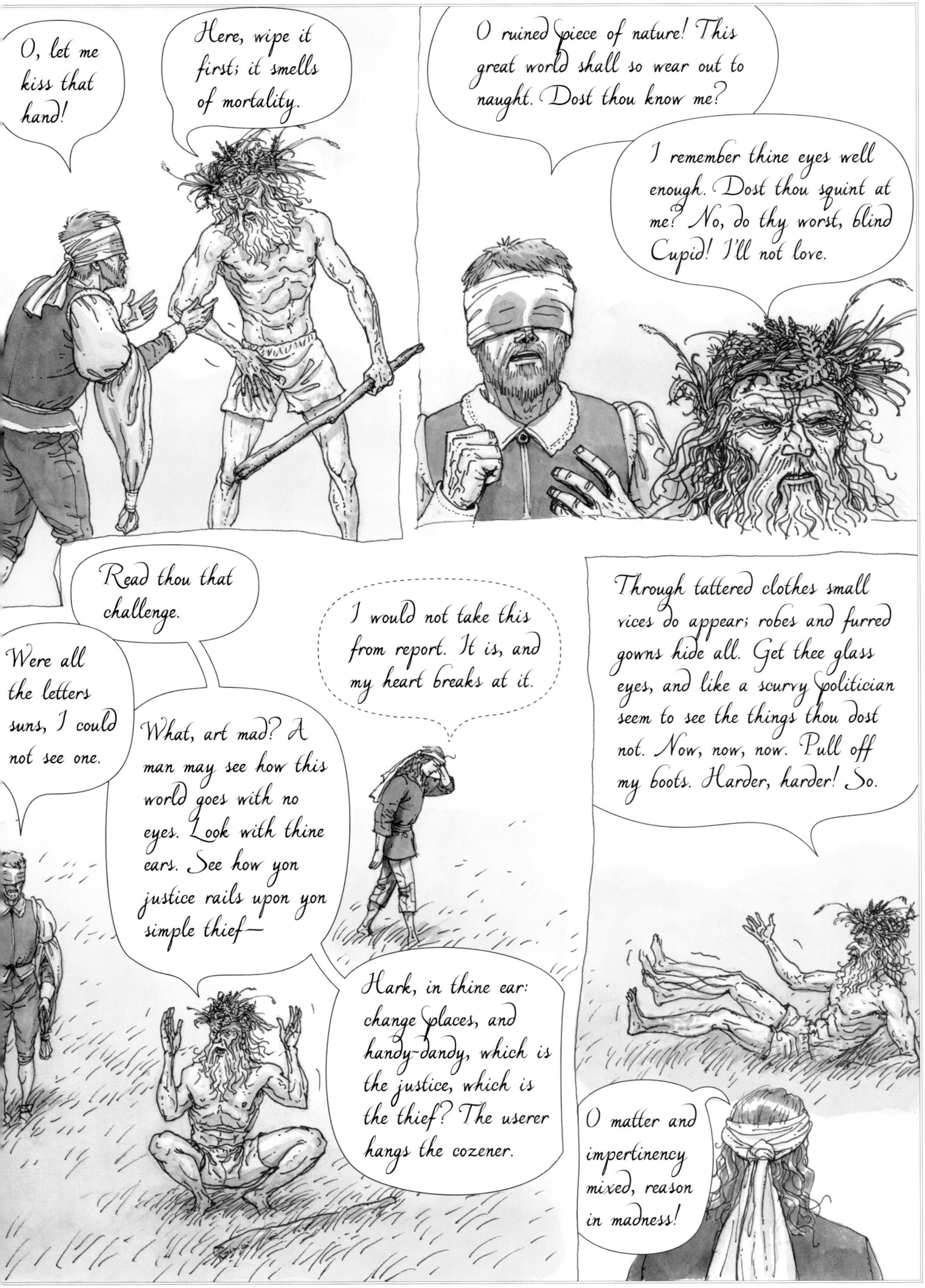
O, let me kiss that hand!
Here, wipe it first; it smells of mortality.
O ruined piece of nature! This great world shall so wear out to naught. Dost thou know me?
I remember thine eyes well enough. Dost thou squint at me? No, do thy worst, blind Cupid! I'll not love.
Read thou that challenge.
Were all the letters suns, I could not see one.
What, art mad? A man may see how this world goes with no eyes. Look with thine ears. See how yon justice rails upon yon simple thief—
I would not take this from report. It is, and my heart breaks at it.
Hark, in thine ear: change places, and handy-dandy, which is the justice, which is the thief? The userer hangs the cozener.
Through tattered clothes small vices do appear; robes and furred gowns hide all. Get thee glass eyes, and like a scurvy politician seem to see the things thou dost not. Now, now, now. Pull off my boots. Harder, harder! So.
O matter and impertinency mixed, reason in madness!

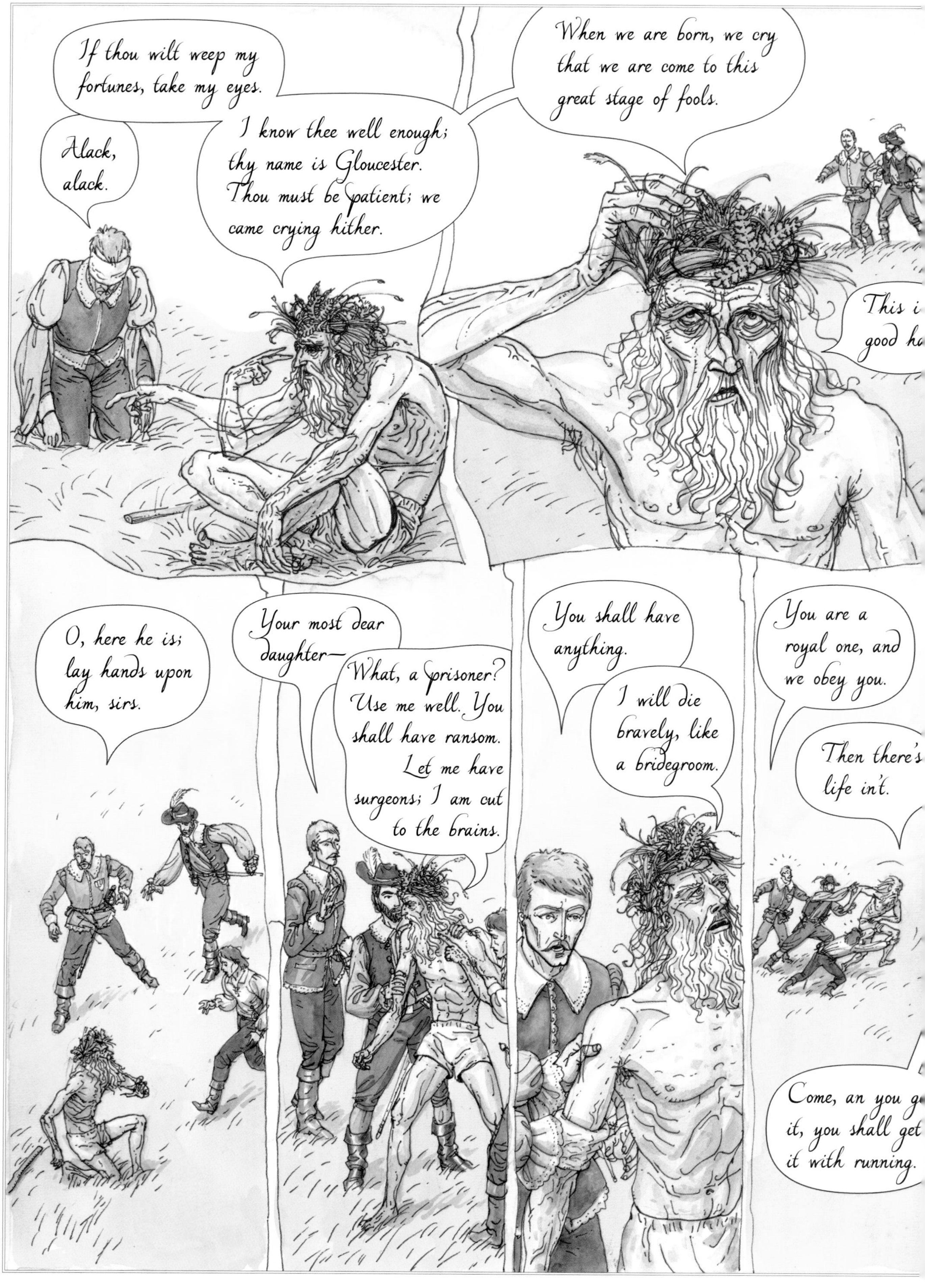
If thou wilt weep my fortunes, take my eyes.
Alack, alack.
I know thee well enough; thy name is Gloucester. Thou must be patient; we came crying hither.
When we are born, we cry that we are come to this great stage of fools.
This i
good h
O, here he is; lay hands upon him, sirs.
Your most dear daughter—
What, a prisoner? Use me well. You shall have ransom. Let me have surgeons; I am cut to the brains.
You shall have anything.
I will die bravely, like a bridegroom.
You are a royal one, and we obey you.
Then there's life in't.
Come, an you g
it, you shall get
it with running.

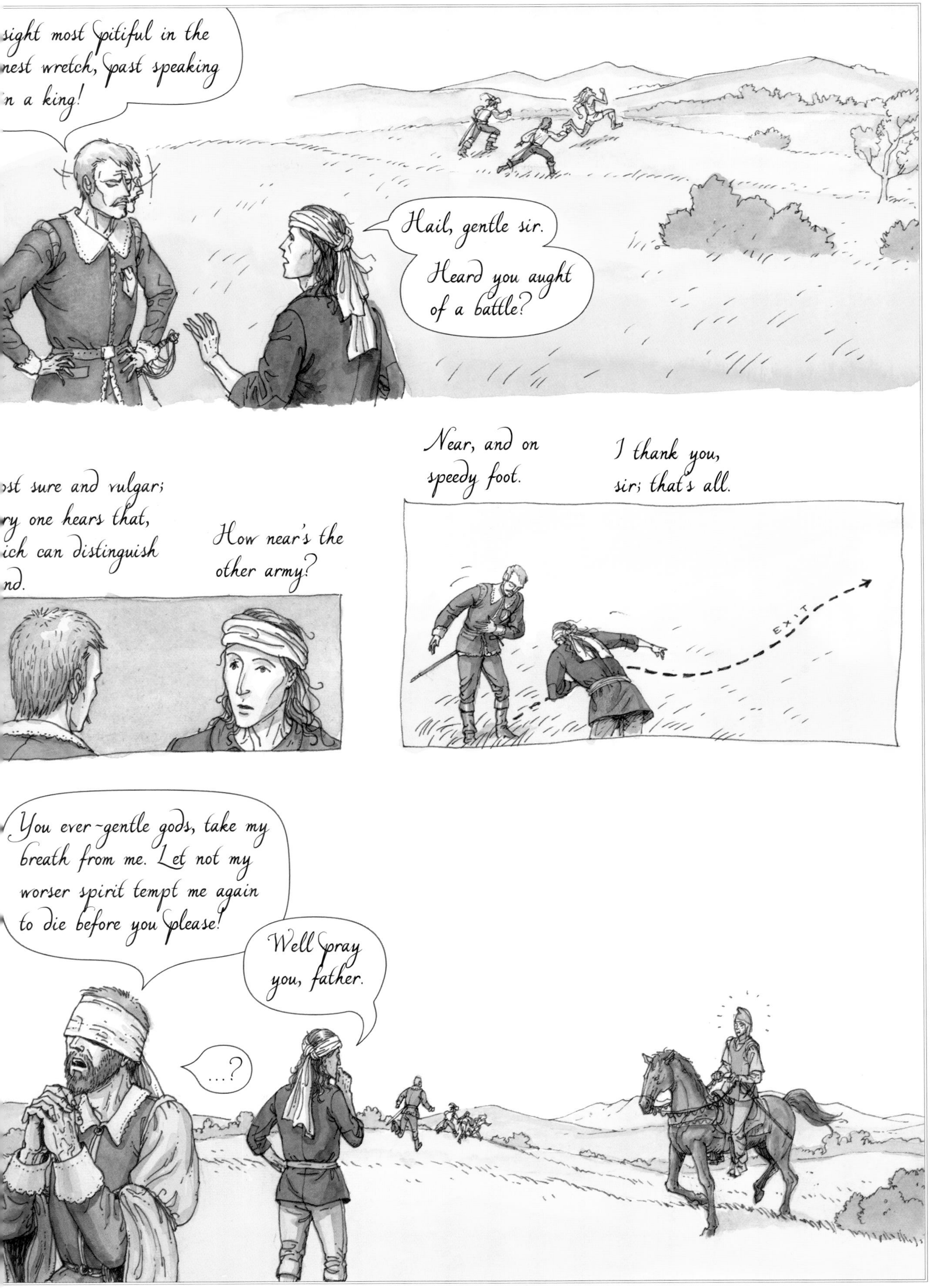

sight most pitiful in the nest wretch, past speaking n a king!
Hail, gentle sir.
Heard you aught of a battle?
ost sure and vulgar; ry one hears that, ich can distinguish nd.
How near's the other army?
Near, and on speedy foot.
I thank you, sir; that's all.
EXIT
You ever-gentle gods, take my breath from me. Let not my worser spirit tempt me again to die before you please!
Well pray you, father.
...?

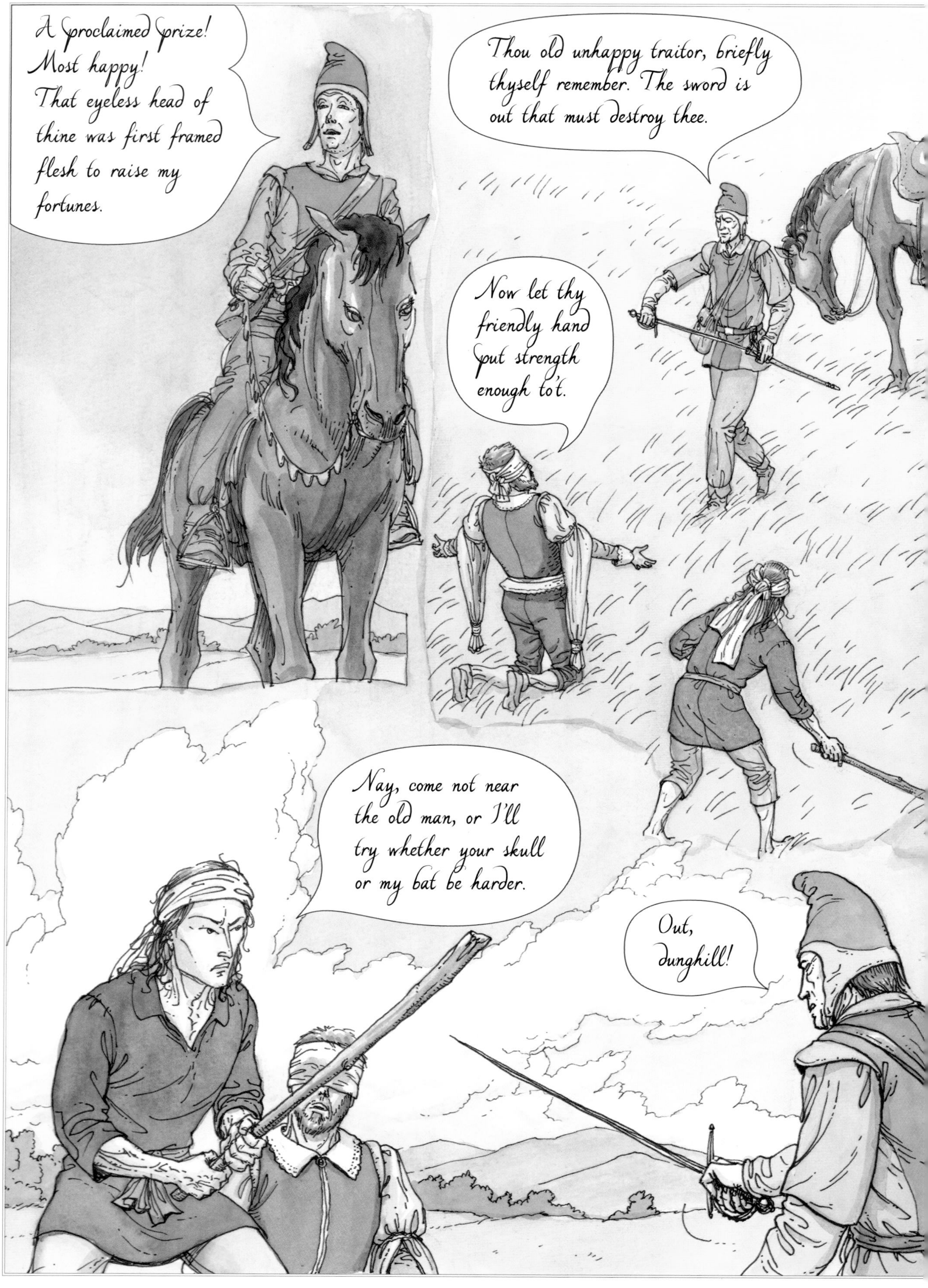
A proclaimed prize! Most happy! That eyeless head of thine was first framed flesh to raise my fortunes.
Thou old unhappy traitor, briefly thyself remember. The sword is out that must destroy thee.
Now let thy friendly hand put strength enough to't.
Nay, come not near the old man, or I'll try whether your skull or my bat be harder.
Out, dunghill!

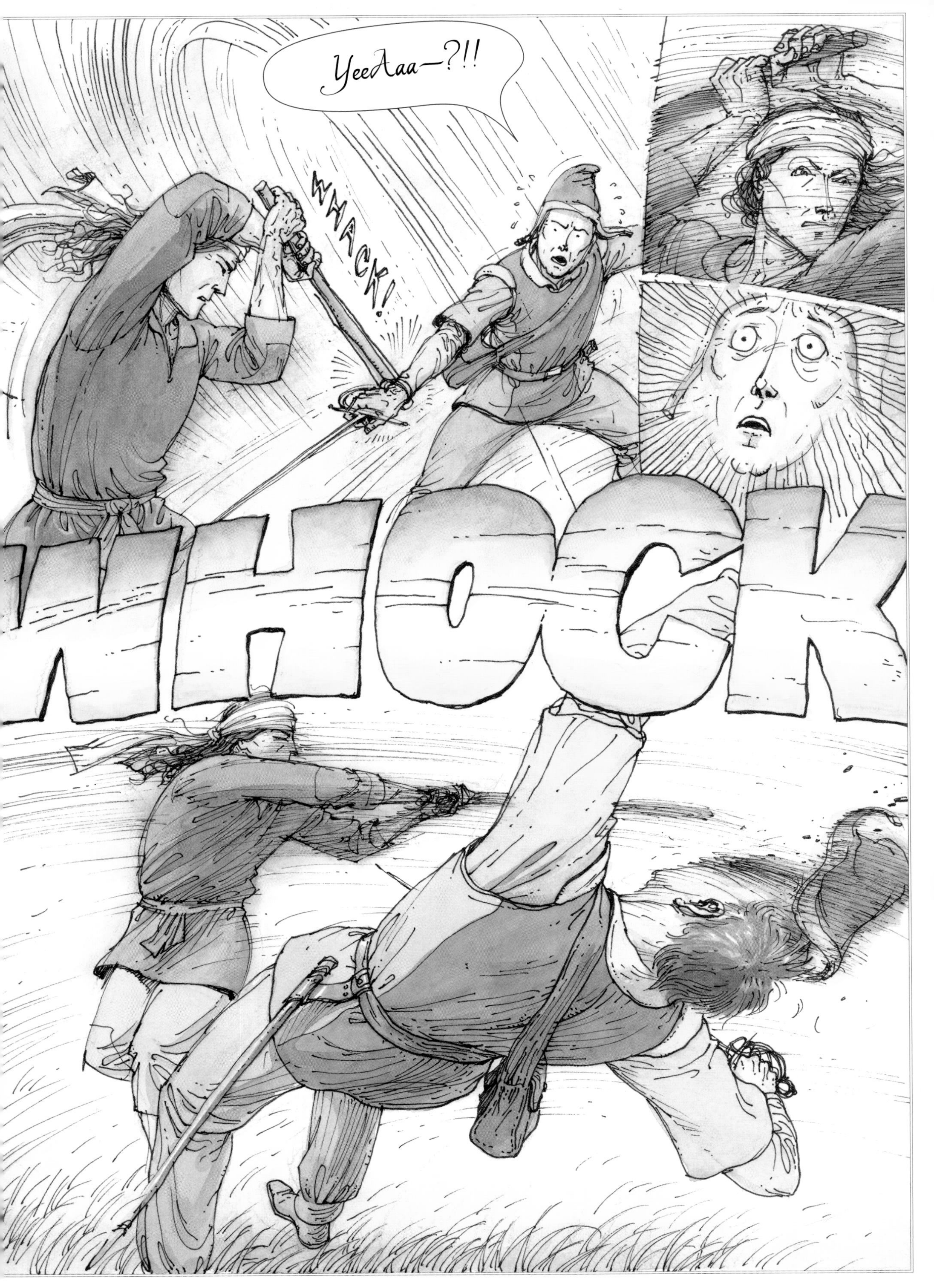
YeeAaa—?!!
WHACK!
WHOCK

Unh... Ngg—

Slave, thou hast slain me.

Villain, take my purse. If ever thou wilt thrive, bury my body, and give the letters which thou find'st about me to Edmund, Earl of Gloucester.

Seek him out among the British army.

O, untimely death!

...✳

I know thee well: a serviceable villain, as duteous to the vices of thy mistress as badness would desire.

What, is he dead?

Sit you down, father, rest you. Let's see his pockets. These letters that he speaks of may be my friends.

Leave, gentle wax, and manners blame us not. To know our enemies' minds, we'd rip their hearts; their papers is more lawful.

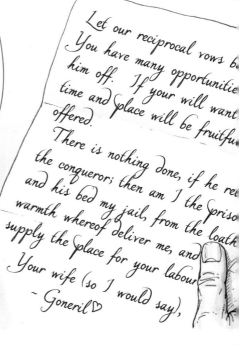

Let our reciprocal vows be remembered. You have many opportunities to cut him off. If your will want not, time and place will be fruitfully offered. There is nothing done, if he return the conqueror; then am I the prisoner, and his bed my jail, from the loathed warmth whereof deliver me, and supply the place for your labour.

Your wife (so I would say),

~ Goneril ♡

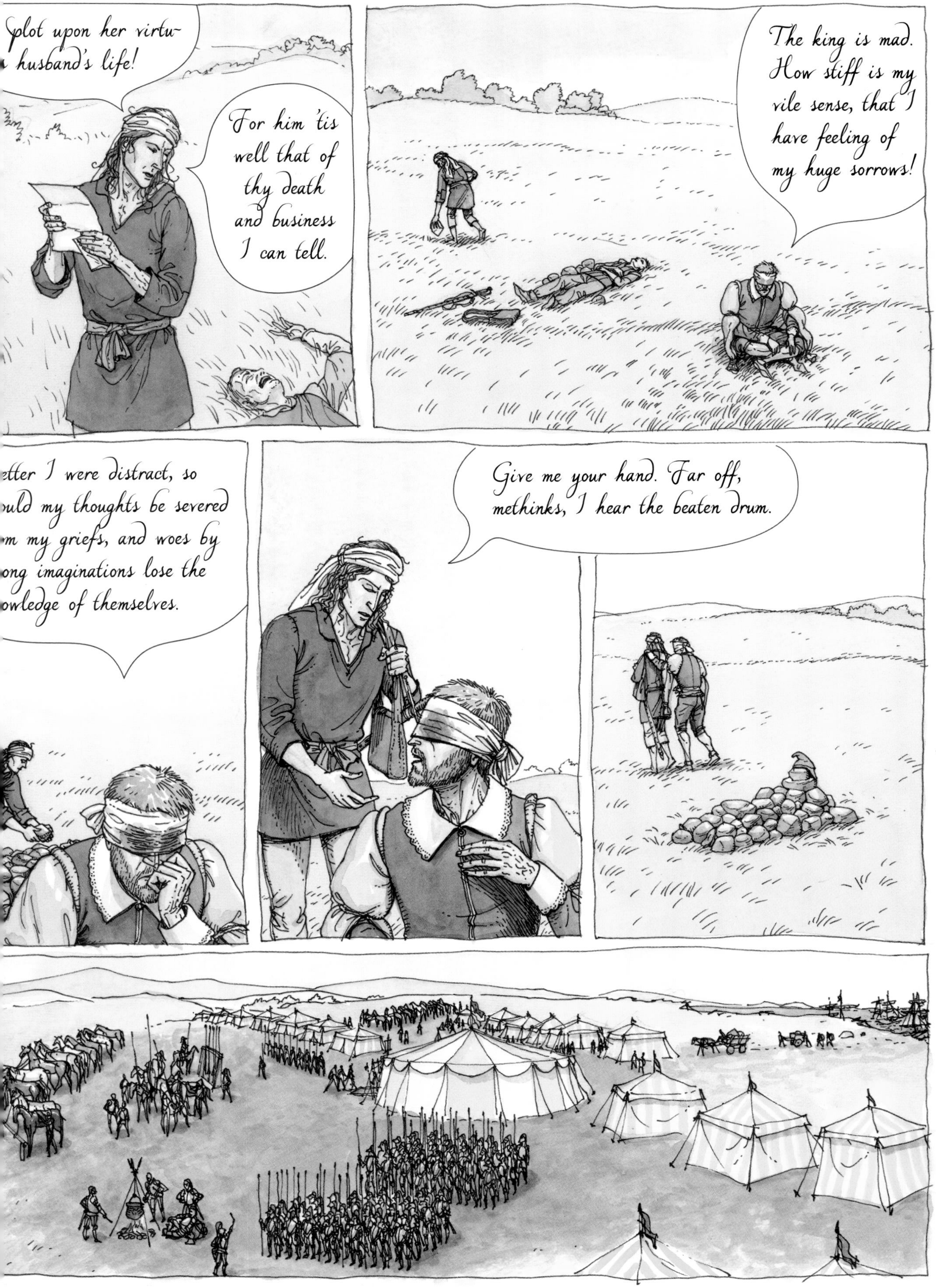
plot upon her virtu-
husband's life!
For him 'tis well that of thy death and business I can tell.
The king is mad. How stiff is my vile sense, that I have feeling of my huge sorrows!
etter I were distract, so
uld my thoughts be severed
m my griefs, and woes by
ong imaginations lose the
owledge of themselves.
Give me your hand. Far off, methinks, I hear the beaten drum.

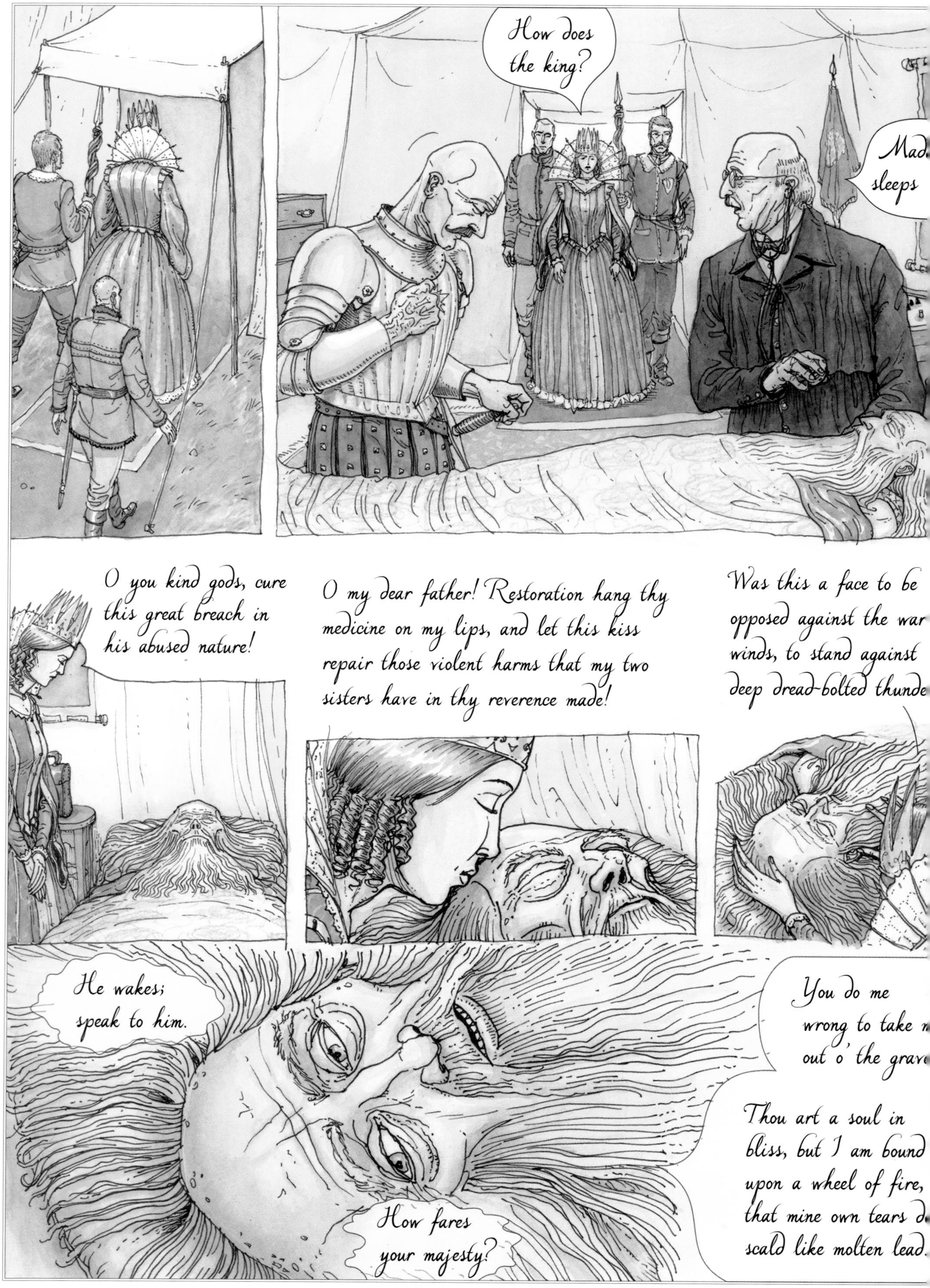
How does the king?
Mad. sleeps
O you kind gods, cure this great breach in his abused nature!
O my dear father! Restoration hang thy medicine on my lips, and let this kiss repair those violent harms that my two sisters have in thy reverence made!
Was this a face to be opposed against the war winds, to stand against deep dread-bolted thunde
He wakes; speak to him.
How fares your majesty?
You do me wrong to take out o' the grave
Thou art a soul in bliss, but I am bound upon a wheel of fire, that mine own tears d scald like molten lead.

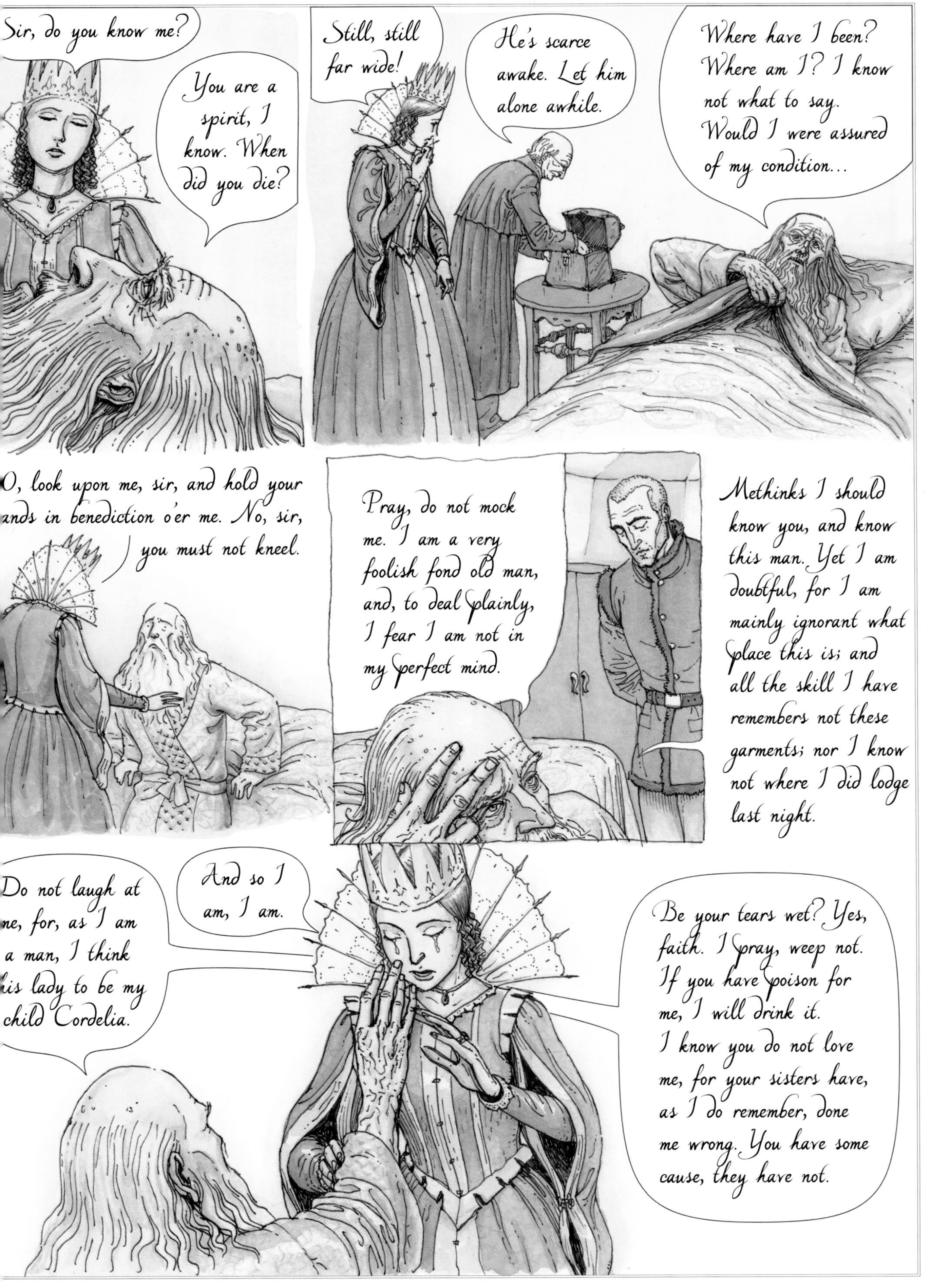

Sir, do you know me?
You are a spirit, I know. When did you die?
Still, still far wide!
He's scarce awake. Let him alone awhile.
Where have I been? Where am I? I know not what to say. Would I were assured of my condition...
O, look upon me, sir, and hold your ands in benediction o'er me. No, sir, you must not kneel.
Pray, do not mock me. I am a very foolish fond old man, and, to deal plainly, I fear I am not in my perfect mind.
Methinks I should know you, and know this man. Yet I am doubtful, for I am mainly ignorant what place this is; and all the skill I have remembers not these garments; nor I know not where I did lodge last night.
Do not laugh at ne, for, as I am a man, I think is lady to be my child Cordelia.
And so I am, I am.
Be your tears wet? Yes, faith. I pray, weep not. If you have poison for me, I will drink it. I know you do not love me, for your sisters have, as I do remember, done me wrong. You have some cause, they have not.

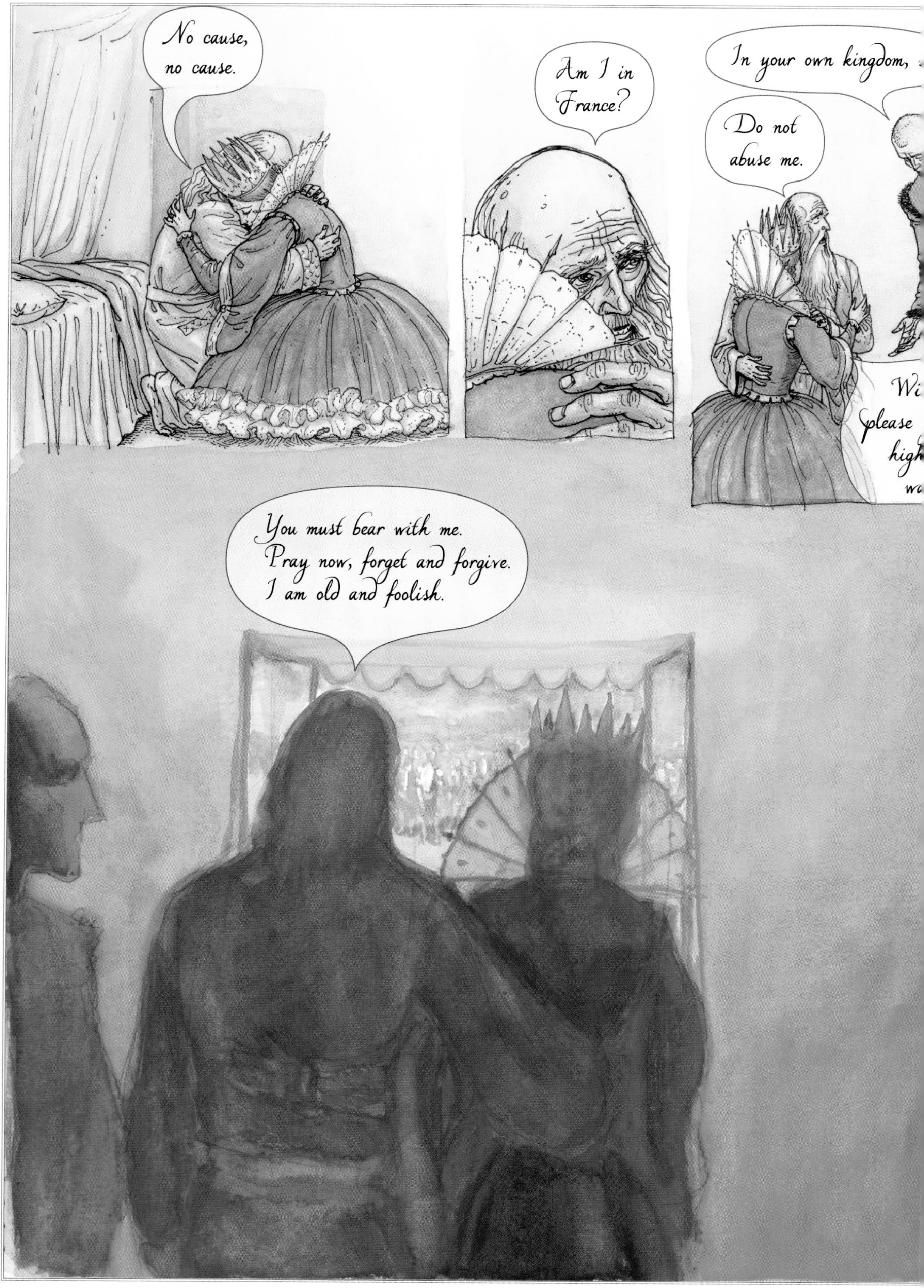
No cause, no cause.
Am I in France?
In your own kingdom,
Do not abuse me.
You must bear with me. Pray now, forget and forgive. I am old and foolish.

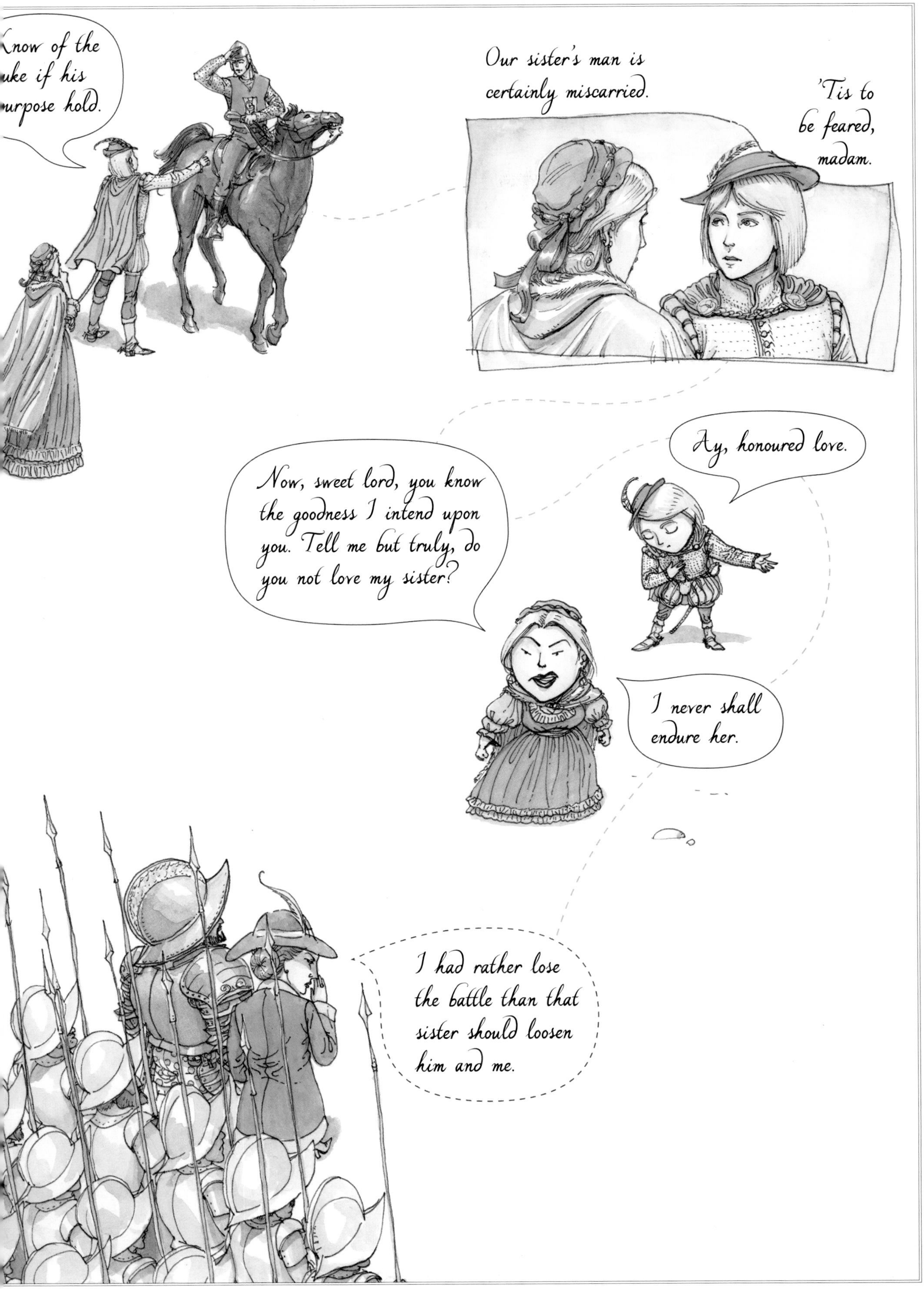

know of the
uke if his
urpose hold.
Our sister's man is certainly miscarried.
'Tis to be feared, madam.
Now, sweet lord, you know the goodness I intend upon you. Tell me but truly, do you not love my sister?
Ay, honoured love.
I never shall endure her.
I had rather lose the battle than that sister should loosen him and me.

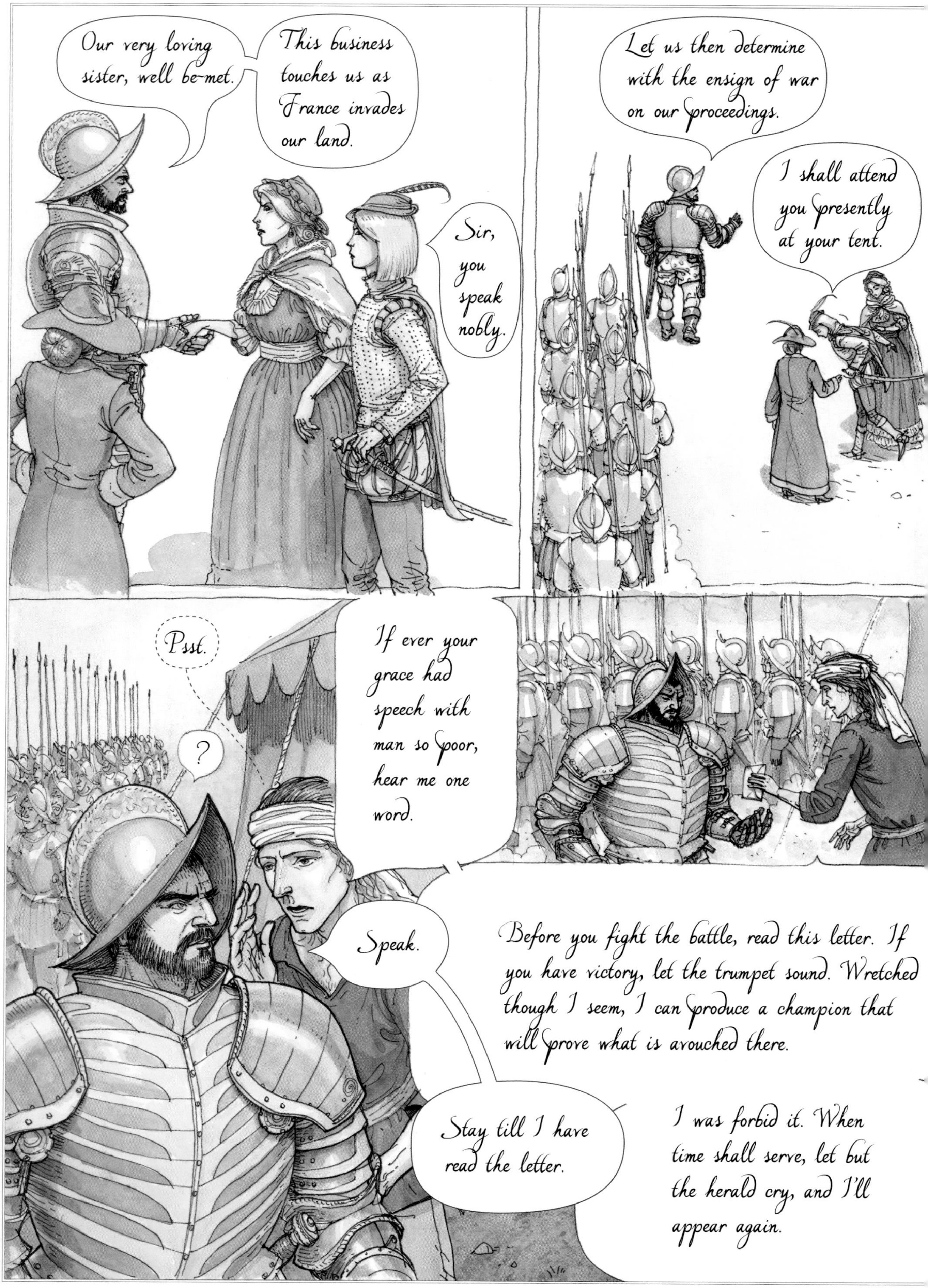

Our very loving sister, well be-met.
This business touches us as France invades our land.
Sir, you speak nobly.
Let us then determine with the ensign of war on our proceedings.
I shall attend you presently at your tent.
Psst.
?
If ever your grace had speech with man so poor, hear me one word.
Speak.
Before you fight the battle, read this letter. If you have victory, let the trumpet sound. Wretched though I seem, I can produce a champion that will prove what is avouched there.
Stay till I have read the letter.
I was forbid it. When time shall serve, let but the herald cry, and I'll appear again.

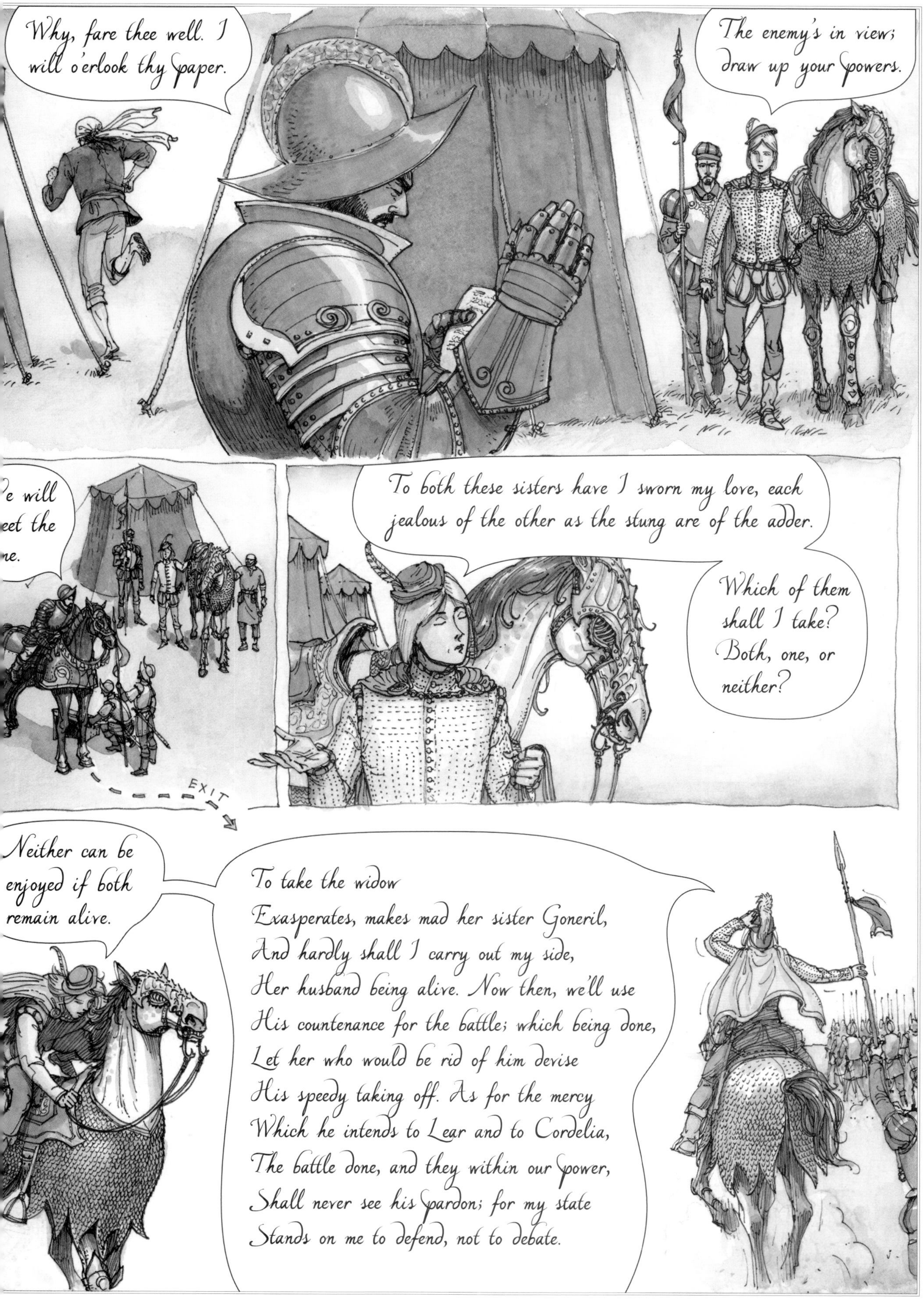
Why, fare thee well. I will o'erlook thy paper.
The enemy's in view; draw up your powers.
EXIT
To both these sisters have I sworn my love, each jealous of the other as the stung are of the adder.
Which of them shall I take? Both, one, or neither?
Neither can be enjoyed if both remain alive.
To take the widow
Exasperates, makes mad her sister Goneril,
And hardly shall I carry out my side,
Her husband being alive. Now then, we'll use
His countenance for the battle; which being done,
Let her who would be rid of him devise
His speedy taking off. As for the mercy
Which he intends to Lear and to Cordelia,
The battle done, and they within our power,
Shall never see his pardon; for my state
Stands on me to defend, not to debate.

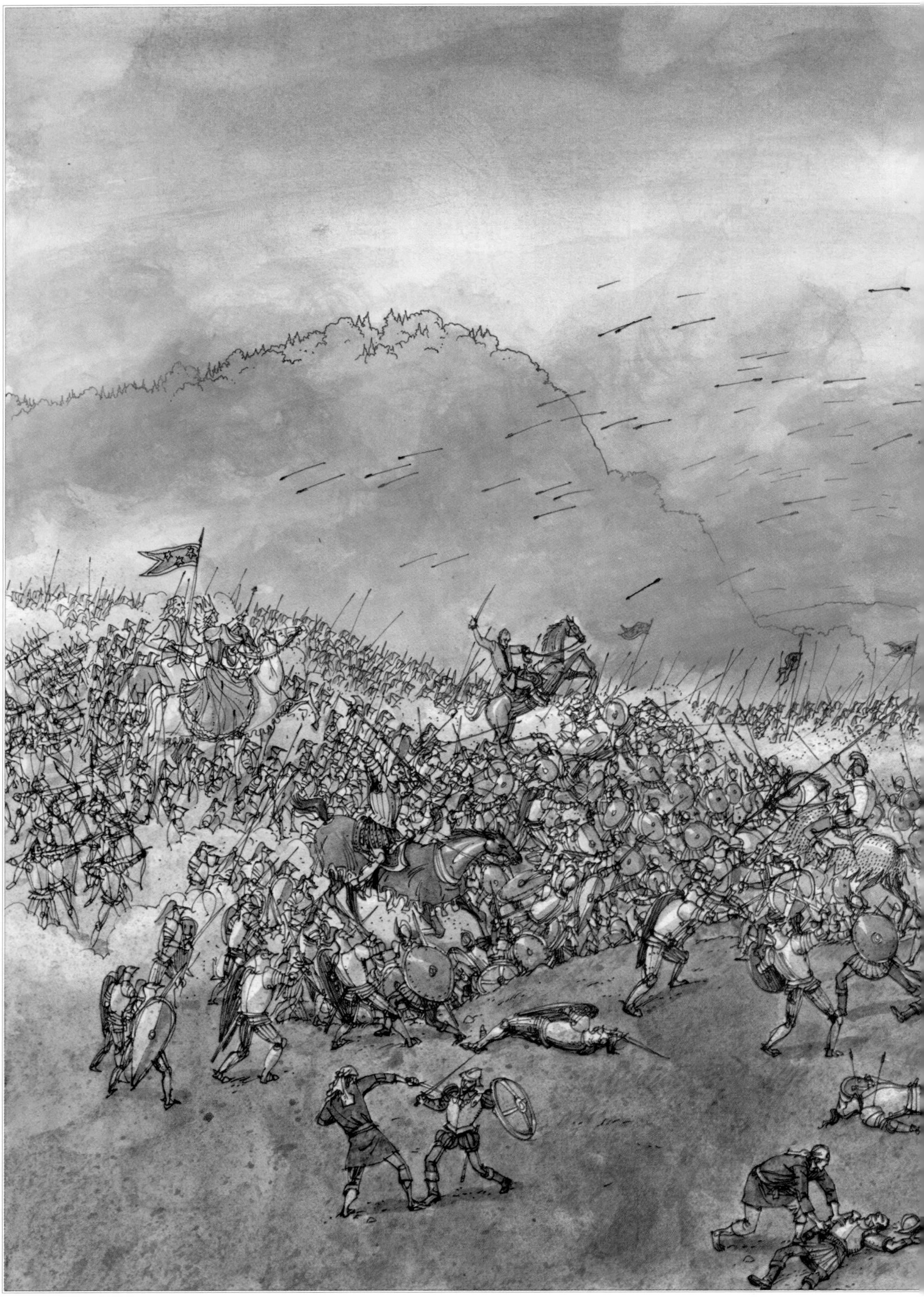

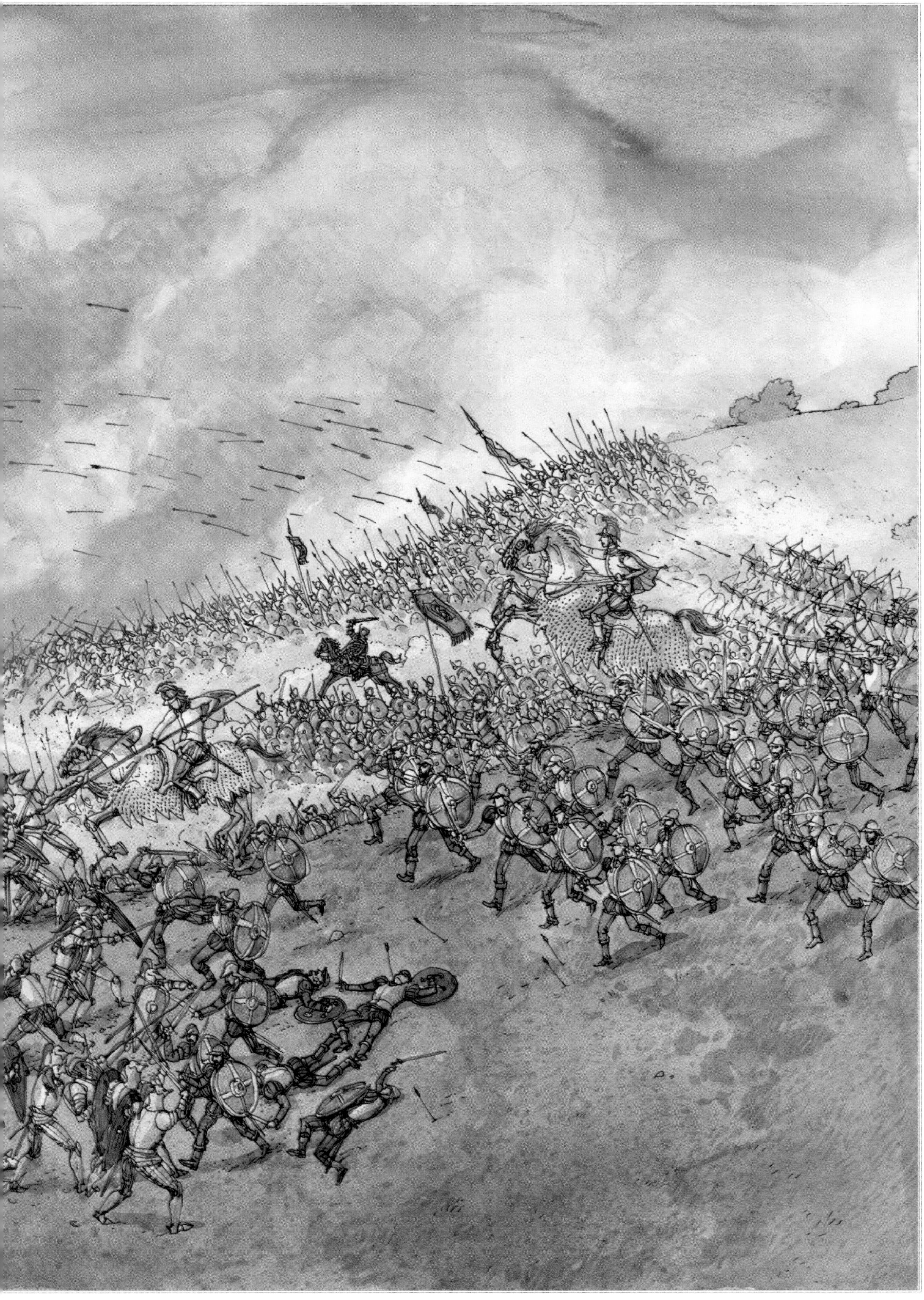

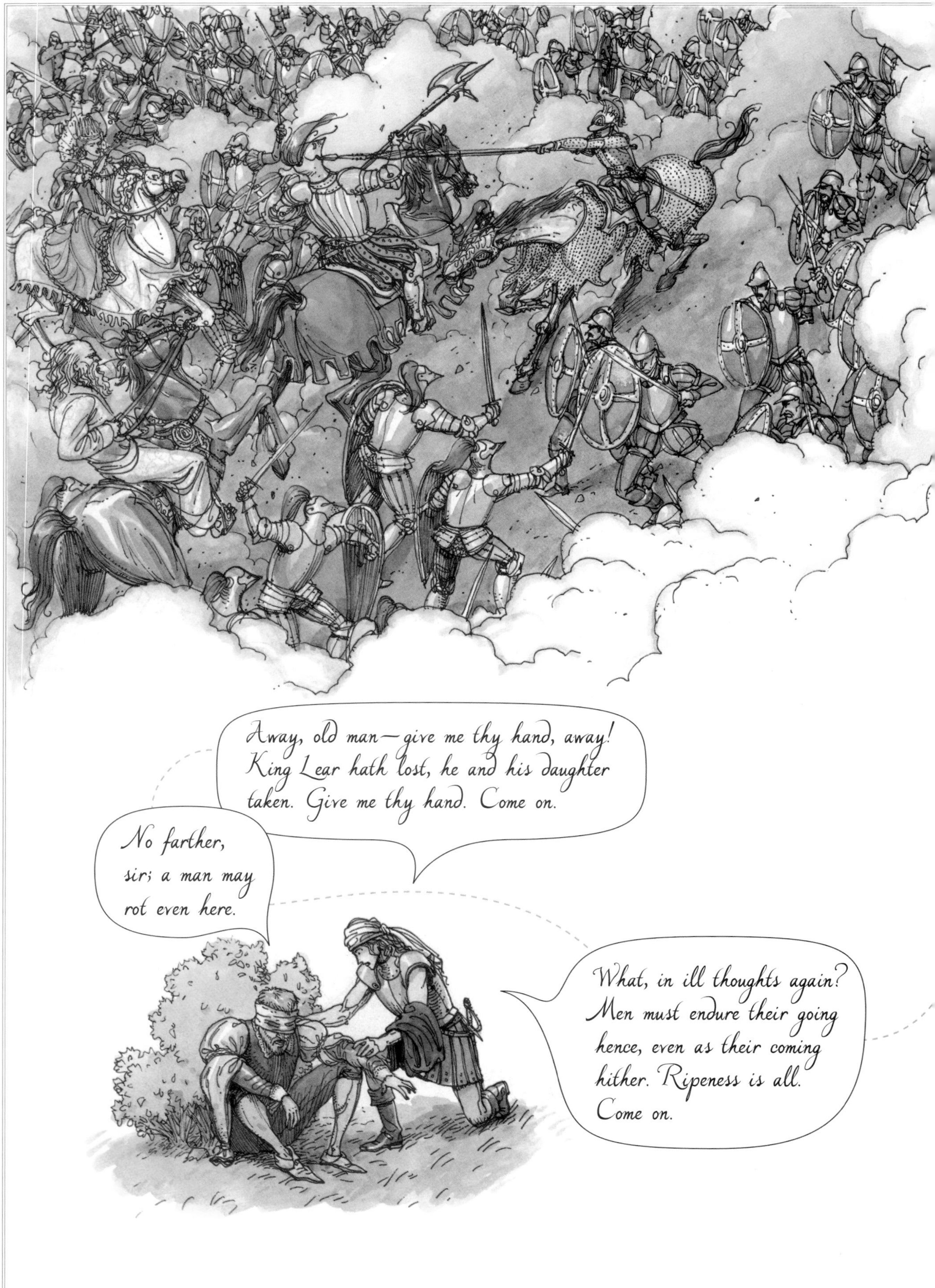
Away, old man—give me thy hand, away! King Lear hath lost, he and his daughter taken. Give me thy hand. Come on.
No farther, sir; a man may rot even here.
What, in ill thoughts again? Men must endure their going hence, even as their coming hither. Ripeness is all. Come on.

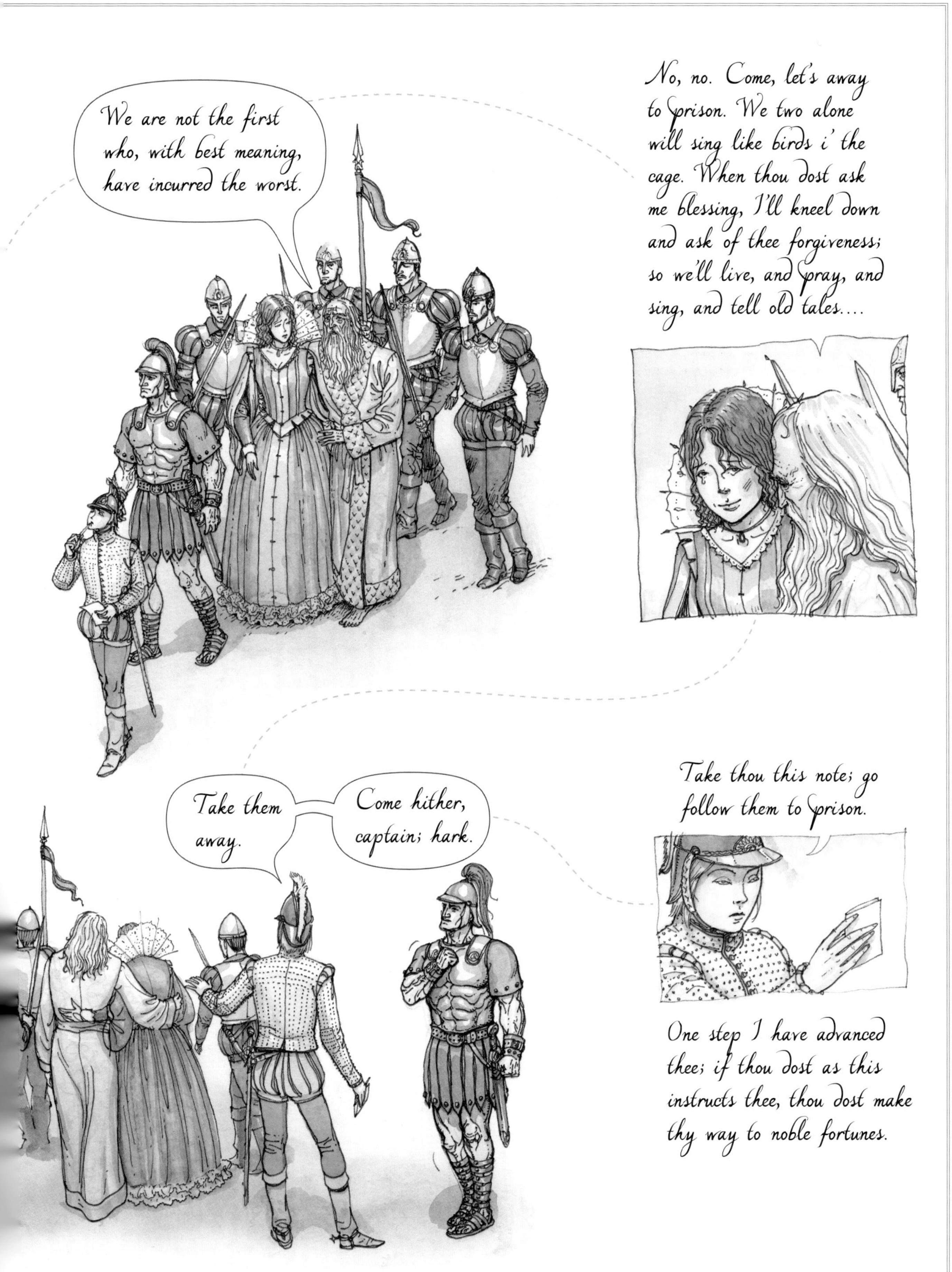
We are not the first who, with best meaning, have incurred the worst.
No, no. Come, let's away to prison. We two alone will sing like birds i' the cage. When thou dost ask me blessing, I'll kneel down and ask of thee forgiveness; so we'll live, and pray, and sing, and tell old tales....
Take them away.
Come hither, captain; hark.
Take thou this note; go follow them to prison.
One step I have advanced thee; if thou dost as this instructs thee, thou dost make thy way to noble fortunes.

I'll do it, my lord.

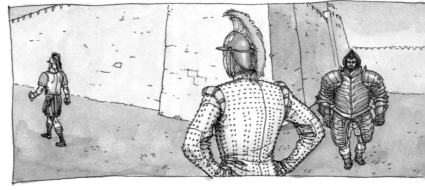

Sir, you have shown today your valiant strain, and fortune led you well. You have the captives that were the opposites of this day's strife. We do require then of you, so to use them as we shall find their merits and our safety may equally determine.

Sir, I thought it fit to send the old and miserable king to some retention and appointed guard. With him I sent the queen, and they are ready to-morrow, or at further space, to appear where you shall hold your session.

Sir. At this time we sweat and bleed; the question of Cordelia and her father requires a fitter place.

Sir, by your patience, I hold you but a subject of this war, not as a brother.

That's as we list to grace him. Methinks our pleasure should have been demanded, ere you had spoke so far.

......

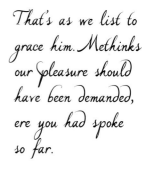

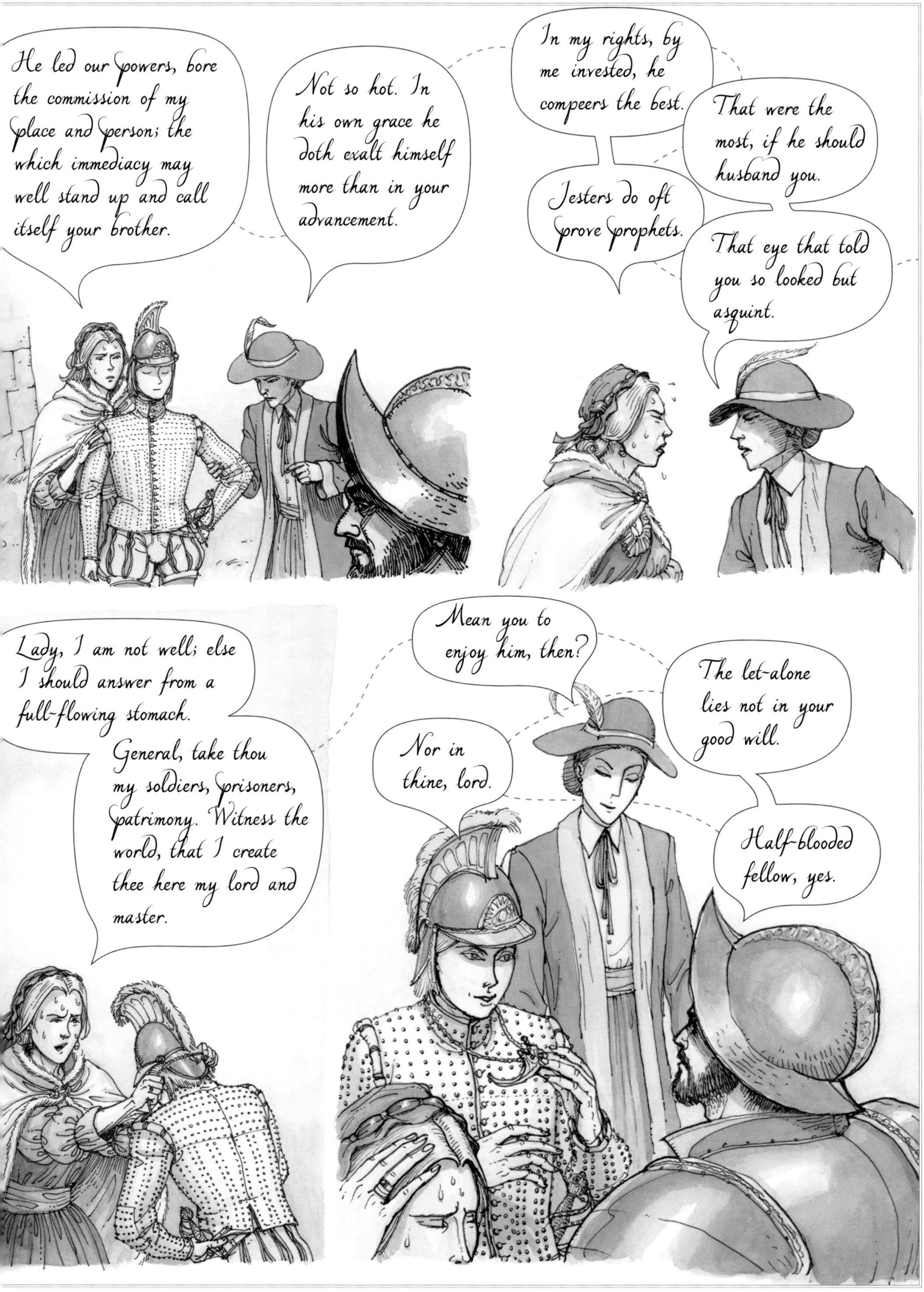

He led our powers, bore the commission of my place and person; the which immediacy may well stand up and call itself your brother.
Not so hot. In his own grace he doth exalt himself more than in your advancement.
In my rights, by me invested, he compeers the best.
That were the most, if he should husband you.
Jesters do oft prove prophets.
That eye that told you so looked but asquint.
Lady, I am not well; else I should answer from a full-flowing stomach.
General, take thou my soldiers, prisoners, patrimony. Witness the world, that I create thee here my lord and master.
Mean you to enjoy him, then?
The let-alone lies not in your good will.
Nor in thine, lord.
Half-blooded fellow, yes.

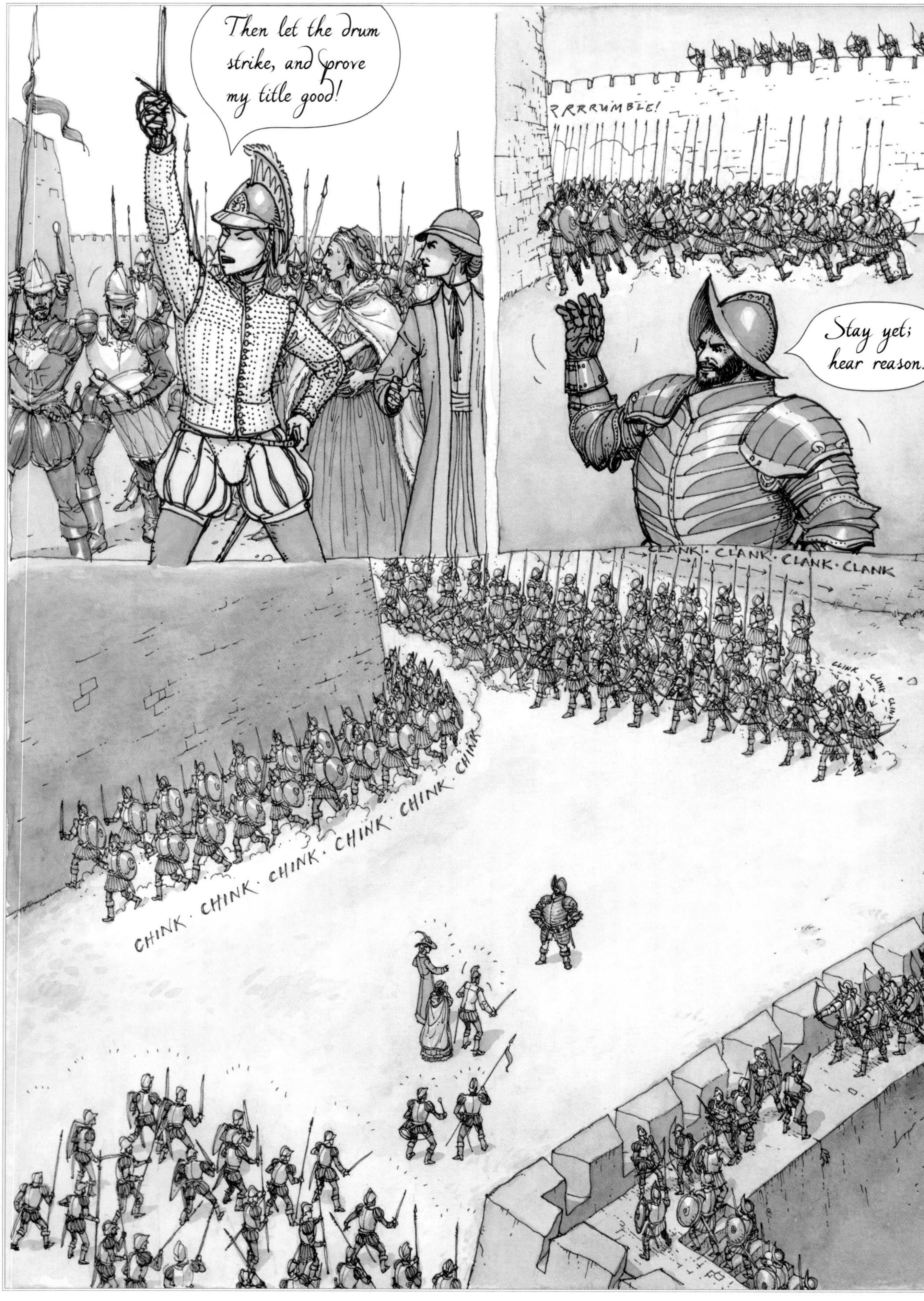
Then let the drum strike, and prove my title good!
RRRRUMBLE!
Stay yet; hear reason.
CLANK · CLANK · CLANK · CLANK
CLINK CLINK CLINK
CHINK · CHINK · CHINK · CHINK · CHINK CHINK

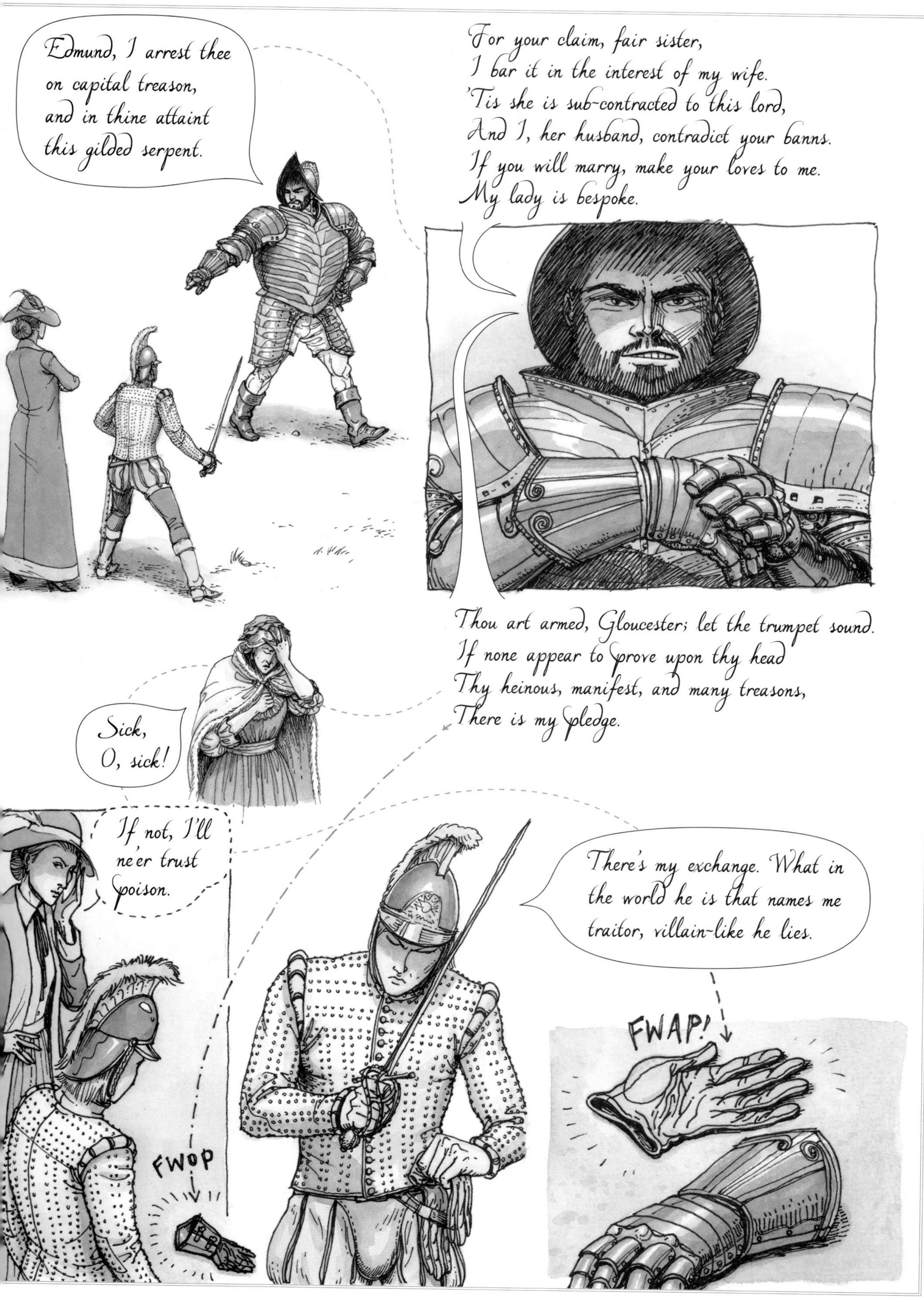

Edmund, I arrest thee on capital treason, and in thine attaint this gilded serpent.
For your claim, fair sister, I bar it in the interest of my wife. 'Tis she is sub-contracted to this lord, And I, her husband, contradict your banns. If you will marry, make your loves to me. My lady is bespoke.
Thou art armed, Gloucester; let the trumpet sound. If none appear to prove upon thy head Thy heinous, manifest, and many treasons, There is my pledge.
Sick, O, sick!
If not, I'll ne'er trust poison.
There's my exchange. What in the world he is that names me traitor, villain-like he lies.
FWOP
FWAP!

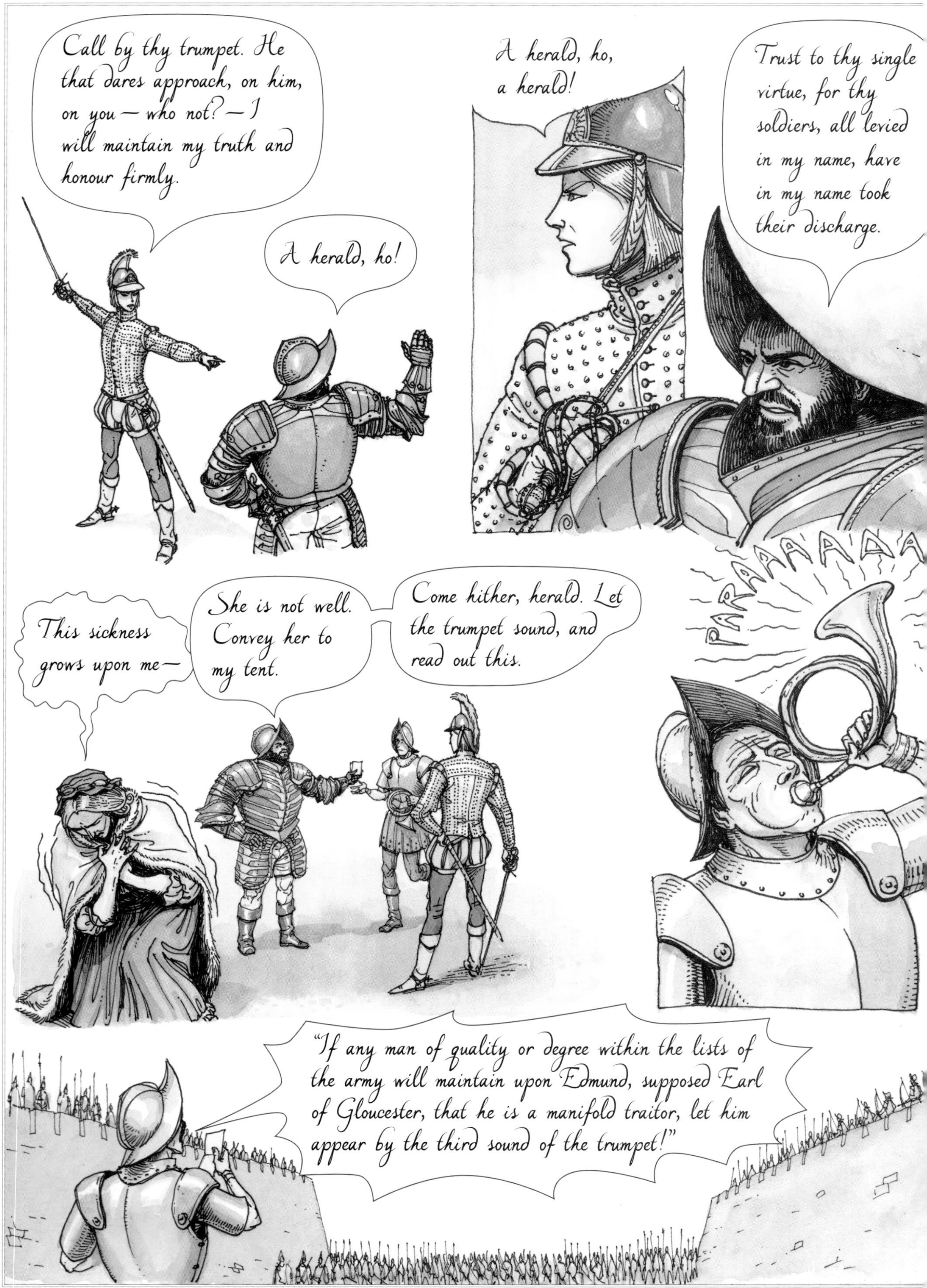
Call by thy trumpet. He that dares approach, on him, on you — who not? — I will maintain my truth and honour firmly.
A herald, ho!
A herald, ho, a herald!
Trust to thy single virtue, for thy soldiers, all levied in my name, have in my name took their discharge.
PARAAAAAA
This sickness grows upon me—
She is not well. Convey her to my tent.
Come hither, herald. Let the trumpet sound, and read out this.
"If any man of quality or degree within the lists of the army will maintain upon Edmund, supposed Earl of Gloucester, that he is a manifold traitor, let him appear by the third sound of the trumpet!"

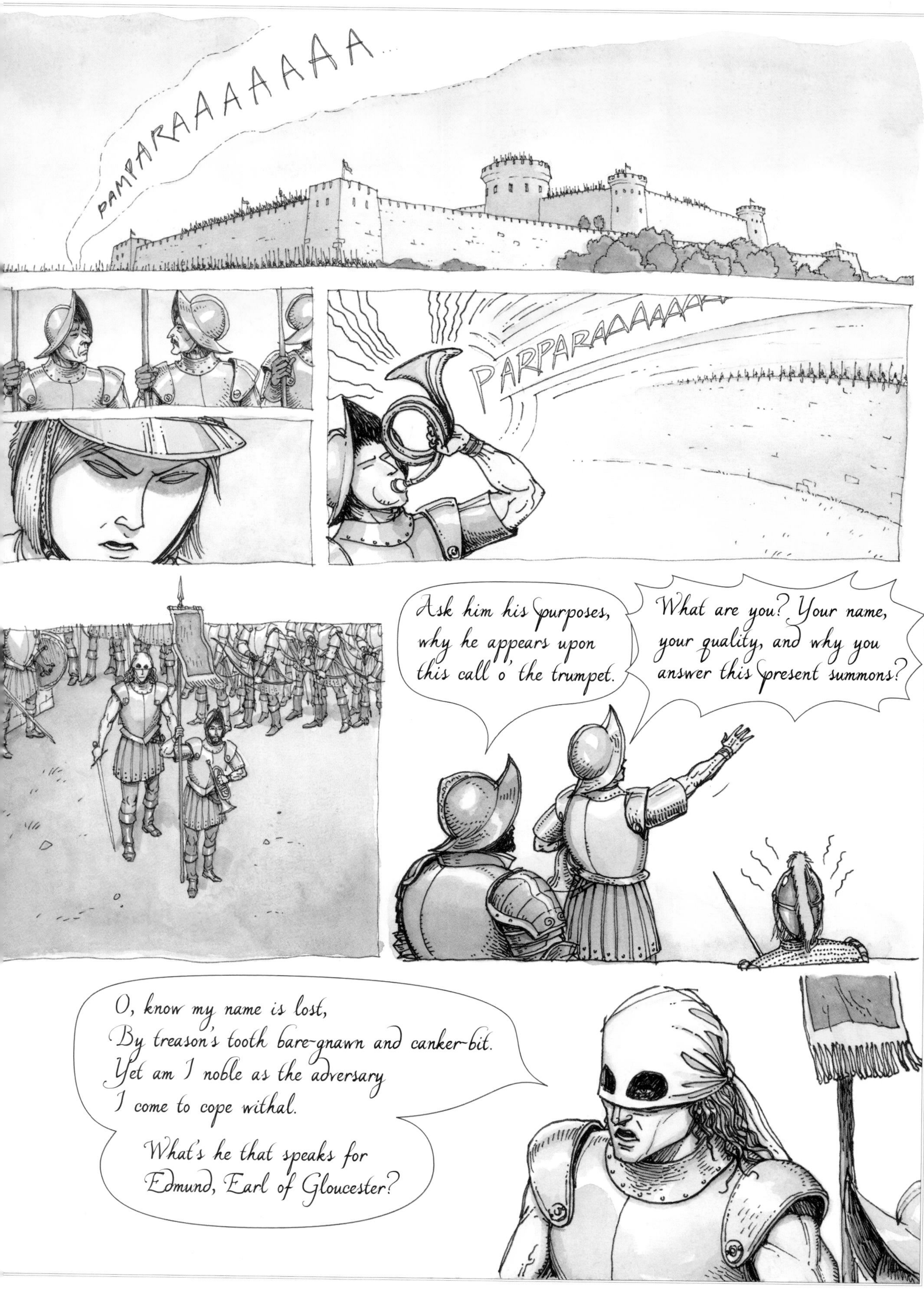
PAMPARAAAAAAAA...
PARPARAAAAAAA
Ask him his purposes, why he appears upon this call o' the trumpet.
What are you? Your name, your quality, and why you answer this present summons?
O, know my name is lost,
By treason's tooth bare-gnawn and canker-bit.
Yet am I noble as the adversary
I come to cope withal.
What's he that speaks for Edmund, Earl of Gloucester?

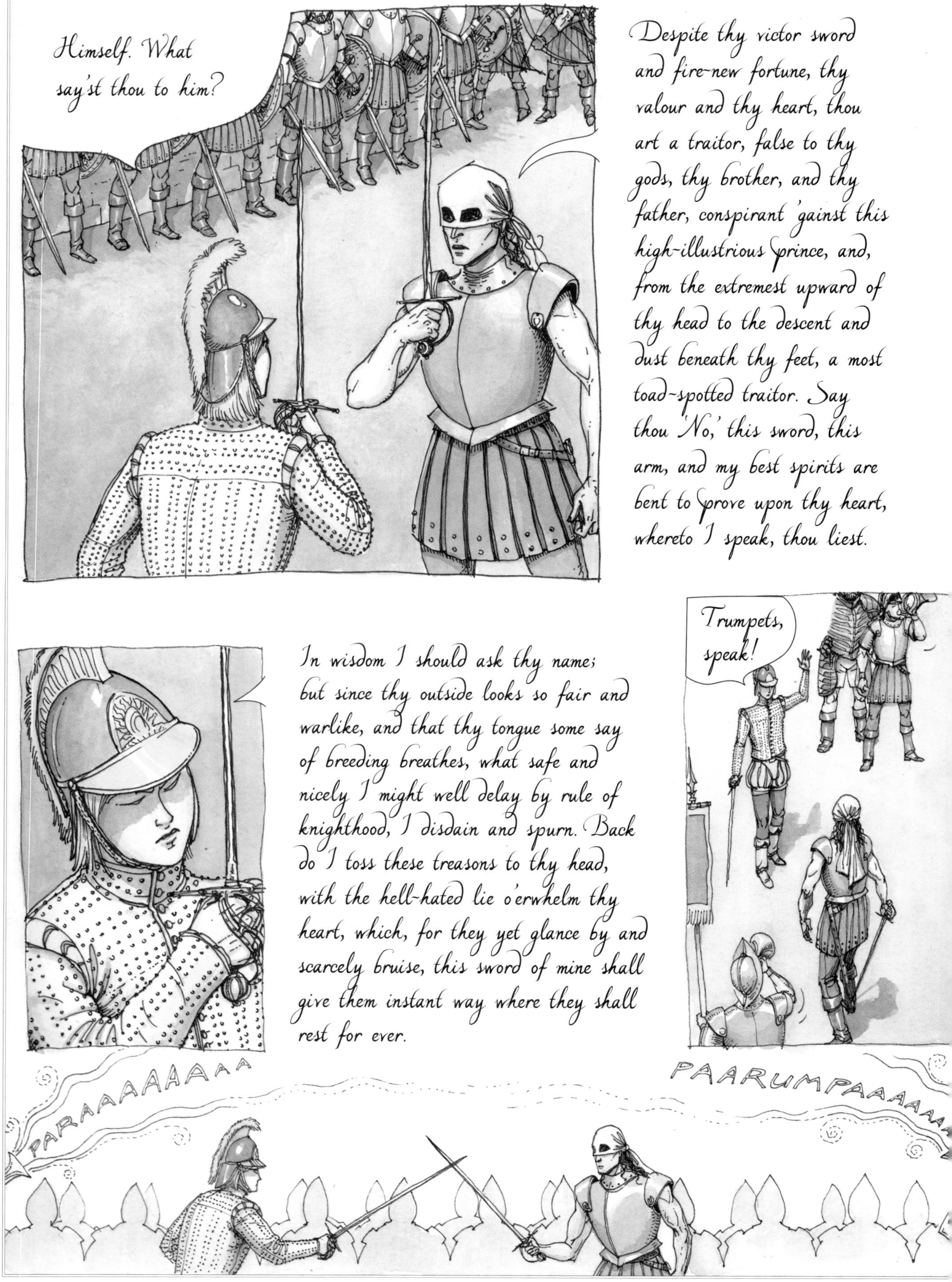
Himself. What say'st thou to him?
Despite thy victor sword and fire-new fortune, thy valour and thy heart, thou art a traitor, false to thy gods, thy brother, and thy father, conspirant 'gainst this high-illustrious prince, and, from the extremest upward of thy head to the descent and dust beneath thy feet, a most toad-spotted traitor. Say thou 'No,' this sword, this arm, and my best spirits are bent to prove upon thy heart, whereto I speak, thou liest.
In wisdom I should ask thy name; but since thy outside looks so fair and warlike, and that thy tongue some say of breeding breathes, what safe and nicely I might well delay by rule of knighthood, I disdain and spurn. Back do I toss these treasons to thy head, with the hell-hated lie o'erwhelm thy heart, which, for they yet glance by and scarcely bruise, this sword of mine shall give them instant way where they shall rest for ever.
Trumpets, speak!
PARAAAAAAAAaa
PAARUMPAAAAAAA

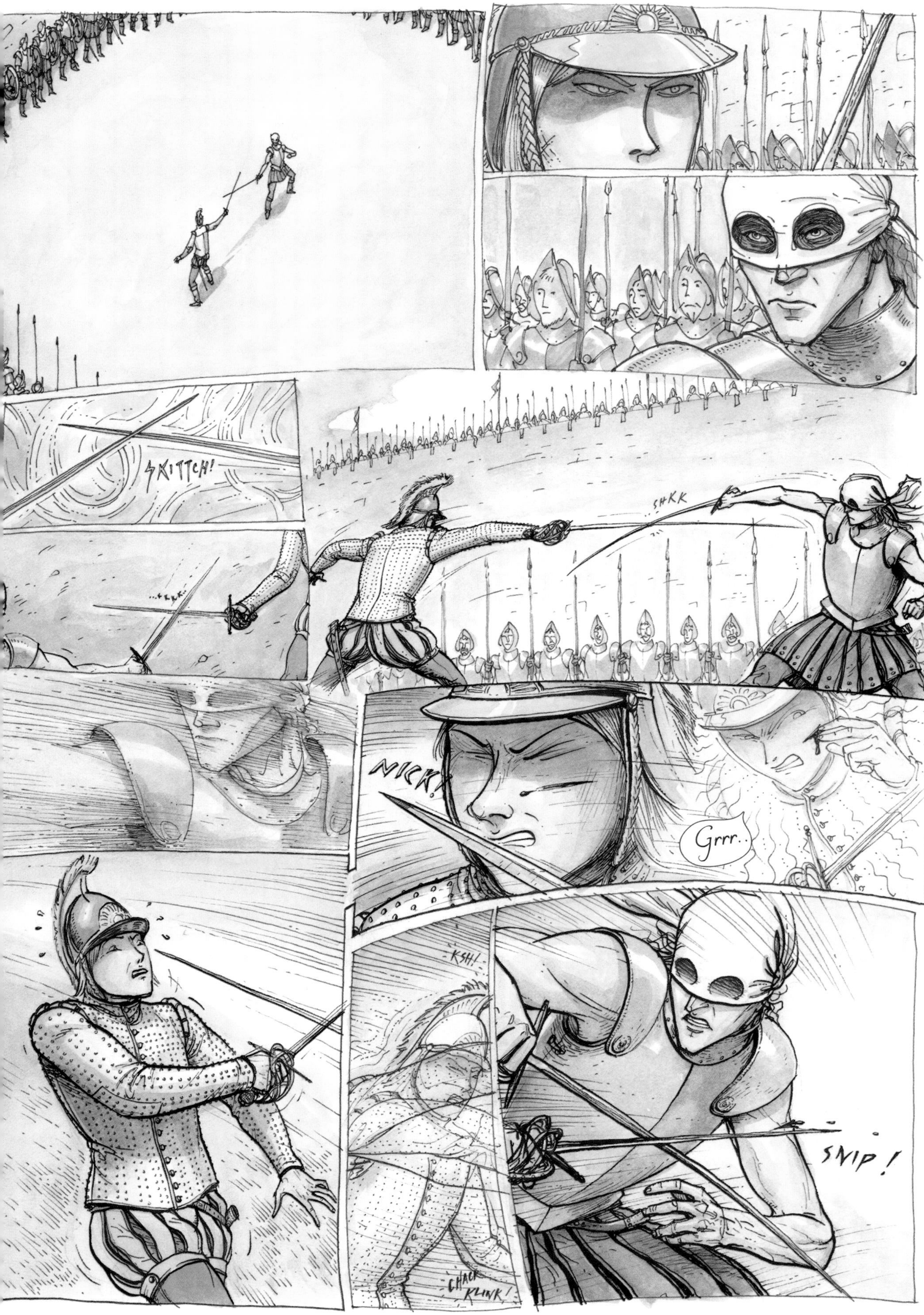
SKITTCH!
SHKK
...SHKK
NICK!
Grrr..
KSH!
SNIP!
CHACK
KLINK!

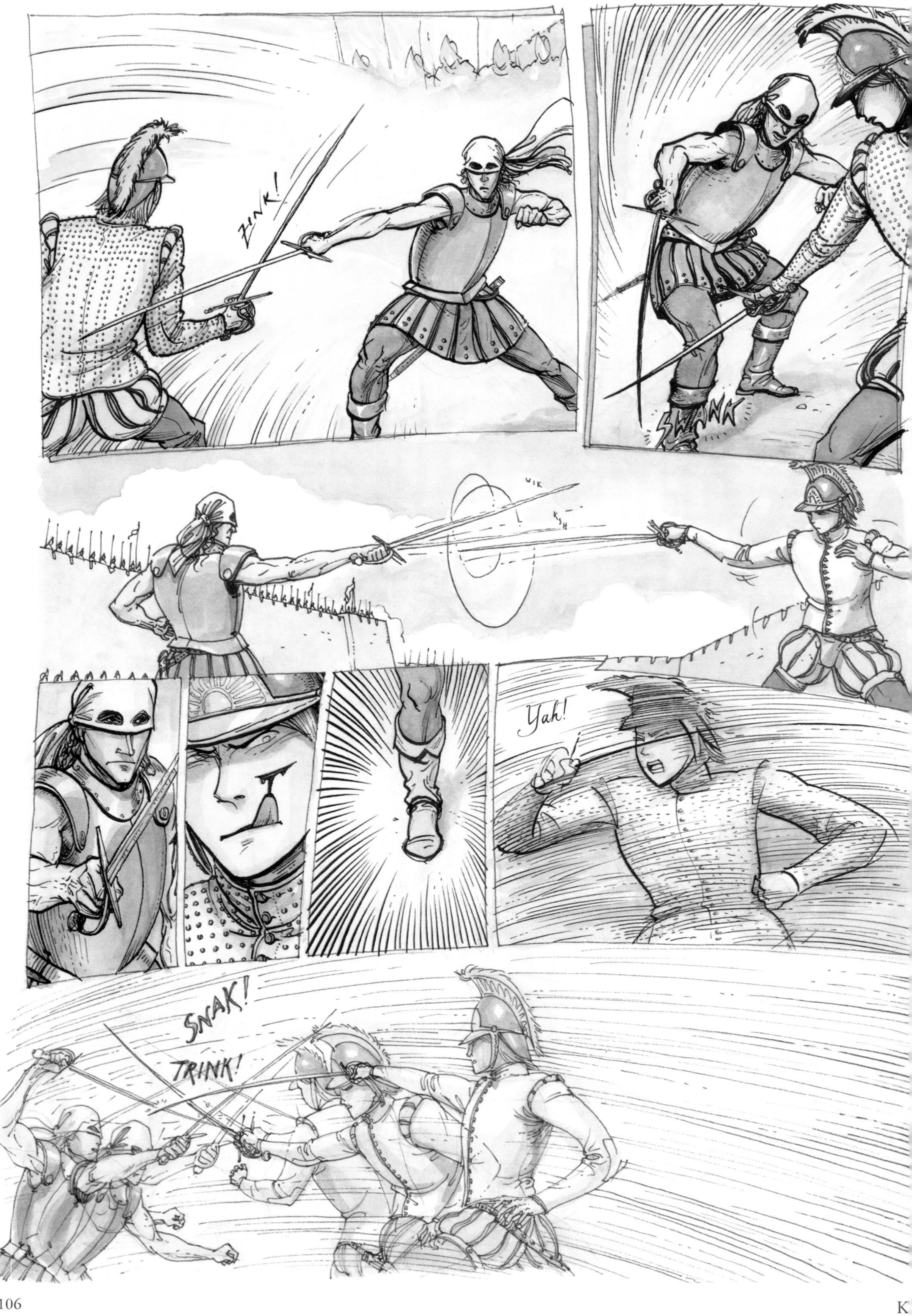
ZINK!
SWANK
WIK
KSH
Yah!
SNAK!
TRINK!

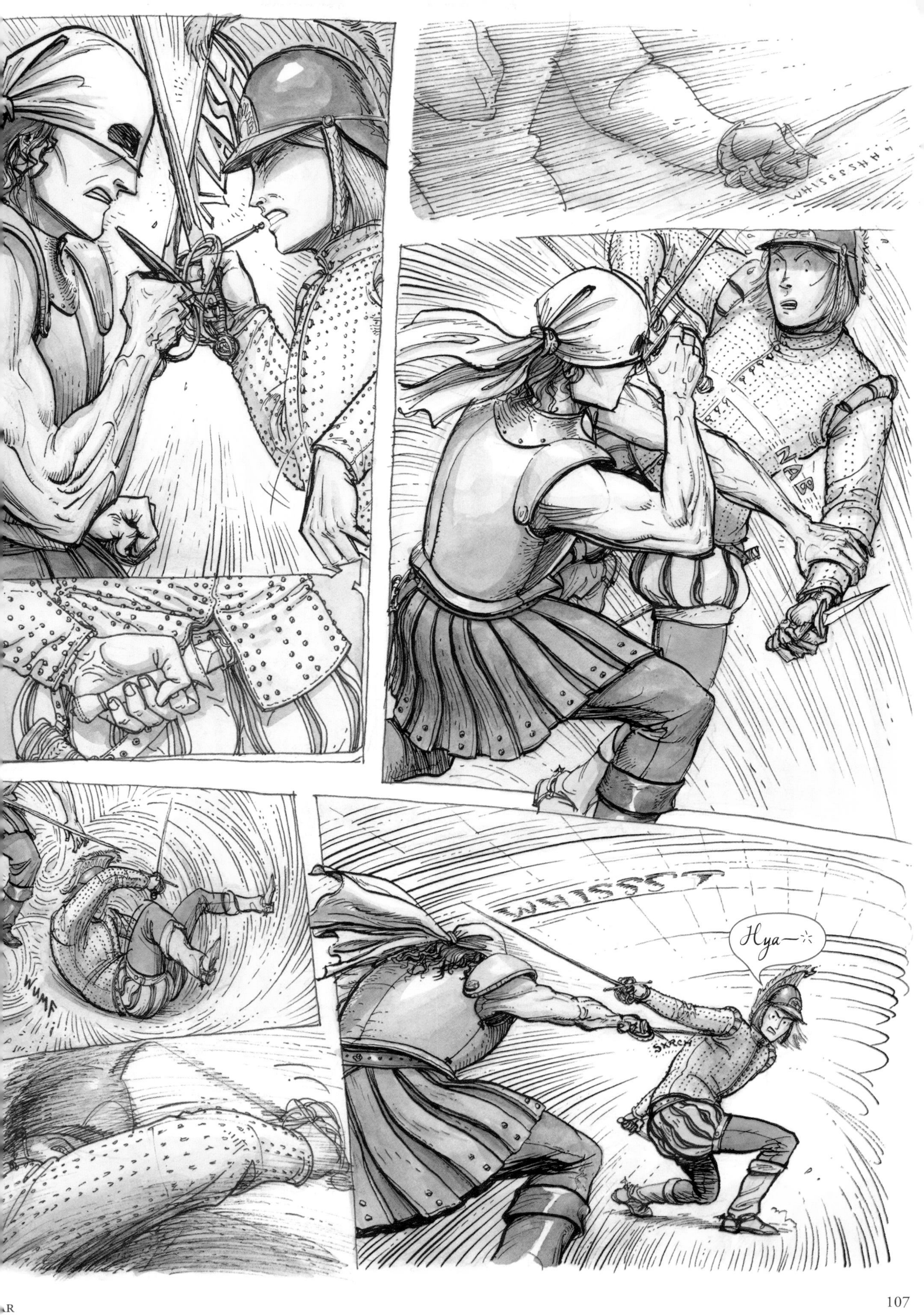
WHISSSSHH
NAB
WUMF
WHISSST
Hya—
SKRCH

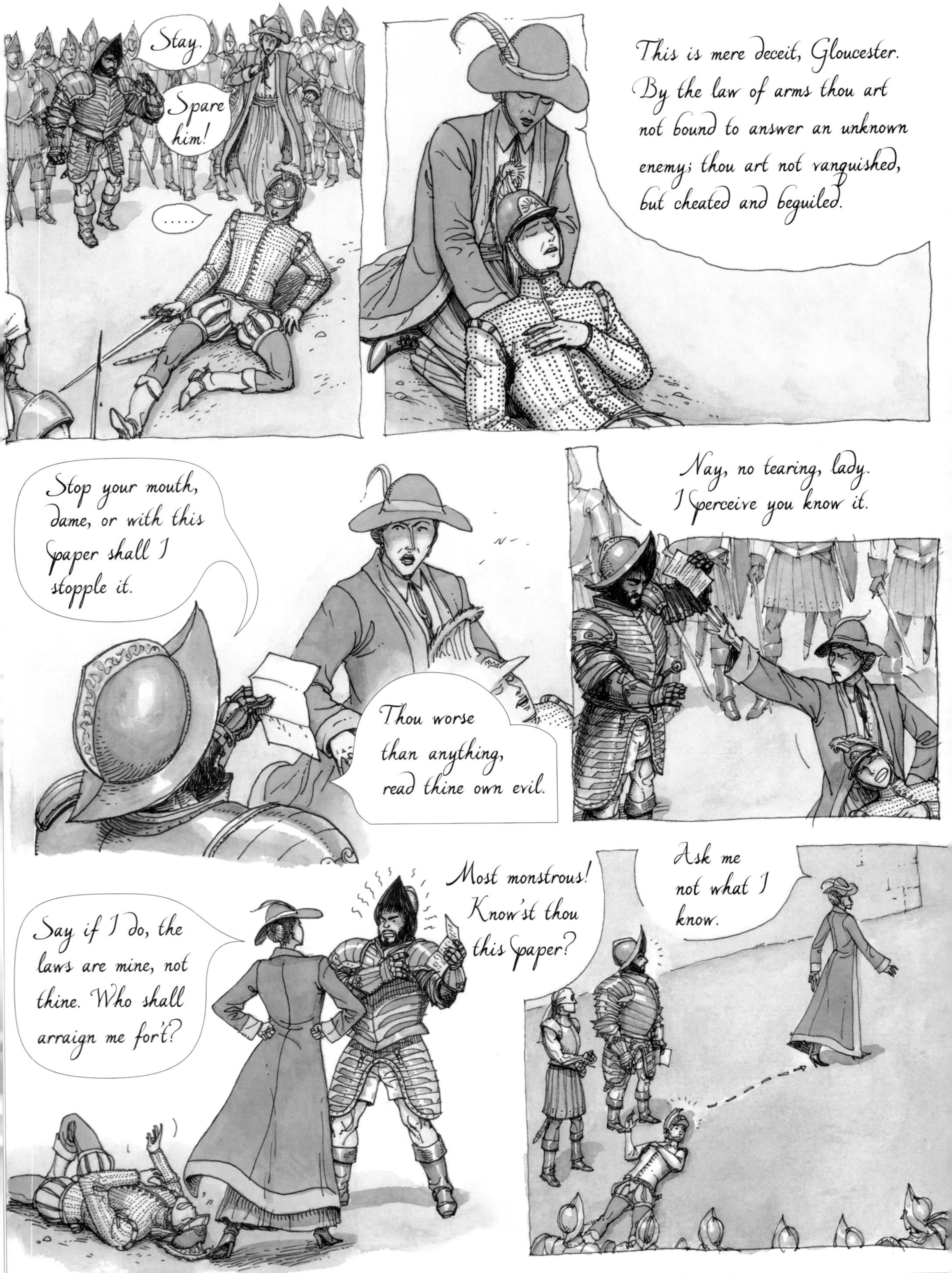
Stay.
Spare him!
.....
This is mere deceit, Gloucester. By the law of arms thou art not bound to answer an unknown enemy; thou art not vanquished, but cheated and beguiled.
Stop your mouth, dame, or with this paper shall I stopple it.
Thou worse than anything, read thine own evil.
Nay, no tearing, lady. I perceive you know it.
Say if I do, the laws are mine, not thine. Who shall arraign me for't?
Most monstrous! Know'st thou this paper?
Ask me not what I know.

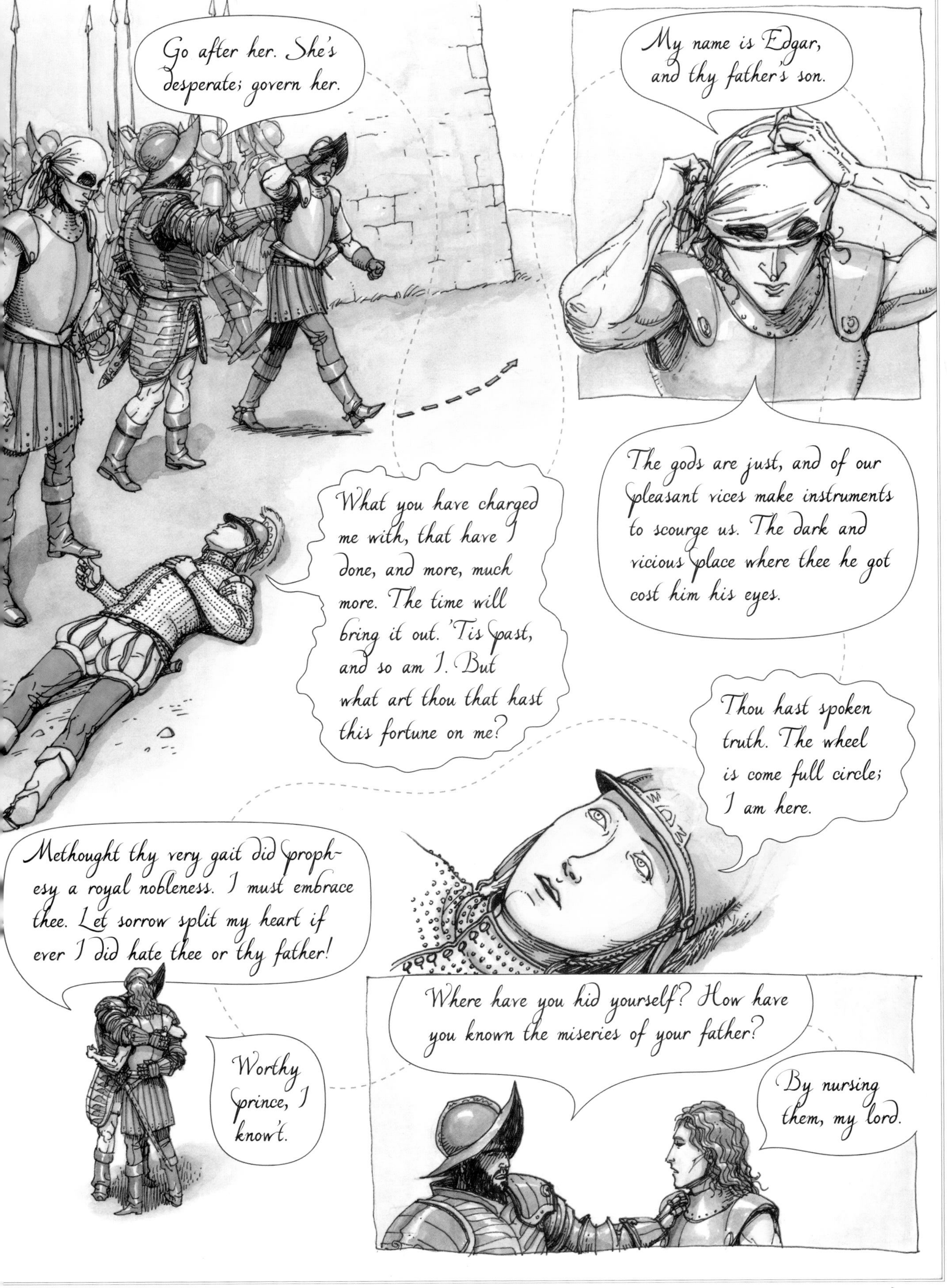
Go after her. She's desperate; govern her.
My name is Edgar, and thy father's son.
What you have charged me with, that have I done, and more, much more. The time will bring it out. 'Tis past, and so am I. But what art thou that hast this fortune on me?
The gods are just, and of our pleasant vices make instruments to scourge us. The dark and vicious place where thee he got cost him his eyes.
Thou hast spoken truth. The wheel is come full circle; I am here.
Methought thy very gait did prophesy a royal nobleness. I must embrace thee. Let sorrow split my heart if ever I did hate thee or thy father!
Worthy prince, I know't.
Where have you hid yourself? How have you known the miseries of your father?
By nursing them, my lord.

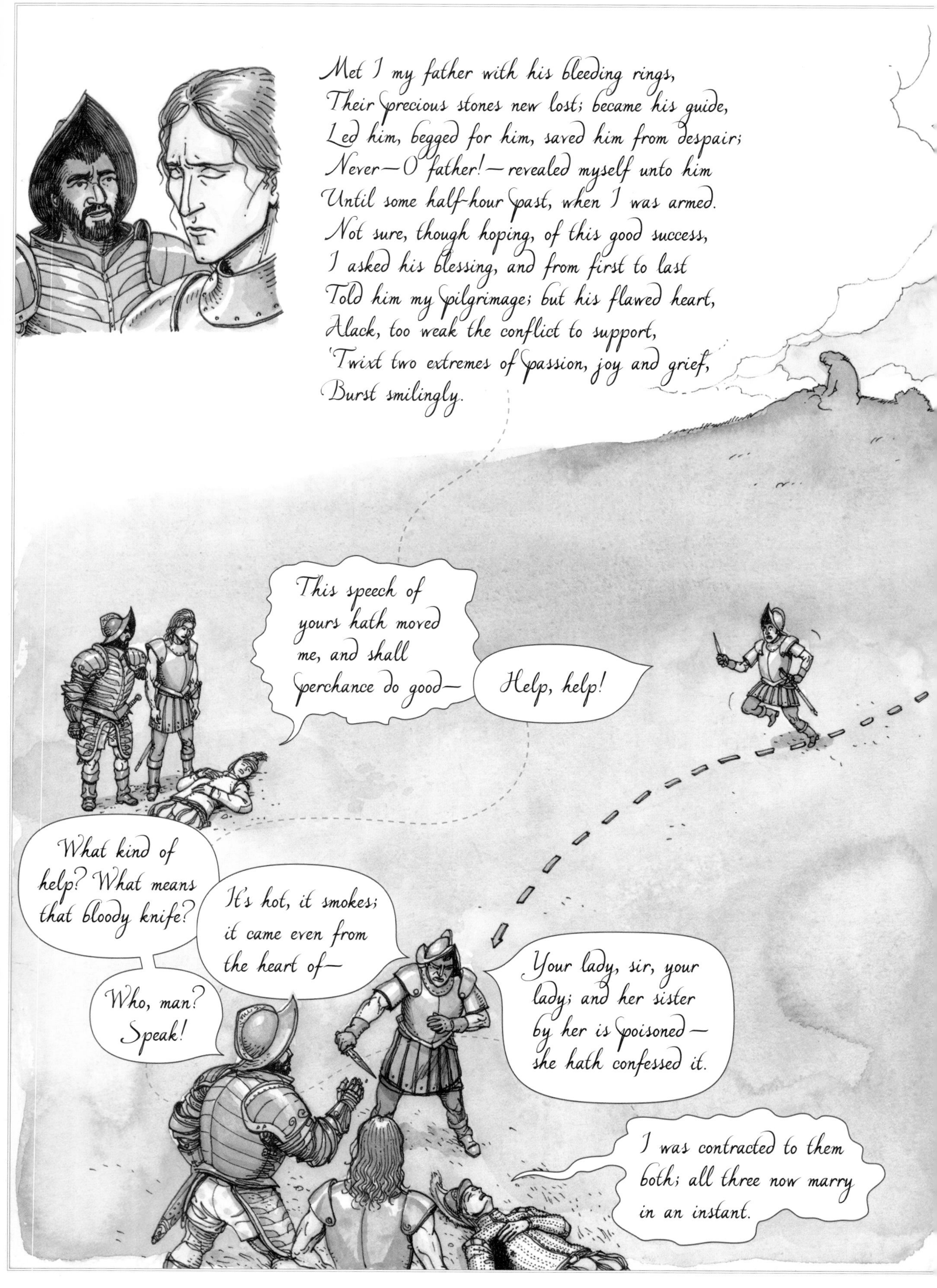
Met I my father with his bleeding rings,
Their precious stones new lost; became his guide,
Led him, begged for him, saved him from despair;
Never—O father!—revealed myself unto him
Until some half-hour past, when I was armed.
Not sure, though hoping, of this good success,
I asked his blessing, and from first to last
Told him my pilgrimage; but his flawed heart,
Alack, too weak the conflict to support,
'Twixt two extremes of passion, joy and grief,
Burst smilingly.
This speech of yours hath moved me, and shall perchance do good—
Help, help!
What kind of help? What means that bloody knife?
It's hot, it smokes; it came even from the heart of—
Who, man? Speak!
Your lady, sir, your lady; and her sister by her is poisoned—she hath confessed it.
I was contracted to them both; all three now marry in an instant.

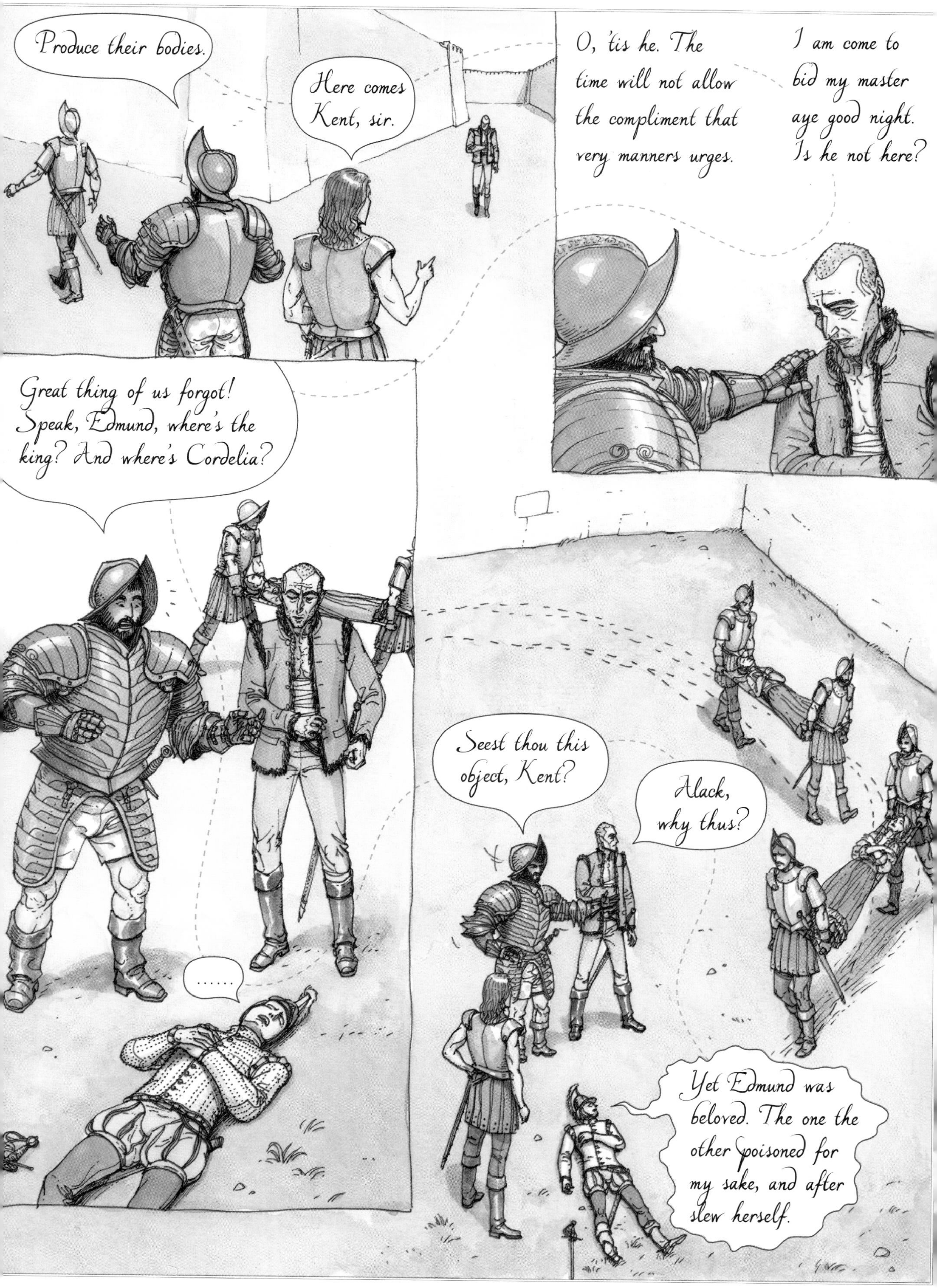
Produce their bodies.
Here comes Kent, sir.
O, 'tis he. The time will not allow the compliment that very manners urges.
I am come to bid my master aye good night. Is he not here?
Great thing of us forgot! Speak, Edmund, where's the king? And where's Cordelia?
......
Seest thou this object, Kent?
Alack, why thus?
Yet Edmund was beloved. The one the other poisoned for my sake, and after slew herself.

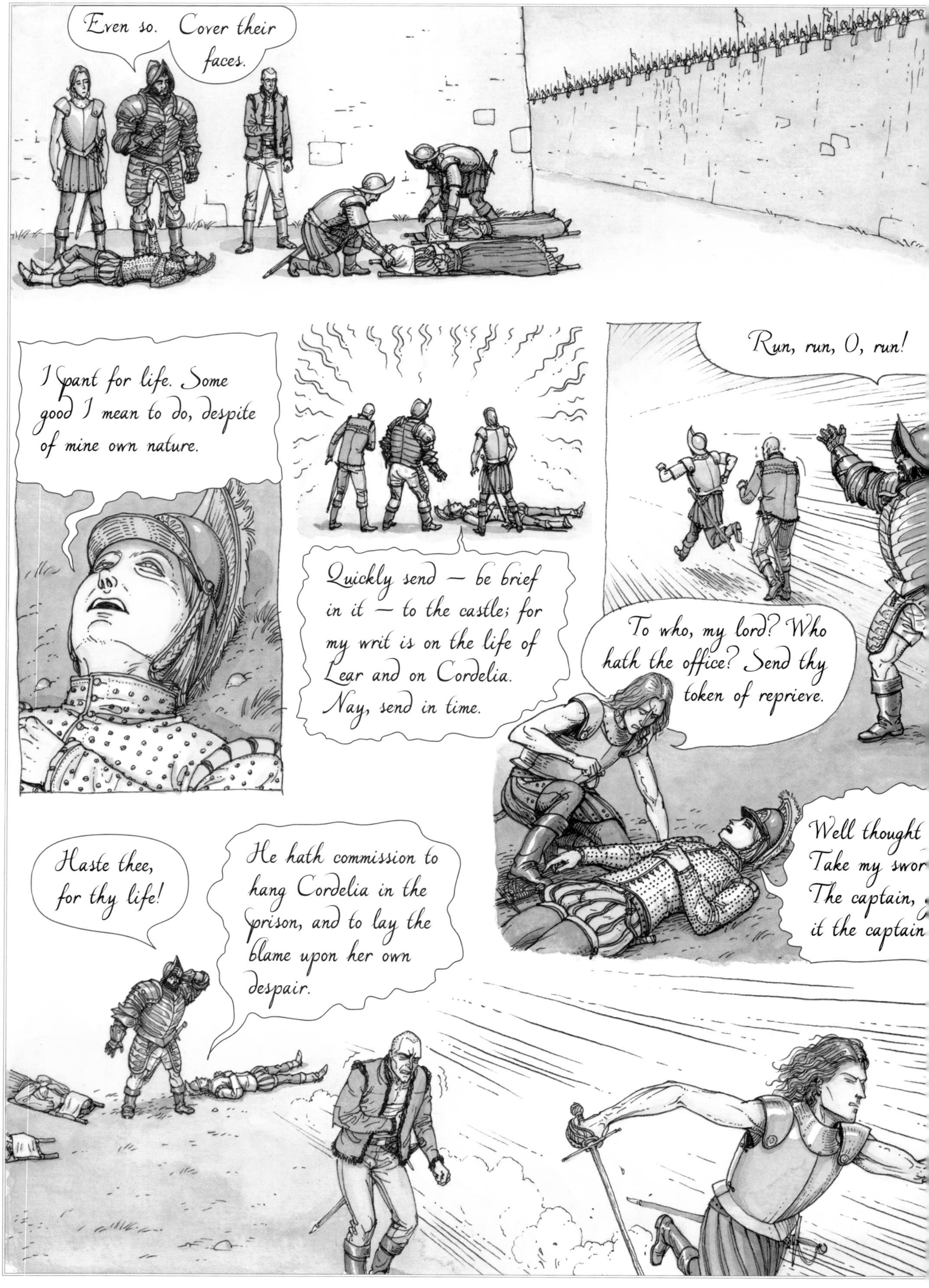
Even so. Cover their faces.
I pant for life. Some good I mean to do, despite of mine own nature.
Quickly send — be brief in it — to the castle; for my writ is on the life of Lear and on Cordelia. Nay, send in time.
Run, run, O, run!
To who, my lord? Who hath the office? Send thy token of reprieve.
Well thought
Take my swor
The captain,
it the captain
Haste thee, for thy life!
He hath commission to hang Cordelia in the prison, and to lay the blame upon her own despair.

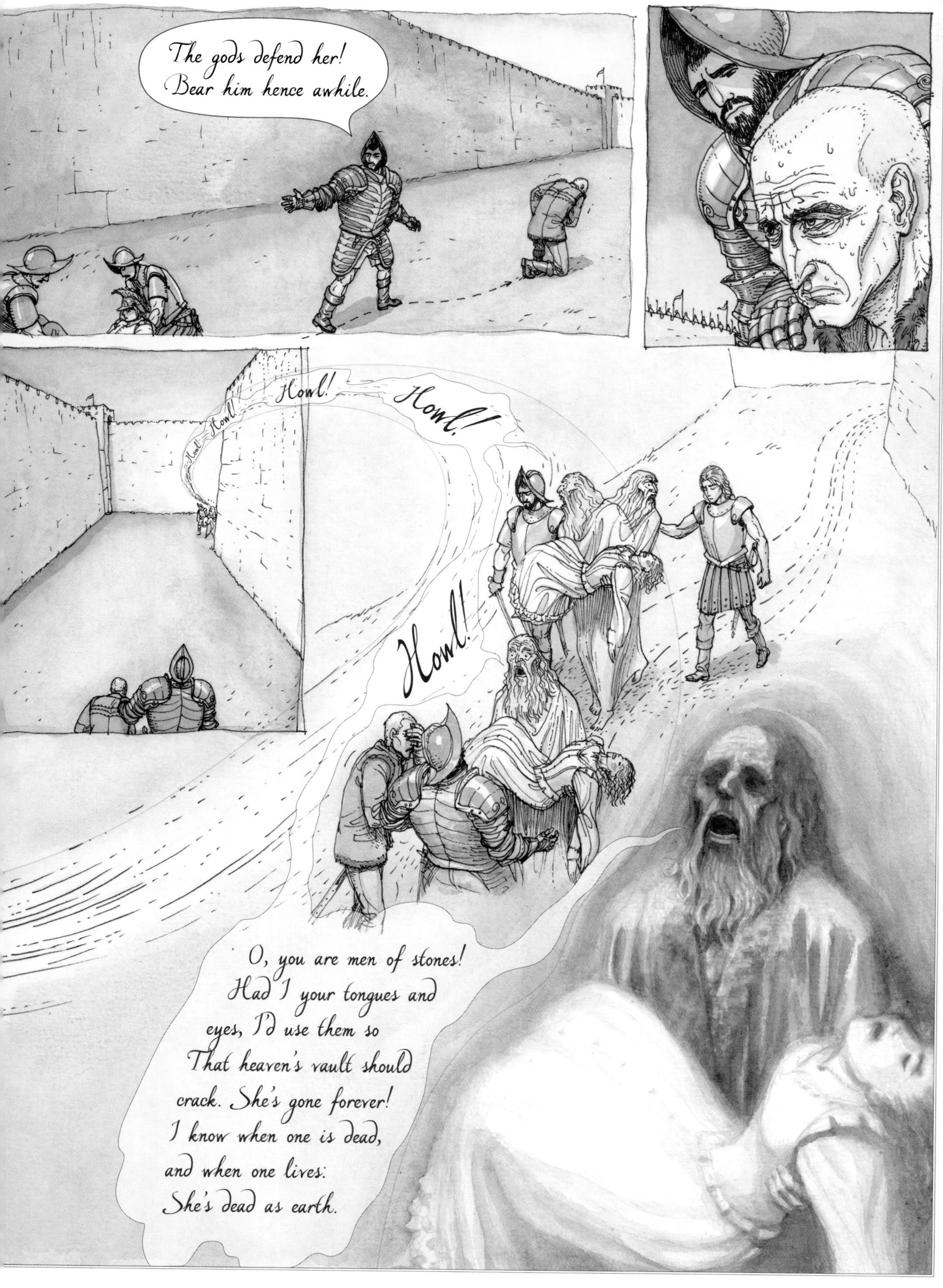
The gods defend her!
Bear him hence awhile.
Howl!
Howl!
Howl!
Howl!
Howl!
O, you are men of stones!
Had I your tongues and
eyes, I'd use them so
That heaven's vault should
crack. She's gone forever!
I know when one is dead,
and when one lives.
She's dead as earth.

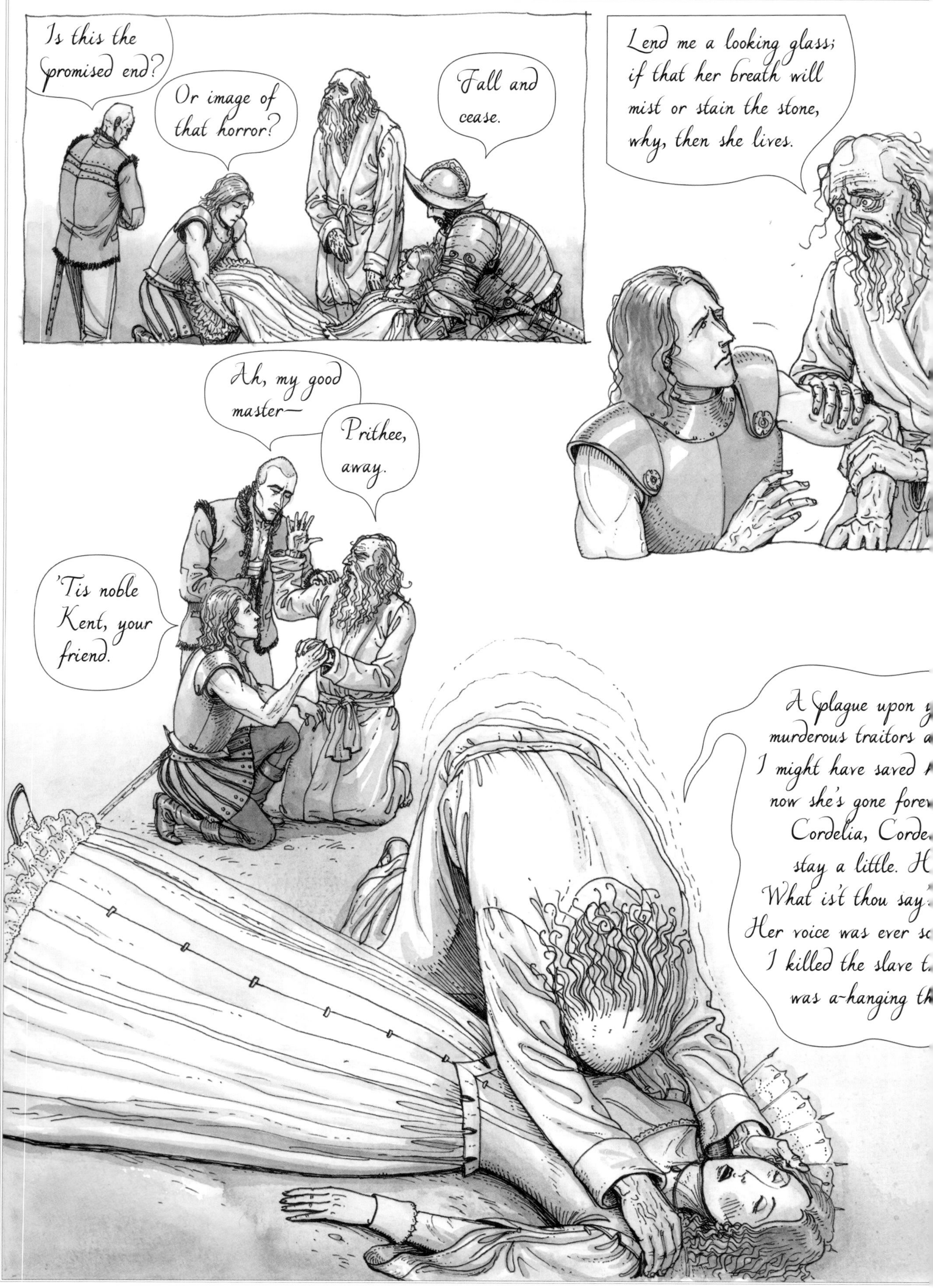
Is this the promised end?
Or image of that horror?
Fall and cease.
Lend me a looking glass; if that her breath will mist or stain the stone, why, then she lives.
Ah, my good master—
Prithee, away.
'Tis noble Kent, your friend.
A plague upon
murderous traitors
I might have saved
now she's gone
Cordelia,
stay a little.
What is't thou
Her voice was ever
I killed the slave
was a-hanging

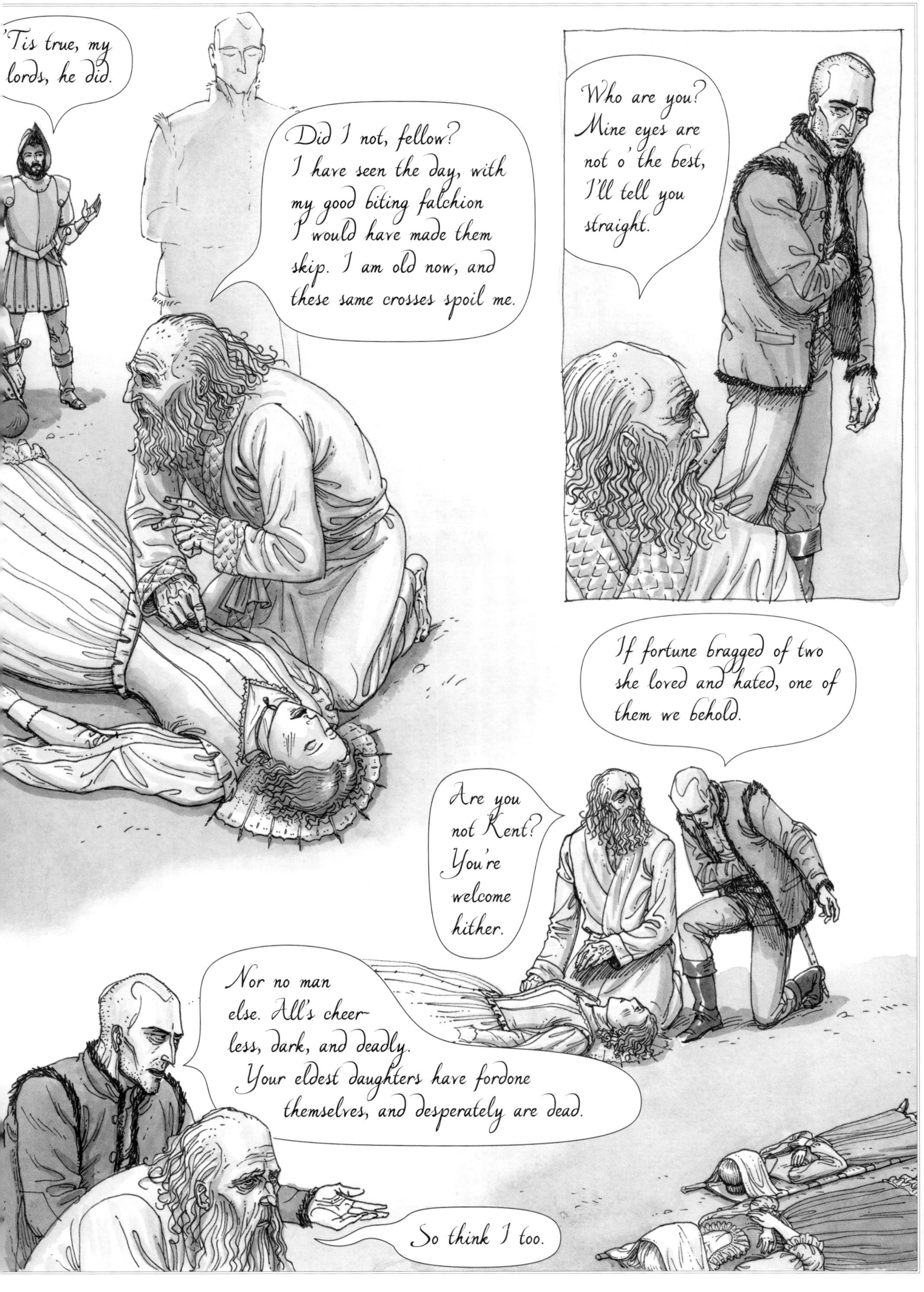
'Tis true, my lords, he did.
Did I not, fellow? I have seen the day, with my good biting falchion I would have made them skip. I am old now, and these same crosses spoil me.
Who are you? Mine eyes are not o' the best, I'll tell you straight.
If fortune bragged of two she loved and hated, one of them we behold.
Are you not Kent? You're welcome hither.
Nor no man else. All's cheer-less, dark, and deadly. Your eldest daughters have fordone themselves, and desperately are dead.
So think I too.

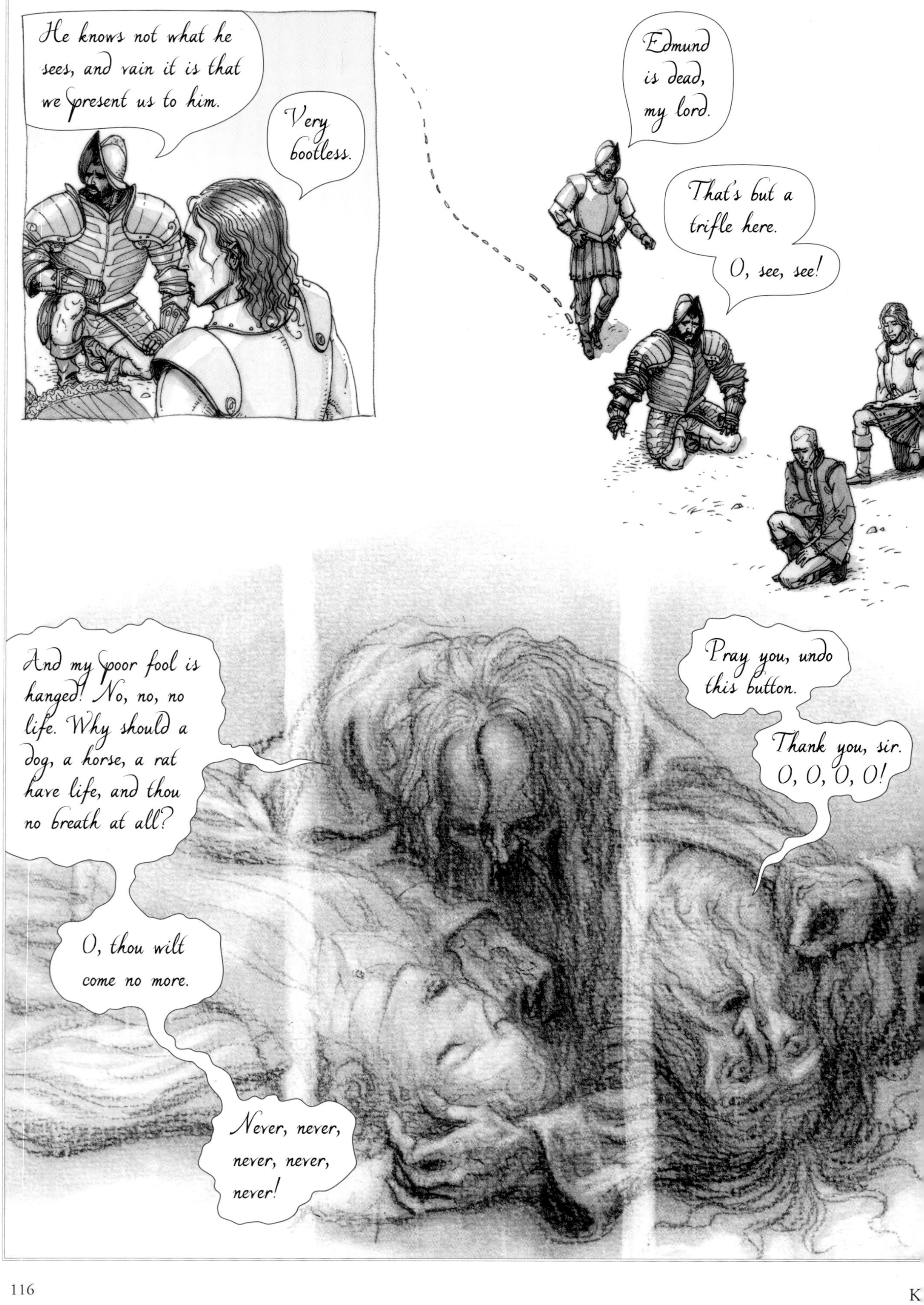
He knows not what he sees, and vain it is that we present us to him.
Very bootless.
Edmund is dead, my lord.
That's but a trifle here.
O, see, see!
And my poor fool is hanged! No, no, no life. Why should a dog, a horse, a rat have life, and thou no breath at all?
O, thou wilt come no more.
Never, never, never, never, never!
Pray you, undo this button.
Thank you, sir.
O, O, O, O!

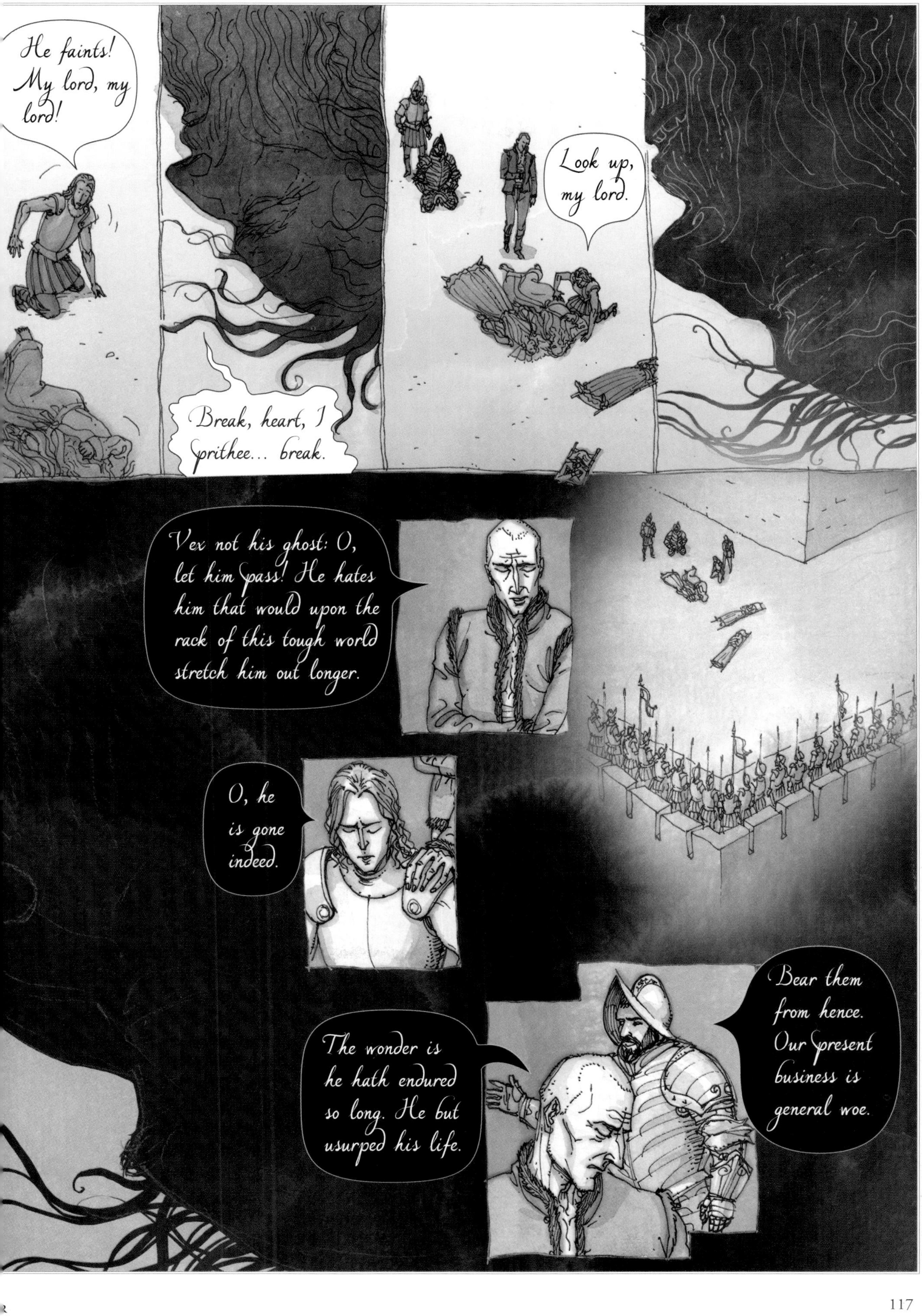
He faints! My lord, my lord!
Break, heart, I prithee... break.
Look up, my lord.
Vex not his ghost: O, let him pass! He hates him that would upon the rack of this tough world stretch him out longer.
O, he is gone indeed.
The wonder is he hath endured so long. He but usurped his life.
Bear them from hence. Our present business is general woe.

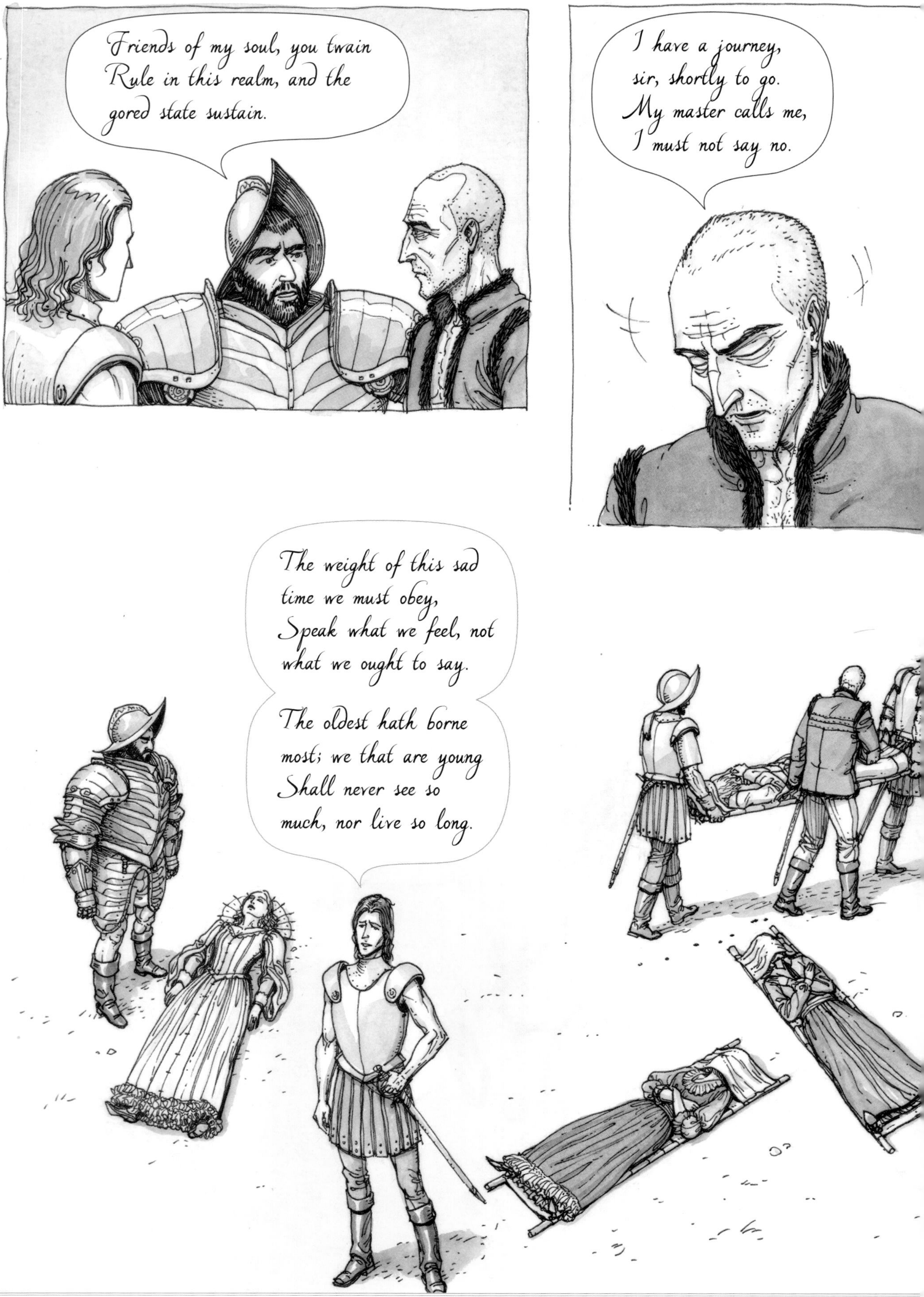
Friends of my soul, you twain Rule in this realm, and the gored state sustain.
I have a journey, sir, shortly to go. My master calls me, I must not say no.
The weight of this sad time we must obey, Speak what we feel, not what we ought to say.
The oldest hath borne most; we that are young Shall never see so much, nor live so long.

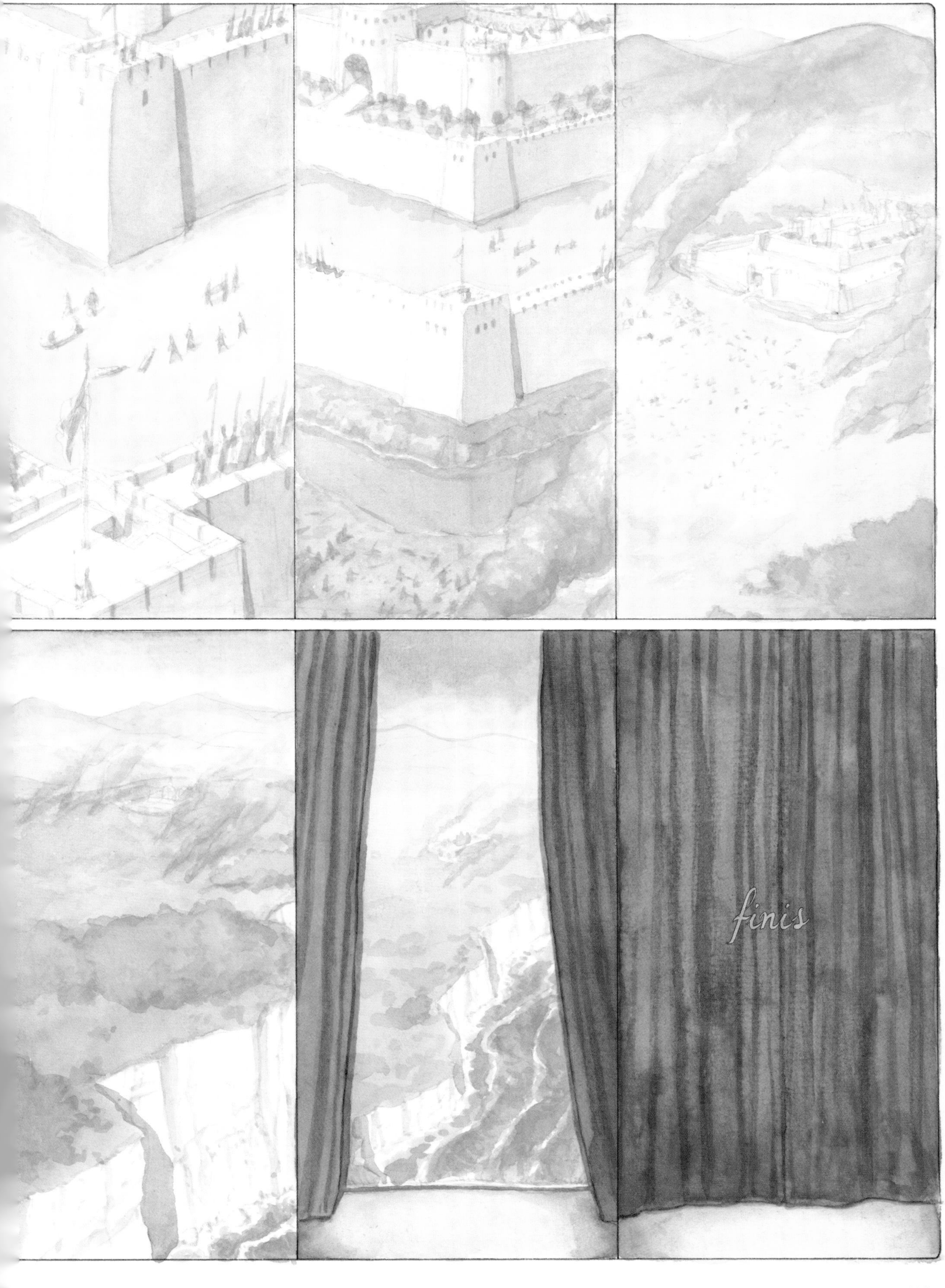
finis

Shakespeare's plays are remarkably rich. Every word of *King Lear*'s original text reveals something about the play's themes, symbols, or characters. In order to adapt it to the graphic novel format, though, I had to cut a lot of material that was less essential to the narrative. Included here are notes on some of the alterations I made to the text, insight into the ideas imparted by those passages, and themes I think deserve particular attention. I hope these notes will help to reveal the depth of this play, and the nature of the challenges and opportunities involved in retelling it.

PAGE 1 – Note the eclipse, which Gloucester refers to on p 13. A recurring theme of the play is the question of whether astronomical phenomena affect human actions or destinies.

PAGE 2 – I've shortened this exchange between Gloucester, Edmund, and Kent. In the original text, Gloucester makes another joke about Edmund's illegitimate parentage, and Edmund and Kent exchange courtesies. The most notable line is Edmund's *"Sir, I shall study deserving."* Deserving does not come naturally to Edmund, and he is only academically interested in it.

PAGES 2-4 – Shakespeare's text gives no indication as to whether Lear's map is pre-divided or not. The play is often performed using a pre-divided map, which makes Lear's "test" for his daughters a sham (no matter how flattering their speeches, their shares are already determined, as Lear assumes all of his daughters are suitably obedient). I chose to leave the illustrations ambiguous on this point. I also chose to have the map depict America, mainly to establish that I'm taking liberties with the play's historical grounding.

PAGE 5 – "Nothing" is a central theme in the play, and makes its first appearance here as the spark that ignites Lear's anger.

PAGE 12 – Note the use of "nothing" again.

PAGE 15 – In the last panel, I cut two lines: Lear says *"What's that?"* and Kent replies *"Authority."* The nature of authority is another big theme in this play.

PAGE 19 – More references to "nothing."
– In the original text the fool has several more choice words for Lear, continuing to mock him for dividing his crown.

PAGE 22 – I cut a nice section here in which Goneril chides Albany for his *"milky gentleness."*

PAGE 32 – For the sake of a better visual transition to Edgar, I've cut a section in which Kent takes out a letter from Cordelia and peruses it, which establishes that they are in communication and may be plotting something.

PAGE 50 – I cut *"the younger rises when the old doth fall,"* which is a nice statement of another recurring theme.

PAGE 51 – There were two pieces of Lear's dialogue I considered use on this page, but I couldn't really fit them both. I chose the one I think is more thematically important, and sacrificed *"Thou think'st 'tis much that this contentious storm invades us to the skin; so 'tis to thee, but where the greater malady is fixed, the lesser is scarce felt."*

PAGE 53 – I cut Edgar's fictitious origin (*"A serving-man, proud in heart and mind... that slept in the contriving of lust, and waked to do it"*), which is entertaining in its own right, and is possibly intended to ape Oswald.

PAGE 55 – I cut a nice little speech by Gloucester about the betrayal by his son, which highlights the parallels between his story and Lear's. I think the parallels are clear enough without that passage.

PAGE 64 – Another major theme in this play is (in)justice. It makes a direct appearance in this scene when Cornwall says *"Pinion him like a thief; bring him before us. / Though we may not pass upon his life / Without the form of justice, yet our power / Shall do a curtsy to our wrath, which men / May blame but not control."*

PAGE 65 – "True" is used here to mean loyal, but elsewhere in the play it is used by other characters to show various meanings and perceptions of truth. For example, Cordelia's *"so young, my lord, and true,"* Lear's *"thy truth then be thy dower,"* and Cornwall's *"True or false, it hath made thee Earl of Gloucester."*

PAGE 71 – In order to fit this scene on one page, I had to cut a lot of dialogue. Edgar begins the original scene with a rather long monologue, the gist of which is that things can't get any worse: *"The lamentable change is from the best, the worst returns to laughter"*. He repents voicing such a sentiment, however, when he sees his blinded father: *"O gods, who is't can say 'I am the worst'? / I am worse than e'er I was. And worse I may be yet. The worst is not / the worst as long as we can say 'this is the worst.'"* When Gloucester hears that a madman is there, his speech indicates that he almost recognized his son: *"In the last night's storm I such a fellow saw, / Which made me think a man a worm. My son / Came then into my mind, and yet my mind / Was then scarce friends with him. I have heard more since."*

– A bit later, Gloucester delivers a wonderfully rich speech: *"Let the superfluous and lust-dieted man / That stands your ordinance (resists heaven's command), that will not see / Because he does not feel, feel your power quickly. So distribution should undo excess, / And each man have enough. Dost thou know Dover?"* This seems to reflect on Lear, both his emotional blindness and the social woes he has overlooked, as in own realization *"I have ta'en too little care of this."* Some scholars favor a reading of the play in which Dover is seen as a symbol for a more progressive, less class-bound society, and this speech of Gloucester's is a mainstay of their argument.

PAGE 73 – Goneril's original line is *"I have been worth the whistling,"* a somewhat confusing reference to a dog who is (or is not) worth calling home.

PAGE 75 – *"And the Queen"* is my own addition, as it seems odd to me that the text says LaFar is in charge, but he never appears in the play.
– Some of my favorite imagery that appears throughout Shakespeare's plays is that of the natural elements as representations of characters' mental or emotional states. The storm in this play, which crescendo's with Lear's grief, is the quintessential example. Another nice one appears in this conversation between Kent and the Gentleman: *"You have seen sunshine and rain at once; her smiles and tears / Were like, a better way."* I

omitted it in favor of the king / rebel image, which seemed more indicative of the approaching conflict.

PAGE 76 – I left out a passage in which the doctor goes on to say, essentially, that rest will cure Lear. This comes up a few times in the play, possibly suggesting that Shakespeare's view of health may have been that rest restores order and no medical meddling is needed.

PAGE 77 – I cut a line of Regan's, which I think unnecessary, though it does clarify why she wants Gloucester dead: *"It was great ignorance, Gloucester's eyes being out, / To let him live; where he arrives he moves / All hearts against us, and now, I think, is gone … to descry the strength o' th' army."*

PAGE 79 – I changed "bourne" to "cliff" for clarity, and removed a passage in which Edgar invents an elaborate fantasy of seeing a demon on the top of the cliff, implying that malignant supernatural powers tried to aid Gloucester's suicide but good powers thwarted the attempt.

PAGE 80 – In Lear's speech I changed "cause" to "crime" and "luxury" to "lechery," for clarity. His rant goes on much longer, and includes a venomous attack on female sexuality, which I preferred to leave out, especially since the rest of the speech is more entertaining and (madly) astute.

PAGE 81 – There's more great eye/sight imagery in this exchange between Lear and Gloucester.
L: *"Read."*
G: *"What, with the case of eyes?"*
L: *"O ho, are you there with me? No eyes in your head, nor no money in your purse? Your eyes are in a heavy case, your purse in a light; yet you see how this world goes."*
G: *"I see it feelingly."*

PAGE 83 – I cut Edgar's description of himself as a poor man ready to lend a hand, which juxtaposes interestingly with Oswald's very different "friendly hand" on the next page.

PAGE 87 – I took out *"And the exchange my brother!"* since the text of the letter makes this clear, and removing it streamlined the transition to the next line.

PAGE 88 – I removed an exchange between Cordelia and Kent, in which Cordelia asks Kent to remove his disguise and reconcile with Lear. Kent puts her off, saying *"Yet to be known shortens my made intent,"* meaning that he still has plans and reasons for wanting to stay incognito. Although it's implied that Kent is contriving in the background throughout the play, in the end his mysterious plots all fail to materialize. He has virtually no effect on the final outcome. Kent's failure is ultimately an important piece of the tragedy; but I don't find it thematically satisfying, as Shakespeare provides no explanation for it. I decided to show that he was wounded in the big battle, which crippled his ability to carry out his plans and protect his master. This fits a facet of Kent's personality established early in the play – that he relies too much on his physical capabilities.

PAGE 91 – I cut *"he's full of alteration and self-reproving,"* which parallels nicely with Lear as we've just seen him, similarly altered and self-reproving.

PAGE 92 – "Touches" = concerns. The crux of Albany's speech is that he has decided to join his forces with Regan's because the French army is invading. His speech, though, indicates that his sympathy would be with Lear, if Lear were not allied with Cordelia and the French. Regan wants to take him to task for this, but Goneril forestalls their argument (presumably because she knows Albany's cooperation is quite delicate at this point, and she has lost her control over him). The full speech reads: *"Our very loving sister, well bemet, / For this I hear: the king is come to his daughter, / With others whom the rigor of our state/ Forced to cry out. Where I could not be honest / I never yet was valiant. For this business, / It touches us as France invades our land, / Not bolds the king, with others whom, I fear, / Most just and heavy causes make oppose."*

PAGE 97 – Lear goes on at some length about what a nice time he and Cordelia can have in prison. He's clearly reconciled with his daughter, but perhaps not with reality – *"...and laugh / At gilded butterflies, and hear poor rogues / Talk of court news, and we'll talk with them too, / Who loses and who wins, who's in, who's out, / And take upon's the mystery of things / As if we were God's spies; and we'll wear out / In a walled prison packs and sects of great ones / That ebb and flow by th'moon."*

PAGE 98 – I used the shorter Folio line here for the captain's answer, but the Quarto reads *"I cannot draw a cart, Nor eat dried oats. If it be man's work, I'll do't,"* which I think is great characterization.

– Panel 4: Albany doesn't have a line here, but I made him start to issue an order so I could suggest that his intention is to settle matters with Lear right away, and that Edmund has to stall him.

PAGE 100 – Edmund's *"Let the drum strike and prove my title good"* (to which I added "then" for rhythm) is instead said by Regan in the Folio – *"Let the drum strike and prove my title thine"* – but I prefer the Quarto version suggesting that Edmund feels he already has the power of Regan's army. Albany is, of course, about to disabuse him of this notion, and this is really Albany's moment of triumph. As I see it, Albany, having been forewarned by Edgar, is leaving nothing to chance; so I have him bringing in his army to make sure Edmund is trapped. Visually in this scene I'm paying homage to *Ran*, the spectacular film by Akira Kurosawa which is based on *King Lear*. In Kurosawa's version of the big battle scene, the armies move rapidly around the field in centipede-like rivers of armored men, to great visual effect.

PAGE 109 – In the original text, Edmund ends his *"Who art thou"* speech with *"If thou'rt noble, I do forgive thee."* This is rather ironic, since his own nobility is the product of lies and treason.
– Edgar's comment about *"The dark and vicious place where thee he (be)got"* suggests contempt for his father's sexual relations with women. Lear also seems to have little respect for women (see p114 note), and the majority of female characters in this play are pretty rotten. By the end, all of them are dead. To see Shakespeare treat women in a more positive light, you might want to read *Twelfth Night* and *The Merchant of Venice*.

PAGE 110 – Edgar also recounts meeting Kent after the battle, but doesn't provide any more clues as to exactly what Kent's plans were or how they failed.

PAGE 114 – I cut out the sexist part of Lear's lament here. The full line is *"Her voice was ever soft, an excellent thing in women."* (Sigh.)

PAGE 115 – In the original text Kent explains that he was disguised as Lear's servant, Caius. Since this is the only time a name is mentioned for Kent's alter-ego, and since Lear doesn't seem to really comprehend what Kent is saying, I chose to omit this exchange. Some theatrical productions, however, do make this an emotional moment of reunion. ✍

This is a work of fiction. Names, characters, places, and incidents are either products of the author's imagination or, if real, are used fictitiously.

Copyright © 2007 by Gareth Hinds

All rights reserved. No part of this book may be reproduced, transmitted, or stored in an information retrieval system in any form or with any means, graphic, electronic, or mechanical, including photocopying , taping, and recording, without prior written permission from the artist.

First edition 2007

ISBN 978-1893131-06-4 (paperback)

Printed in Canada

This book was typeset in Learscript4, © 2007 by Gareth Hinds
All rights reserved.
The endmatter was set in Adobe Caslon Pro.

THECOMIC.COM
Cambridge, MA

visit us at www.thecomic.com or www.garethhinds.com